BEHAVIOR
THERAPY
WITH
DELINQUENTS

BEHAVIOR THERAPY WITH DELINQUENTS

Compiled and Edited by

JEROME S. STUMPHAUZER, Ph.D.
University of Southern California
School of Medicine
Los Angeles, California

CHARLES C THOMAS · PUBLISHER
Springfield · Illinois · U.S.A.

Published and Distributed Throughout the World by
CHARLES C THOMAS • PUBLISHER
BANNERSTONE HOUSE
301-327 East Lawrence Avenue, Springfield, Illinois, U.S.A.

© *1973, by* CHARLES C THOMAS • PUBLISHER
ISBN 0-398-02668-8
Library of Congress Catalog Card Number: 72-88457

With THOMAS BOOKS *careful attention is given to all details of manufacturing and design. It is the Publisher's desire to present books that are satisfactory as to their physical qualities and artistic possibilities and appropriate for their particular use.* THOMAS BOOKS *will be true to those laws of quality that assure a good name and good will.*

Printed in the United States of America
N-1

For

BILL, CAESAR, WAYNE, DICK, CURLEY JOE,
DANA, ED, TOM, JIM, DANNY, EUGENE,
TAMMY, GARY, DIANNE, JAMEY, JULIE,
HANS, JOHN, RALPHETTA, JIMMY, RUSSELL,
MARCO, HAVA, HENRY, GENE, VIC, AND
DAVID

CONTRIBUTORS

EDUARDO AZCARATE, Ph.D., Children's Hospital, Washington, D.C.

C. J. BIRTLES, M.Sc., University of Liverpool, England.

BARBARA R. BISHOP, Ph.D., Camarillo State Hospital, California.

KENNETH S. BOWERS, Ph. D., University of Waterloo, Canada.

G. DUANE BROWN, Ph.D., West Virginia University.

ROY E. BUEHLER, Ph.D., Contra Costa County Mental Health Services, California.

JOHN D. BURCHARD, Ph.D., University of Vermont.

JOSEPH R. CAUTELA, Ph.D., Boston College.

WILLIAM J. DeRISI, Ph.D., California Youth Authority.

JEAN M. FURNISS, M.S., Washtenaw County Juvenile Department, Michigan.

H. M. HOLDEN, M.D., Tavistock Clinic, London.

LOIS E. HORTON, Ph.D., Burlington, Massachusetts.

GILBERT L. INGRAM, Ph.D., Federal Correctional Institution, Tallahassee, Florida.

RONALD B. JAMIESON, LL.D., Honolulu, Hawaii.

CARL F. JESNESS, Ph.D., California Youth Authority.

LOREN KARACKI, Robert F. Kennedy Youth Center, West Virginia.

SAMUEL L. KIMBLES, Ph.D., Intercommunity Child Guidance Center, Whittier, California.

D. A. KOLB, Ph.D., Massachusetts Institute of Technology.

ROBERT B. LEVINSON, Ph.D., United States Bureau of Prisons, Washington, D.C.

MALCOLM J. MACCULLOCH, M.D., University of Liverpool, England.

DONALD H. MEICHENBAUM, Ph.D., University of Waterloo,

vii

Canada.

GERALD R. PATTERSON, Ph.D., Oregon Research Institute.

ELERY L. PHILLIPS, Ph.D., University of Kansas.

ROBERT R. ROSS, Ph.D., University of Waterloo, Canada.

ROBERT L. SCHWITZGEBEL, Ed.D., Ph.D., Claremont Graduate School, California.

SALEEM A. SHAH, Ph.D., Center for Studies of Crime and Delinquency, Washington, D.C.

RICHARD B. STUART, D.S.W., University of Michigan.

JEROME S. STUMPHAUZER, Ph.D., University of Southern California School of Medicine.

ROLAND G. THARP, Ph.D., University of Hawaii.

GAYLORD L. THORNE, Ph.D., Research and Program Evaluation Division, State of Oregon.

VERNON O. TYLER, Ph.D., Western Washington State College.

RALPH J. WETZEL, Ph.D., University of Arizona.

C. WILLIAMS, M.Sc., Institute of Subnormality, Lea Hospital, England.

PREFACE

BEHAVIOR THERAPY may be defined as the systematic application of the psychological principles of learning in the modification of human deviant behavior. Behavior therapy has witnessed a phenomenal growth in the last ten years, yet it is only recently that behavior therapy has been reported with juvenile delinquents. The goal of this volume has been to bring together several major reports of behavior therapy with delinquents in one reference volume. The editor's task has been to bring some organization to this growing area, to evaluate these contributions, to review related research, and to stimulate students and practitioners in still more effective application of the principles of learning in modifying the behavior of delinquents.

More specifically, this text is intended as a reference book for those many individuals who are charged with the responsibility of changing the behavior of young criminals: probation officers, psychologists, psychiatrists, social workers, teachers, institutional staff juvenile courts, and police agencies. It may serve as a supplementary textbook for courses in juvenile delinquency, criminology, police science, and behavior therapy. Although it deals specifically with young offenders, the principles apply to adult criminals as well.

The book has been organized in four parts with an introduction to each section by the editor. These introductory remarks include discussion and evaluation of the papers in that section, review of related papers, and suggestions for further work. Part One contains introductory papers—papers introducing the reader to behavior therapy and papers discussing basic scientific, ethical, and practical issues. In Part Two some basic research papers are presented. While experimental in nature, it is hoped that these research reports may stimulate applied treatment programs. Behavior therapy is being applied extensively in institutions for delinquents, and chapters describing such programs are found in Part Three. Finally, behavior therapy as it has been applied in the community is presented in Part Four.

The origin of this volume may, in part, be traced to a review paper, "Behavior modification with juvenile delinquents: a critical review," which served as partial fulfillment for the Ph.D. degree from the Department of Psychology of Florida State University. It was published in a privately circulated technical bulletin series of the Federal Correctional Institution for Youthful Offenders, Tallahassee, Florida: *FCI Technical and Treatment Notes*, 1970, 1, whole no. 2. Professors Wallace A. Kennedy and Edwin I. Megargee were instrumental in the inception of the review and its subsequent development.

The editor wishes to express his gratitude to each of the authors, journals, and publishers who graciously granted permission to reproduce articles here; they are acknowledged at the beginning of each chapter. In addition the editor would like to thank Drs. Bishop and Kimbles who prepared chapters exclusively for this volume.

J.S.S.

CONTENTS

BEHAVIOR
THERAPY
WITH
DELINQUENTS

PART
ONE

Delinquency and
Behavior Therapy

Prison is a good place for murderers, thieves and drug pushers.

Unfortunately, it's also a good place to become a murderer, a thief or a drug pusher.

And that's just what's happening.

Every year, thousands of young men and women are arrested and sent to prison for petty larceny or smoking pot or joy-riding in a stolen car.

And every year thousands of kids with a little problem on their minds come out of jail with a big chip on their shoulders.

Kids who once might have been helped by us are now beyond the help of anyone.

The answer isn't prison reform. Because the answer isn't prison.

These kids don't need punishment. They need treatment.

By a social worker. Or a psychiatrist. Or a trained counsellor. Or a community center for job development and training.

The National Council on Crime and Delinquency is an organization that's working to prevent juvenile delinquents from becoming adult ones.

Keeping problem children from becoming problem adults isn't just a matter of building a few playgrounds.

We need more understanding. We need more volunteers.

We need more money.

Please send all three to:

The National Council on Crime and Delinquency,
44 East 23rd Street,
New York, N.Y. 10010.

And please hurry.

Every day, kids are being sent to prison to learn a lesson they'll never forget.

This advertisement was prepared by Daniel & Charles, Inc. It was written by Lawrence Dunst, art directed by Murray Smith and photographed by Arnold Beckerman. Reproduced with permission of National Council on Crime and Delinquency.

**Prison isn't a waste of time.
A lot of kids come out learning a trade.**

This illustration is as appeared in *TIME*, June 15, 1970. Reproduced with consent of the National Council on Crime and Delinquency.

INTRODUCTION

JEROME S. STUMPHAUZER

CRIMINAL BEHAVIOR among young people continues to be a major concern for both the general public and the treatment-research community. Tunley (1964) reports that apart from peace and national survival, Americans are more concerned about juvenile delinquency than any other problem. The figures in the Federal Bureau of Investigation's annual *Uniform Crime Reports* are often quoted as suggestive of the extent of the problem in the United States. In 1970, for example, there were more than two million arrests of persons under 21 years of age. It should be emphasized, however, that these figures represent only the amount of *detected* criminal behavior resulting in arrest of American youth and do not represent the actual extent of such crime. Also, as Gibbons (1970) found, police authorities and other agencies often dispose of many juvenile cases far short of actual arrest. The problem of juvenile crime is, of course, not limited to the United States. Prins (1969, p. 132) found for England and Wales, "that there has been more than a twofold increase in the total number of indictable and nonindictable offenses (for all ages) known to the police over the last two decades."

Much of our correctional process seems to be ineffective in that many juveniles that have been arrested commit crimes again. The rate of this recidivism for juvenile parolees was found to be 43 to 73 percent by Arbuckle and Litwack (1960), while former Attorney General Kennedy (1964) suggested the rate was about 50 percent. It seems, then, that at least half of arrested delinquents are arrested again.

The costs of crime, both in money and wasted human resources, are staggering. In California alone, over *one billion dollars* a year is spent by the major agencies which deal with crime and law enforcement, courts, prosecution, and corrections. The $3500 cost to keep a youthful offender in an institution, suggested by Kennedy in 1964, is probably now a very conservative estimate. In addition, there is the great waste of human resources represented by juvenile crime.

The reported traditional psychotherapeutic treatment of delinquents and youthful offenders gives little promise of success in lessening this national problem. The well-publicized Cambridge-Somerville project found no significant differences between treatment and control groups (McCord, McCord, and Zola, 1959; Powers and Witmer, 1951). Psychiatric treatment of delinquents is reported to have had no effect on number of subsequent court appearances (Teuber and Powers, 1951). Gordon (1962) even found the addition of individual insight therapy to a group treatment program resulted in *less* success than group therapy alone!

There is rightfully a growing concern about the ineffectiveness of our correctional programs and the crime of punishment (Menninger, 1968). If the aim of judicial proceedings, probation, and correctional institutionalization is to change delinquent behavior in a pro-social direction, then they have failed. In fact, much of our present *correctional* programs probably act to *increase* criminal behavior. As the National Council on Crime and Delinquency illustration suggests, "Prison isn't a waste of time, a lot of kids come out learning a trade," i.e. they learn to be more sophisticated criminals. As will be seen in Part Two (Buehler, Patterson, and Furniss), peers in institutions are more consistent and effective in shaping *anti*social behavior, than institutional staff are in promoting *pro*social behavior. Many of the chapters will discuss the inherent problems in present traditional programs and have suggestions for the vast changes needed.

The learning theories and experiments of I.P. Pavlov (1927), C.L. Hull (1943) and B.F. Skinner (1953) have been extended over the last few decades and applied to human deviant behavior. This approach, termed *behavior therapy, behavior modification, reinforcement therapy, or conditioning therapy,* has been rapidly gaining coverage in the literature. At this writing, four journals are devoted exclusively to behavior therapy: *Behavior Research and Therapy*, the *Journal of Applied Behavior Analysis*, *Behavior Therapy*, and the *Journal of Behavior Therapy and Experimental Psychiatry*. The reader is referred to these journals for a more thorough view of current developments in this field.

Ullman and Krasner (1965, p. 1) suggest that the behavior therapist is likely to concern himself with these following questions.

1. What behavior is maladaptive, that is, what subject behaviors should be increased or decreased. 2. What environmental contingencies currently support the subject's behavior (either to maintain his undesirable behavior or to reduce the likelihood of his performing a more adaptive response). 3. What environmental changes, usually reinforcing stimuli, may be manipulated to alter the subject's behavior.

Behavior therapy may be defined as the systematic application of the psychological principles of learning in the modification of human deviant behavior. Several papers which review behavior modification and therapy are currently available: Bandura (1961, 1967), Gelfand and Hartman (1968), Grossberg (1964), Werry and Wollershein (1967), and Krasner (1971). While this book deals chiefly with juvenile delinquents, some references are available for behavior therapy with delinquent military recruits (Coleman and Baker, 1969) and with adult prisoners (Clements and McKee, 1968).

The following is a list of seventeen major principles of learning and behavior therapy. While some are more or less pure principles of learning and are applied directly in treatment, others are obviously hybrid principles, relying on other more basic principles. The editor will refer to these principles in the introduction to each section of the book, in reference to each chapter, with the hope that readers will develop an understanding of the principles of behavior therapy and how they may be applied to change delinquent behavior. It is also hoped that readers will be stimulated to new use of these principles, as this is still a new and developing field, and it will become obvious that all these principles have not yet been applied fully with delinquents. Further introduction and discussion of some of these principles will be made by Shah, in Chapter 1.

1. Principle of Positive Reinforcement
The presentation of a positive stimulus (positive reinforcement) as the consequence of a response will increase the strength (frequency) of that response.

2. Principle of Negative Reinforcement
The removal of an aversive stimulus, as the consequence of a response, will increase the strength (frequency) of that response. A response is negatively reinforced if it results in termination or avoidance of an aversive stimulus.

3. Principle of Punishment
Punishment decreases the strength (frequency) of the response which it follows. This term refers to two basic operations: (a) the first form of punishment occurs when an aversive stimulus is presented as the consequence of a response, and (b) the second form of punishment occurs when the opportunity for positive reinforcement is withheld or withdrawn as the consequence of a response (time-out from positive reinforcement).

4. Principle of Extinction
This refers to a process whereby a conditioned response is reduced to its preconditioned frequency or strength, often approaching a zero magnitude or level. The process of extinction in the case of respondent conditioning involves continuing presentation of the conditioned stimulus without any further pairing with the unconditioned stimulus. With operant conditioning, extinction results when responding is no longer followed by reinforcement.

5. Principle of Shaping
Desired behavior may be produced by selectively reinforcing responses that gradually *approximate* or are a part of it.

6. Principle of Chaining
A procedure in which one operant response leads to another. The procedure involves a "linking" of the three-term operant paradigm (e.g. discriminative stimulus, response, reinforcement), which permits the development of a series of connected operants of indefinite length.

7. Principle of Social Reinforcement
Social reinforcement is the response contingent attention and/or approval of another person. When a given response meets with social reinforcement (positive reinforcement), it tends to increase in frequency. When a response is followed by withdrawal of social reinforcement (time-out from positive reinforcement), it tends to decrease in frequency.

8. Principle of Respondent Conditioning

Respondent behavior is stimulus-elicited behavior. When a neutral stimulus is paired with an unconditioned stimulus, the result is that after a number of pairings, the neutral stimulus will itself come to elicit the response formerly elicited only by the unconditioned stimulus.

9. Principle of Aversive Conditioning

When a positive stimulus (e.g. drinking alcohol) is repeatedly paired with an unconditioned aversive stimulus (e.g. electric shock), the result is that the positive stimulus will come to elicit the response formerly elicited by the aversive stimulus (avoidance behavior).

10. Principle of Reciprocal Inhibition

If a response inhibitory of anxiety can be made to occur in the presence of anxiety-evoking stimuli, it will weaken the bond between these stimuli and anxiety. In *systematic desensitization,* the response inhibitory of anxiety and usually complete relaxation and the anxiety provoking stimuli are the fears and phobias of the patient.

11. Principle of Counterconditioning

In autonomic, respondent emotional reactions, there are certain responses which are incompatible: if one occurs, the other is precluded. Counterconditioning is the process whereby a new conditioned response, which is incompatible with the conditioned response to be eliminated, is associated with the conditioned stimulus. If counterconditioning has been effected, the presentation of the conditioned stimulus will elicit the *new* conditioned response, rather than the original maladaptive conditioned response.

12. Principle of Implosive Therapy

A sufficient condition for the extinction of anxiety is to re-present, reinstate, or symbolically reproduce the stimuli (cues) to which the anxiety response has been conditioned, in the absence of primary reinforcement. If a conditioned stimulus (e.g. phobic object) is presented without an accompanying unconditioned stimulus (primary reinforcement), an intense emotional reaction (anxiety) will be generated; and, with repeated presentations of these anxiety-eliciting stimuli, the reaction will subside and cease altogether (extinction).

13. Principle of Negative Practice

Practicing a tic, stammer, or undesirable habit such as nail biting, over and over again, leads to the extinction of the response in the absence of the "unconditioned stimulus of anxiety." There is inhibition or fatigue associated with having made the response, so that performing the response may be painful and not performing it avoids an aversive situation, that is, becomes a positively reinforced behavior.

14. Principle of Assertive Training

It is hypothesized that anxiety and the *expression* of resentment are incompatible, so that if the person can assert himself, anxiety will be inhibited. With an unassertive patient, the behavior therapist provides the motivation by pointing out the irrationality of the fears and encouraging the individual to insist on his legitimate human rights by (a) reasoning with him, (b) by assigning tasks as part of a therapy program, or (c) through practice or role playing directly in the therapeutic situation.

15. Premack Principle

This principle states that if one behavior (e.g. watching television) is of higher probability than another behavior, (e.g. studying) then, for example, studying can be made more probable (i.e. to have a higher frequency) by making watching television contingent upon it.

16. Principles of Stimulus Deprivation and Satiation

The reinforcing properties of a stimulus may be manipulated by depriving a person of that stimulus (stimulus deprivation) or by making it so abundant that he becomes satiated.

17. Principle of Modeling and Imitation

Behavior may be learned simply as a function of *observing* the behavior of others and the consequences to their behavior without the observer's performing any overt responses himself or receiving any direct reinforcement during the acquisition period.

EXPERIMENTAL DESIGN

Well-designed behavior therapy is, by nature, experimental research as well as treatment; this has been lauded as one of its strongest points by its advocates. Claims of "science" and "rigor" are found in nearly every report of behavior therapy. Yet the design and evaluation of these therapies is often far from scientific or rigorous. Simply attaching the label "behavior therapy," or using a principle of learning in treatment does not mean the results are clear, replicable, or defensible as scientific. The early history of behavior therapy is replete with ill-controlled case studies or demonstration projects typically and yet ironically found in the kind of psychotherapy which research behavior therapy is said to replace. Patterson (1971) named that period the "whoopee phase" of behavior therapy and asked for its end. This calls for a few words on research design. Paul (1969, P. 35) suggests that "... there is really only one principle of design: the experiment should be designed so that the effects of the independent variables can be evaluated unambiguously." Paul went on to trace the history of behavior modification research as follows *(behavior modification* here used as an all-encompassing, generic term, referring to the total field of behavior influence and change) : (a) prior to 1920, the case study method appeared to be the *only* method; (b) the period from 1920 to the mid-1940's became the "demonstration era," when percentage of "successes" began to appear; (c) in the late 1940's, and related to World War II, the "scientific era" began and continued to the early 1960's with sophisticated methodology and evaluation; (d) the last stage, the "experimental era," started in the 1960's, with a firm methodological foundation and clarification of obstacles met in the past. Campbell and Stanley (1963) differentiate several experimental designs for research and go into considerable detail in exploring common threats to valid inference. The concern basically is whether or not the researchers can indeed make the treatment inferences they intend to, within the limitations of their research design. Campbell and Stanley described pre-experimental designs, true experimental designs, quasi-experimental designs, and correlational or ex post facto designs. The behavior therapy presented in this book will be evaluated, in part, by its place within these research designs and the inferential limitations thereof.

PRE-EXPERIMENTAL DESIGNS. The lowest level of pre-experimental design is the one-shot *case study,* in which an individual, or group of individuals receive a treatment and some observation is taken after treatment. Too often in psychotherapy research, especially in the psychiatric literature, this is the only design used. This kind of total absence of experimental control is almost of no scientific value, i.e. the research cannot say, within the limits of his casestudy design, that his treatment was causing the effect found, or even that there was *any* effect! Questions as elementary as, "How would these people do, had they not received this treatment," cannot be ignored. Somewhat better than that design, but still called a "bad example" by Campbell and Stanley, is the *one-group pretest—post-test design,* in which there is a measure before and after the treatment. Another pre-experimental design is the *static group comparison,* in which one group has a treatment and then is compared to another, which has none. There is one measure of comparison after the treatment. There is no measure suggesting that the groups were equivalent before the treatment.

TRUE EXPERIMENTAL DESIGNS. The two necessary aspects of true experimental designs, according to Campbell and Stanley are (a) randomized assignments to treatment groups and (b) the use of control groups. In the *pretest—post-test control group design,* subjects are randomly assigned to groups; one group receives the treatment; both groups are measured before and after. More complicated, but praised for its consideration of external validity, is the *Solomon four-group design.* Not only are the effects of the treatment determined, but so are the effects of the measures themselves. This is achieved by adding to the pretest—post-test design just described, an experimental and a control group lacking the pretest. The final true experimental design discussed by Campbell and Stanley is the *post-test only control group design.* There is randomization, which presumably assures lack of initial bias, and a control group. Campbell and Stanley neglected one important true experimental design—the *individual baseline design,* or *experimental analysis of behavior.* They neglected it perhaps because it was 1963 and this design is a relatively recent development, or perhaps because they were dealing mainly with research in education, although baseline designs are commonly used today in educational research. These individual baseline designs, best represented in *The Journal of the Experimental Analysis of Behavior,* and *The Journal of Applied Behavior Analysis* and thoroughly discussed by Sidman (1960, 1962), do demonstrate experimental control over behaviors within individual subjects. Many proponents of this approach vehemently disavow any need to rely on group data or statistics. Typically a measure of the behavior is made over several time-periods before any intervention is made and this is called a base-rate or baseline. An intervention is then made and its effect continually measured. The intervention is taken out and later replaced, to determine reversibility or true experimental control of the behavior by the intervention being manipulated.

QUASI-EXPERIMENTAL DESIGNS. These designs are used when full control over the scheduling of experimental stimuli is, for some reason, not possible. For example, in the *time-series experiment,* there is a periodic measurement and at some point an experimental change is introduced, while in the *equivalent time-sample design,* there is repeated introduction of the treatment along with repeated measurement. There are also a number of other quasi-experimental designs listed by Campbell and Stanley, but full discussion is beyond the limits of this introduction.

CORRELATION AND EX POST FACTO DESIGNS. Correlation literally means the degree to which two measures co-relate or co-vary. It is an index of how much the measures vary together. Correlation, however, does not imply causation, i.e. that one caused the other. As Campbell and Stanley point out though, when causation produces mean differences in experiments, this does imply correlation. In ex post facto designs, measures are made after the fact and then there is some attempt to go back and match subjects, as might be done by studying community success and then matching subjects from high-school records.

Experimental design, and the limits therein, must be considered when attempting any kind of treatment or program evaluation; this not only includes behavior therapy and psychotherapy, but also interventions like arrest, probation, and imprisonment. Without this kind of self-evaluation, we are left only to our guesses about the successes or failures of our programs. Curiously enough, these guesses are often considered "professional judgment," and even more alarming, are accepted as such. Does jail work? Does probation work? Does psychotherapy work? How do we know? And compared to what?

PREVIEW OF PART ONE

Part One of this book provides a further introduction to behavior therapy and airs some of the controversial issues surrounding its use in general and in particular with delinquents.

In Chapter 1, Shah presents an introduction to behavior therapy, especially as it applies to criminal offenders. He discusses some of the principles of learning and behavior modification. The reader is referred to Ullman and Krasner (1965, pp. 30-34) for a summary of fifteen major techniques. In general, Shah presents a positive and optimistic view of behavior therapy with delinquents.

The chapters by Holden and Kimbles are more critical of behavior therapy and are included in this volume in the hope of providing the reader with knowledge of some of the controversy surrounding behavior therapy. They effectively bring out some of the basic ethical, theoretical, and practical issues related to this particular form of the control of human behavior. Holden's paper (Ch. 2) was part of a symposium on behavior and aversion therapy in the treatment of delinquency, held at the Institute for the Study and Treatment of Delinquency, London, England, in 1964. In the first paper, Jones (1965) reviewed behavior modification techniques in general and suggested aversive conditioning as potentially relevant to the treatment of delinquents. For most of the specific techniques that he reviewed, Jones doubted the direct applicability to delinquency. Instead, new approaches might be designed for treating this group of individuals. It seemed that little such work had been done up to that time and no examples were cited. Gelder (1965), while addressing himself to what behavior therapy can contribute to the treatment of delinquency, concluded on a half-hearted note (p. 375) that "behavior therapy may find a small but important place" in treatment, and results are not so bad that the approach should be discarded. Gelder cited one research study, that of Tyler (1965). Holden, in the paper reproduced here, responded harshly to even the weak support given behavior therapy by Jones and Gelder. He did aptly criticize the earlier papers for skirting the actual subject of the conference: the treatment of delinqunets by these methods. A psychiatrist, Holden responded to these "dangerous goods" on ethical grounds. Terming aversion therapy a "highly refined form of torture," he went on to warn us of the horrors of *1984* and *Brave New World*. Holden found it too short a step from "pocket do-it-yourself superegos" to "Thought Police." Finally, Holden chose not to accept the "dangerous gift" of behavior therapy and excluded it from "medical matters" and even from the title "therapy."

Kimbles, in Chapter 3, specifically takes issue with the use of behavior therapy with black delinquents. Many of his points are valid and need further exploration. For example, Tracy (1971) recently found that mature behavior for whites and blacks may not be the same thing. The editor suggests that the decision-making process regarding what behavior is to be modified, does need to be examined. In many cases the target behaviors are, of course, defined by the courts (e.g. car stealing) and by other social agencies such as the school. But what about less well-defined "anti-social" behaviors such as those Kimbles discusses: manipulativeness, hustling, opportunism? Should these behaviors be modified in a ghetto delinquent? Who decides on the "should"—the behavior therapist, the court, the school, the probation officer, parents? If a black or disadvantaged delinquent were "modified" so that he later had white middle-class values (behaviors), what would happen to him when he returned to the ghetto? He might, in fact, be unable to cope within that soicety. His new behaviors, perhaps defined as *adaptive* by many of us, might actually be *maladaptive* when he returns home to his neighborhood. Behavior therapists must take into account the environment in which the youth lives, and Kanfer and Saslow (1965, 1969) have repeatedly stressed this point in their discussions of what constitutes a thorough behavioral analysis. It must include an analysis of the social milieu of the person. In one behavior therapy program, headed by Irwin Sarason in Seattle (Sarason, 1966), modeling techniques were used, in part, to teach the delinquents how to "manipulate" in contacts with police so as not to be arrested. (See Stumphauzer (1972) for a discussion of training in social manipulation.) The editor must take issue with the idea presented by Carkhuff and Berenson (1969) and Kimbles that shaping restricts the repertoire of the person. In fact, shaping is often employed to develop *new* behaviors *not* previously present in the person's repertoire, that is, *expanding* the behavioral repertoire. The number of behaviors is not specifically limited by shaping.

Since the advent of behavior therapy, the issues raised by Holden have been aired repeatedly and most often by those supporting a psychodynamic view. They are still heard today and Kimbles has here added some other social and therapeutic issues.

McConnell (1970) has pushed the case for behavior therapy even further in suggesting we use any and all methods available to us to "brainwash" the behavior of criminals. R.L. Schwitzgebel (1969) has even given us "a belt from a Big Brother," to monitor the behavior of delinquents from afar, and several years before 1984 at that! Many have attempted to answer the critics of behavior therapy. B.F. Skinner (1966), the founder and articulate leader of modern behaviorism, finds the center of conflict in the development of Western society. On the one hand, Western democracy has fostered the growth of a modern science of human behavior. On the other hand, the so-called "democratic philosophy" seems to dictate that this scientific knowledge *should not* be applied to human affairs. Skinner goes on to suggest, optimistically, that behavioral control is inevitable, desirable, and necessary if man is to control his world and finally himself. London (1970) finds that behavior therapists have really not yet had much large-scale control over the behavior of others, but we seem to be headed in that direction, and he suggests (p. 194) that "the moral imperative which confronts today's behavior modifiers is the recognition of the power which tomorrow will bestow." London ends his discussion of moral issues by suggesting that behavior modifiers are in a better position than most people to help search for a natural basis for morality. Morality with a basis in natural (scientific) events would presumably provide for the control of human behavior, and therefore behavior therapy. Skinner (1971), in *Beyond Freedom and Dignity*, suggests that we *are* under the control of the environment and should make full use of this reality by designing the culture we want. The prerequisite, according to Skinner, is that we abandon ". . . autonomous man—the inner man, the homunculus, the possessing demon, the man defended by the literatures of freedom and dignity . . . .Only then can we turn from the inferred to the observed, from the miraculous to the natural, from the inaccessible to the manipulable." (pp. 200-201) Skinner (1972) summarized his position by saying "control exists. . .the thing to do it to improve it."

The issue of control is dealt with in a different manner by

Bishop in her paper here (Ch. 4). One of the recurring criticisms of behavior therapy is that there is too great a reliance on external controls of others, that control needs to come from within the person and not from, as Kimbles states, the powerful other who manipulates from a distance. Bishop explores the idea that before *internal* or *self-control* can develop (and lack of self-control does seem a major problem in much of delinquency), first there must be *external* control. If delinquents do not have sufficient internal control ("conscience" or self-control), to stop their repeated antisocial behavior, then some societal (external) agent will step in to provide external controls on behavior—arrest, incarceration, probation, etc. Are these the most effective means available to develop self-control? Bishop raises serious doubt and suggests alternatives based in the principles of learning. I might add a personal observation to her discussion of the transitional period of control from external and internal. I am currently working with a twelve-year-old who could be termed a "predelinquent." In the months we have been working with him, we have seen many vivid examples of this transitory phase. He now says, "good boy" to himself and sometimes kisses his own hand when he has done something well; and at times when he has misbehaved, he not only says, "bad boy," but slaps his own face!

In the final chapter of this section, Burchard explores a few other important issues in the application of behavior therapy to delinquency. Through years of such work himself, Burchard has witnessed the phenomenal growth of behavior therapy, but here he expresses some serious second thoughts. His first concern is: what, in fact, constitutes behavior therapy. I would add to Burchard's discussion a concern often voiced over *who* is a behavior therapist. That is, a great many people—some of them apparently untrained and unqualified—call themselves behavior therapists. While there are some local and national organizations of behavior therapists (e.g. The Association for the Advancement of Behavior Therapy and the Behavior Therapy Research Society), there is currently no set of standards or legal regulation stipulating who is qualified to practice behavior therapy, or call themselves behavior therapists. Secondly, Buchard focuses on the particular manner in which behavior therapy should be applied with delinquents. Finally he explores the difficulty in achieving and demonstrating generalization of behavior therapy results. Increasingly, the *Journal of Applied Behavior Analysis* is focusing its attention on generalization (Donald Baer, personal communication, October 17, 1970). The results of Bishop and Stumphauzer (unpublished) suggest that one variable important in obtaining generalization is *awareness* (explicit instructions). Greater conditioning effects and generalization were found with a subject who was told specifically what the contingencies were. Also, Stumphauzer (Ch. 9) found generalization through the use of imitative learning. Awareness and observational learning may help in achieving generalization; further research on this key topic is needed.

REFERENCES

Arbuckle, D., and Litwack, L. A.: A study of recidivision among juvenile delinquents. *Federal Probation, 24:*44-46, 1960.

Bandura, A.: Psychotherapy as a learning process. *Psychological Bulletin, 58:* 143-159, 1961.

Bandura, A.: Behavioral psychotherapy. *Scientific American, 216:*2-8, 1967.

Bishop, B. R., and Stumphauzer, J. S.: Control of thumb-sucking by withdrawal and representation of television cartoons. Florida State University, unpublished manuscript.

California Bureau of Criminal Statistics: *California Criminal Justice Digest 1960-1970,* July, 1970.

Campbell, D. T., and Stanley, J. C.: *Experimental and Quasi-experimental Designs for Research.* Chicago, Rand McNally, 1963.

Clements, C. B., and McKee, J. M.: Programmed instruction for institutionalized offenders: contingency management and performance contracts. *Psychological Reports, 22:*957-964, 1968.

Coleman, A. D., and Baker, S. L.: Utilization of an operant conditioning model for the treatment of character and behavior disorders in a military setting. *American Journal of Psychiatry, 125:*1395-1403, 1969.

Gelder, M.: Can behavior therapy contribute to the treatment of delinquency? *British Journal of Criminology, 5:*365-376, 1965.

Gelfand, D., and Hartman, D.: Behavior therapy with children: a review and evaluation of research methodology. *Psychological Bulletin, 69:*204-215, 1968.

Gibbons, D. C.: *Delinquent Behavior.* Englewood Cliffs, New Jersay, Prentice-Hall, 1970.

Gordon, S.: Combined group and individual psychotherapy with adolescent delinquents. *Corrective Psychiatry and Journal of Social Therapy, 8*:195-200, 1962.

Grossberg, J.: Behavior therapy: a review. *Psychological Bulletin, 62*:73-88, 1964.

Hull, C. L.: *Principles of Behavior.* New York, Appleton-Century-Crofts, 1943.

Jones, H. G.: The techniques of behavior therapy and delinquent behavior. *British Journal of Criminology, 5*:355-365, 1965.

Kanfer, F. H., and Saslow, G.: Behavioral analysis: An alternative to diagnostic classification. *Archives of General Psychiatry, 12*:529-538, 1965.

Kanfer, F. H., and Saslow, G.: Behavioral diagnosis. In C. M. Franks (Ed.): *Behavior Therapy: Appraisal and Status.* New York, McGraw-Hill, 1969, 417-444.

Kennedy, R. F.: Halfway houses pay off. *Crime and Delinquency, 10*:4-7, 1964.

Krasner, L.: Behavior therapy. *Annual Review of Psychology, 22*:483-532, 1971.

London, P.: Moral issues in behavior modification. In R. H. Bradfield (Ed.): *Behavior Modification: The Human Effort.* San Rafael, California, Dimensions Publishing Company, 1970, 185-196.

McConnell, J. M.: Criminals can be brainwashed—now. *Psychology Today, 3*:14-18, 1970.

McCord, W., McCord, J., and Zola, I.: *Origins of Crime.* New York, Columbia University Press, 1959.

Menninger, K.: *The Crime of Punishment.* New York, Viking Press, 1968.

Patterson, G. R.: Recent trends in behavior modification with children. Paper given at Western Psychological Association Convention, San Francisco, April 23, 1971.

Paul, G. P.: Behavior modification research: Design and tactics. In C. M. Franks (Ed.): *Behavior Therapy: Appraisal and Status.* New York, McGraw-Hill, 1969, 29-62.

Pavlov, I. P.: *Conditioned Reflexes* Anrep, G. V., (Trans.), New York, Liveright, 1927.

Powers, E., and Witmer, H.: *An Experiment in the Prevention of Delinquency.* New York, Columbia University Press, 1951.

Prins, H.A.: Juvenile delinquency—the facts and what can be done about them. *Medical and Biological Illustration,19*:132-138, 1969.

Sarason, I. G.: Verbal learning, modeling, and juvenile delinquency. *American Psychologist, 23*:254-266, 1968.

Schwitzgebel, R. L.: A belt from big brother. *Psychology Today, 2*:45-47, 65, 1969.

Skinner, B. F.: *Science and Human Behavior.* New York, Macmillan, 1953.

Skinner, B. F.: Freedom and the control of men. In R. Ulrich, T. Stachnik, and J. Mabry (Eds.): *Control of Human Behavior*. Glenview, Illinois, Scott, Foresman, 1966, 11-20.

Skinner, B. F.: *Beyond Freedom and Dignity*, New York, Alfred A. Knopf, 1971.

Skinner, B. F.: The Trouble with Freedom. Lecture at University of California, Los Angeles, January 10, 1972.

Stumphauzer, J. S.: Training in social manipulation: The use of behavior therapy. *Crime and Delinquency, 18:*112-113, 1972.

Teuber, H., and Powers, D.: The effects of treatment of delinquents. *Research Publication of the Association of Nervous Mental Disorders, 31:* 139-147, 1951.

Tracy, J. J.: Personality Factors in Delinquent Boys: Differences between Blacks and Whites. Paper presented at Eastern Psychological Asosciation, April, 1971.

Tunley, R.: *Kids, Crime and Chaos: A World Report on Juvenile Delinquency*. New York, Dell, 1964.

Tyler, V. O.: Exploring the Use of Operant Techniques in the Rehabilitation of Delinquent boys. Paper read at American Psychological Association meeting, Chicago, 1965.

Ullman, L. P. and Krasner, L. (Eds.): *Case Studies in Behavior Modification*. New York, Holt, 1965.

Werry, J. S., and Wollershein, J. P.: Behavior therapy with children: a broad overview. *American Academy of Child Psychiatry Journal, 6:*346-370, 1967.

Chapter 1

SOME BASIC PRINCIPLES AND CONCEPTS OF BEHAVIOR MODIFICATION

SALEEM A. SHAH

T HIS DISCUSSION deals with some of the principles and concepts underlying treatment approaches described by the general term *behavior modification*. Some of the key terms and principles will be explained briefly and the conceptualization of behavior will also be discussed. No attempt will be made in this brief discussion to be exhaustive. Later presentations by the panel members will doubtless go into some specific uses of these principles and how they have been applied in certain correctional programs.

By *behavior modification* I refer to the application of principles derived from psychological learning theory to the treatment of maladaptive behaviors. There are two important aspects of this definition. First, the focus upon principles of learning as the basis for treatment methods. When we talk about learning, we refer broadly to the effects of experience upon the organism. There is the further implication that the behaviors referred to cannot be attributed to growth or temporary changes in the organism as a function of drugs or other organic factors. This by no means implies a dichotomy. There is much research which demonstrates that although organic variables may place certain constraints, learning can still take place. The basis of behavior modification, then, is a body of experimental work dealing with the relationship between changes in the environment and changes in the subject's response.

The second aspect of behavior modification is a clear focus

This chapter is from a paper given at the 97th Annual Congress of Corrections, Miami Beach, Florida, August 22, 1967. Reprinted with permission of the author.

upon behavior—whether the behavior is verbal or motor, whether it reflects immediate social needs, or is highly symbolic and idiosyncratic. The behavior should be definable, it should be amenable to observation by another person or by the experimenter's instruments.

The behavior therapist generally asks three main questions in starting a program of treatment: (a) what behavior is maladaptive, i.e. what are the behaviors displayed by the subject which need to be increased, decreased, or otherwise influenced; (b) what environmental factors *currently* maintain the behavior—either to support undesirable behavior or to reduce the likelihood of performing more adaptive responses; and (c) what environmental changes may be manipulated to influence the behavior.

Thus, if the concern is with strengthening the person's ego, we would need to know the behaviors which indicate poor ego functioning, and we also would need to be told what specific things the person would have to do differently in order for one to know that his ego had indeed been strengthened. In other words, we would need to have the concepts made specific and relevant to observable behavior. Likewise, if the concern is to bring about *emotional maturity* or *self-actualization,* we would again need to know what actual behaviors define these terms.

The above should not be taken to imply that treatment consists simply of changing specific and discrete aspects of behavior. Behavior is indeed complex and its modification typically involves addressing a large number of interrelated variables. Further, some degree of understanding and control of the variables influencing one's behavior (which can be one way of defining insight) may also be an element in behavior modification.

GOALS OF BEHAVIOR MODIFICATION WITH OFFENDERS

When treatment involves offenders, one of the main goals is to bring about a cessation of antisocial activities, and in addition, to develop more constructive personal and social adjustment. As implied earlier, the treatment goals could not be said to have been achieved if the period of treatment did no more than provide temporary control, supervision, and restraint for the deviant behavior.

In keeping with the previous requirement for explicit and behavioral criteria, the above treatment and rehabilitation goals could be further defined in terms of absence of law violations, more effective educational, occupational, social, and interpersonal functioning. To accomplish this, the offender will often need to develop a variety of skills in order to compete more adequately in a demanding societal setting.

The manner in which we conceptualize problems and various treatment tasks tends to determine to large extent the particular approaches and procedures used in the treatment and rehabilitative process. The type of intervention applied—be it intensive psychotherapy, remedial education, group counseling, vocational training, etc.—carries implications about the causes of the deviant behavior. If remedial education, firm discipline, and particular work assignments are seen as necessary treatment and rehabilitative needs, then the implication is that the lack of such skills was related directly or indirectly to the person's law violations and related problems. Certainly, there is some expectation that such procedures will influence the deviant behavior; else why use them. However, to the extent the treatment programs do not relate to some understanding of the determinants of the deviant behavior, no guidance is provided for treatment. "Treatment" then becomes a sort of umbrella word meaning all things to all people. It should be borne in mind that simply by labeling certain procedures as "treatment," we do not thereby make them therapeutic.

DEFINITION AND CONCEPTUALIZATION OF BEHAVIOR

Behavior is viewed as involving an interaction between an individual and a particular environment. Behavior is neither fixed nor absolute, and rarely does it involve only the individual. For example, one does not behave on the job as he does at church, at the New Year's party, the poker group, or in the privacy of the home. To varying degrees the environment influences and controls the kind of behavior displayed. It is not surprising, therefore, that certain offenders described as highly impulsive, explosive, and dangerous while they are in the community, may later be described as "model inmates" within the institution. Such observations concerning the variability of behavior are surprising only if one views behavior as a somewhat fixed and unchanging quality of the individual. A conceptualization of behavior which considers only the individual variables would appear then to be both inadequate and erroneous.

Since behavior represents an interaction between the individual and a particular environment, efforts at its modification have to be directed not only at the individual, but also to alterations of the environment. In contrast to the concern with presumed *intrapsychic* factors and with uncovering "causes" of the problem in the person's remote history as in some traditional therapies, behavioral approaches place great emphasis upon understanding the variables *currently* maintaining and influencing the behavior. Much emphasis is also placed upon control and manipulation of various aspects of the physical and social environment to bring about desired changes in behavior.

EVALUATION OF BEHAVIOR AND TREATMENT IMPLICATIONS

When we talk about behavior, to a very large extent we refer to learned behavior. Even when there is clear organic or similar involvement, learning is still very much involved, although within certain constraints. To a very large extent, behavior—be it deviant or adaptive—can be understood in terms of the complex learning principles involved. Maladaptive patterns of learned behavior may stem from certain distortions in the learning process and/or from various gaps or deficits in learning some basic skills.

The above conceptualization of behavior is also important in assessing the adequacy of a person's skills or reperatoire in coping with a particular situation. The person's behavior is inadequate or deficient in reference to some specific task or situation. Inadequacy of behavior, therefore, relates both to the available skills possessed by the individual and also to the complexity and demands of the situation (environment) in which he has to function. An individual may be able, for example, to function quite well as a farm hand in a rural setting, but may find it very difficult to find suitable employment and to function well in a more demanding urban community. Behavioral skills adequate to functioning as a farm hand will not be adequate when a high school education, certain verbal, mechanical, social skills, and more complex community environments are involved. Likewise, satisfactory performance as an athlete, automobile mechanic, dancer, or even as a "con artist," does not necessarily ensure adequate functioning in some different situations, for example, as a musician, carpenter, computer technician, or even as a husband. A college professor's behavioral repertoire, while most adequate in many academic, intellectual, and social situations, may nevertheless be quite inadequate when the task requires performing minor repairs on his automobile or television set. In the latter situations the professor may show exasperated and frustrated behavior. Similarly, the young man described as lazy, shiftless, lacking in ambition, and with low tolerance for frustration, may in certain other situations display a remarkable degree of patience, persistence, interest, and ingenuity, e.g. when working on his hotrod, training as a boxer or ballplayer, courting a girl, or planning a heist.

The absence of repertoires necessary to function adequately in some situations will elicit patterns of behavior related to nonreinforcement and frustration. The behavior may be quite different in situations for which the repertoires are adequate and certain reinforcements are assured.

SOME CHARACTERISTICS OF OPERANT BEHAVIOR

There is a broad range of behavior which has the characteristic of being influenced by its consequences. Particular consequences tend to bring about rather predictable changes in the rate, frequency, and other features of the behavior. For example, if Johnny's whining results in obtaining mother's attention, then this consequence may tend to maintain or even increase the whining. Scolding may at times serve as a consequence which maintains the whining, since in order to scold attention has also to be given. On the other hand, if the whining provokes mother to provide prompt punishment, such as sending Johnny to his room, then such a consequence when consistently applied may decrease the behavior. However, it may be that mother's attention—be it positive or negative—is in some way rewarding to Johnny. In this instance certain forms of punishment may also have no effect on the whining. It could then be that the absence of any response, i.e. completely ignoring the whining, when used consistently may decrease and possibly eliminate the behavior.

It can be seen that even in this obviously simple aspect of behavior, differing consequences tend to have varying effects on the behavior. Much of our behavior is influenced in rather complex fashion by the consequences we experience. Unpleasant or negative consequences tend to decrease the particular behavior they follow, whereas positive or pleasant consequences tend to maintain or increase the behavior. Behavior which has the characteristic of being influenced by its consequences is referred to as *operant behavior.*

Considerable research has been conducted over the past several years to determine how, to what degree, and under what particular set of circumstances, behavior can be influenced and modified by various consequences. Such studies suggest that the social environment plays a major role in shaping and maintaining patterns of behavior—both deviant and adaptive.

It seems often to be assumed that operant behavior is concerned simply with the use of rewards and punishments. In other words, the old and established *law of effect* which was discussed in psychological learning theory several decades ago. This is not correct. Indeed, viewing operant behavior as involving only rewards and punishments is not only a gross oversimplification, but it may also be considered a simple-minded approach to the complex problem of behavior modification.

The operant paradigm has to do with a number of different and complex variables. These include the following:

Contingency rules. These define and provide prior instructions as to the consequences which will follow certain behaviors.

Consequences. These may be reinforcing, punishing, or have no effect whatsoever.

Potentiating Variables. These are variables such as satiation and deprivation which make consequences more or less effective. For example, in order to use food, candy, praise or some other consequence as a reinforcer, there should be some deprivation of them. That is, to make a consequence gain effectiveness as a reinforcer some deprivation may have to be used; to make the consequence lose effectiveness some satiation may be used. We may find, then, that the old saying that you can take a horse to water but you cannot get him to drink, is not necessarily correct. If the horse were fed salt, or allowed to stand in the sun and went without water for a while, one could indeed get him to drink.

Discriminative Events. These determine which particular events will have what sorts of effects upon behavior. For example, a green traffic light allows the discrimination to be made that it is all right to proceed, while a red light directs one to come to a stop. Such influence of the environment upon behavior is also referred to as *stimulus control*. Likewise, father's presence may signify to a child that certain behaviors cannot take place, while grandmother's visit may indicate that whining will be most effective in eliciting desired consequences. Similarly, the ringing bell of the ice-cream man is the discriminative event for bugging mother to buy some ice cream.

Schedules of Reinforcement. These schedules determine what rate and manner is to be used for providing reinforcements. Much research has been done on the several reinforcement schedules which have been discovered, and it can be shown that particular schedules of reinforcement have rather different and characteristic patterns in regard to the durability, frequency, rate, and persistence of the behavior, and also the amenability of the behavior to extinction and other change.

Constant Conditions. Behavior is extremely sensitive to conditions under which it has been established. Thus if these constant conditions are changed, e.g. if noise is suddenly presented or the physical characteristics of the room are changed, there may be disruption of the behavior.

This presentation obviously cannot go into all the variables involved in operant behavior. However, the variables related to *consequences* will be described and their effects indicated.

The consequences to which behavior is exposed may be of three broad kinds: *reinforcement, punishment,* or *extinction,* i.e. no consequence at all.

For an event to be defined as *reinforcing,* it must meet two specific criteria: (a) it must be made contingent upon a particular response, i.e. it will not occur unless the specified behavior occurs, and (b) it must maintain or increase the response that produced it. This would be an example of *positive reinforcement,* such as when Johnny cuts the grass and is rewarded with a dollar.

There is also another form of reinforcement. In this instance some aversive or punishing effects are removed, contingent upon some particular response. For example, when Johnny completes his homework, he is then allowed to leave his room. In this instance, the rewarding consequence, i.e. removing an unpleasant experience, is referred to as *negative reinforcement.*

For an event to be defined as *punishment* it must again meet two specific criteria: (a) it must be made contingent upon a particular response, and (b) it should decrease or otherwise weaken the behavior it follows.

Punishment is also of two types. In the first type, the negative consequence, such as a fine, restriction to the room, or spanking, is made contingent upon some behavior. In the second type, there is removal of some positive and pleasant experience contingent upon a particular response, i.e. fighting by the children may result in the television being turned off.

It can also be arranged that a response which previously had produced a consequence now produces no consequence. Such an absence of any consequence, i.e. having the response achieve no effect upon the environment, defines *extinction.*

It is very important to remember that for a consequence (reinforcing or punishing) to be effective, it should follow rather closely the response or behavior upon which it has been made contingent, i.e. which is to be influenced. There is a general principle which states that other things being equal, *behavior is as shapeable as the consequences are immediate.* Thus the desired effects of a consequence may indeed be lost if the element of timing and related aspects of contingencies are not considered.

Consequences as defined above may have very diverse effects depending upon such factors as their intensity and timing, the certainty of the reinforcement or punishment, the nature and strength of the response being influenced, the schedule of reinforcement being used, and other related variables. Failure to consider these critical factors may well thwart the effectiveness of otherwise sound reinforcement principles. Such situations can lead to erroneous beliefs about the value of the principles involved.

Another very important point to remember about the aforementioned reinforcing and punishing consequences is that they are defined in terms of the *actual behaviors*—not in terms of the *intentions* of the persons governing the consequences. Thus, even though a certain consequence, such as scolding, spanking, or a jail sentence, may be intended as a punishment, if the behavior shows no change the procedure could not be defined as punishment, at least as the term is used in operant terminology. It may also be that quite the opposite terms may be applied depending upon whether the *intentions* or the *consequences* are used for purposes of the definition. For example, a mother's spanking may be defined as punishment since she has punitive intentions and wishes to decrease certain behavior in the child. If, however, the behavior is not so affected, but rather is being maintained by such a consequence, then such operant behavior would actually have to be defined as *reinforcing* despite the clearly punitive intentions of the mother. (It should be noted that for purposes of explaining the above concepts, the examples used are being simplified. Often, even in these seemingly simple cases, a number of variables may be involved and would have to be considered.)

Let me at this point make another important clarification. Since the term "punishment" has popular, philosophical, technical, and other usage, and since discussion of such matters often involves both empirical and ideological aspects, is should clearly be understood that the discussion here is strictly in terms of technical and empirical considerations. Whether or not and under what specific circumstances consequences defined as reinforcing and punishing have certain observable effects, is a scientific and empirical issue. However, regardless of the demonstrated effectiveness of such principles, whether or not they are to be used by society is an important ideological and social policy issue. The point to be kept in mind is that discussion and thinking which tend to confuse empirical considerations and ideological considerations can rarely lead to clarification and clear understanding of the issues.

It should be evident that the above discussion of consequences and their effects upon behavior has obvious relevance to the broad efforts at social regulation of behavior sought by our system of laws, law enforcement, the administration of justice, and of course, our correctional programs. To the extent that such applications are based upon insufficient understanding and knowledge of the principles governing behavior, or if the principles cannot effectively be applied, such efforts are bound to have only limited success.

THE SHAPING OF BEHAVIOR

A general principle which has long been used by skillful teachers, coaches, parents, therapists and others in modifying behavior can technically be referred to as the method of *successive approximation*. In using this method, one has to start with the existing level of performance and then proceed in small steps toward the desired goal, making sure that each step is within reach of the person. The gradation of steps chosen is one designed to almost eliminate failure. Each appropriate or correct move toward the goal is provided prompt external or *extrinsic reinforcements*— such as points, candy, praise, approval, etc. Such evident progress toward the goal and successful achievement may also generate internal or *intrinsic reinforcements* for the individual himself, viz., pride, satisfaction at his accomplishment, a feeling of success, etc.

Educational, rehabilitative and therapeutic efforts have to be carefully adjusted to meet the needs of the particular individuals, and there has to be full awareness of their existing level of functioning. Likewise, lack of interest, motivation, poor work habits, etc. have to be accepted as very much part of the behavioral deficits of certain individuals. Often, we may find that the serious difficulties posed by the client's poor motivation for treatment may further be compounded by equally poor motivation on the part of therapists.

Rather than expecting many correctional clients to bring with them a "love of learning," a thirst for knowledge, a strong desire to rehabilitate themselves, or a ready response to one's desire to help, we need to search for reinforcers which may effectively motivate such persons. Thus, as in the CASE Project, a token economy in the form of a point system and a variety of other extrinsic reinforcers can be used as powerful motivating and reinforcing variables. Gradually, generalized social reinforcers, such as praise, warmth, and encouragement, can also be developed as well as the intrinsic reinforcements, such as pride in passing examinations, getting good grades, experiencing success, and pleasant feelings in noting one's accomplishments.

The point system in the CASE Project was perhaps one of the most important reinforcers for at least two reasons. First, it was firmly imbedded in a complex, well-organized, and controlled system in which various other operant principles were also being used. Secondly, the points could be exchanged for a variety of goods and reinforcers; in short, the points were equivalent to money.

Money is a powerful generalized reinforcer. A generalized reinforcer is one not specifically related to a particular need, but which can be used to obtain a variety of other reinforcements which have meaning and relevance for the particular individual —be they cigarettes, candy, soft drinks, clothes, books, or other purchasable items or services. Money does indeed provide a strong motivation for people to work and can influence a great deal of behavior. Ogden Nash expressed this rather well in one of his couplets when he remarked:

I could spend my life in ease and insouciance,
Were it not for making a living, which is rather a nuisance.

As was noted earlier, operant procedures are not synonymous with behavior modification. Nor is all behavior operant in its characteristics. However, operant procedures have particular relevance for correctional programs, especially institutional programs, because they can most effectively be used where a good deal of environmental control is possible. And where, might one ask, do we have more opportunities for environmental control than in our penal institutions?

Other Behavior Modification Approaches

In addition to the use of operant methods derived in large measure from learning theories originally formulated by B.F. Skinner and his associates, other forms of behavior therapy have applied learning principles derived from Hullian theory and from classical, Pavlovian, or *respondent conditioning*. Wolpe (1958) is perhaps the foremost exponent of a number of therapeutic techniques using respondent conditioning, or counter-conditioning principles. These methods are appropriate for treating the conditions most frequently seen in conventional interview-therapy situations: anxiety reactions, chronic tensions, inhibitions, phobias, psychosomatic reactions, and certain sexual problems. While many of these techniques have generally been used in a one-to-one treatment situation, work has also been done in group settings.

Another related behavior modification approach focuses more upon social-learning principles. It has been found that by providing an appropriate model, the learning process can distinctly be accelerated. Thus, in addition to using some of the aforementioned operant and respondent principles, the desired behavior is also modeled for the client. Bandura (1964, 1967), who has done the most work in this particular area, has found that even long-standing phobias can often be eliminated by having the person observe a graduated sequence of modeled activities beginning with presentations that are easily tolerated.

Conceptualization of the Treatment Tasks

In dealing with many inmates of correctional institutions we are faced with persons who have serious behavioral deficits. Often such behavioral deficits represent the cumulative effects of a variety of environmental deficiencies during the development and socialization process. The behavioral deficits in their repertoires may lead to serious problems in coping with many social situations. Unable to influence the environment because of the absence of socially acceptable repertoires, alternate skills may be developed which do influence the environment although through antisocial behaviors.

A large part of the treatment objectives, therefore, will be concerned with developing skills which could assist in prosocial functioning. The rehabilitative and treatment programs implicit in the conceptualization being discussed relate to an educational or learning model, rather than to a medical model of treatment.

In considering the behavior modification tasks with persons handicapped because of various deficits, certain concepts used in physical rehabilitation and education seem very relevant. We need to develop special devices such as teaching machines, specially designed curricula, programmed texts, social curricula, devices such as Moore's "talking typewriter" (1965) , and other items of educational technology. Such developments can be viewed as *prosthetic devices* to be used in working with persons having educational, vocational, and related handicaps.

Likewise, in working with the physically handicapped, much use is made of *prosthetic training* in order to enable persons to acquire skills which would help them function more effectively in the average physical environment. Examples of such prosthetic training techniques are lipreading and piano feeling for the totally deaf and cane tapping for the blind. Special educational, vocational, and other rehabilitative programs used in correctional and therapeutic settings may be viewed as examples of prosthetic training for persons with handicaps in these areas. Certainly, counseling, psychotherapy, and related procedures attempt to provide training for persons with problems in social, interpersonal areas.

In cases where the physical handicaps are fairly severe and/or cannot otherwise be handled, it may become necessary to provide special environments—*prosthetic environments*—designed to compensate for deficits and/or to facilitate more effective functioning during the training process. Thus, Braille and recorded books and magazines for the blind, standardized traffic light positions and light intensities for the color blind, and special ramps adjacent to steps for persons using wheelchairs, are examples of prosthetic modifications of the physical environment for persons with certain handicaps.

With many segments of our population of incarcerated law violators, it often may be necessary, in order to protect the community and also to facilitate their rehabilitation, to conduct the behavior modification programs within specially designed environments. In such environments the particular tasks have to be very carefully graduated, the reinforcements and their scheduling made optimal, and other variables and contingencies so arranged as to maximize the acquisition of complex skills.

GENERALIZATION OF BEHAVIOR

Since the ultimate social criteria for evaluating the effectiveness of correctional programs relate to the actual functioning of the individual in the community after release, it is most essential that the modification of behavior achieved in the institution be generalized to the free social environment. Therefore, the task for correctional institutions is not only to remove major behavioral deficits and to correct distorted patterns of behavior, but also to strengthen the new behaviors so that they can be maintained in the face of drastic changes in the environment, weak and uncertain reinforcement schedules, and a number of other stressful and disruptive influences in the community.

A variety of behavioral principles can be used to gradually strengthen the newly learned skills so as to make them persistent and capable of being maintained with minimal environmental reinforcement. Most essential to such generalization of changes to the community are a variety of facilities for carefully graduating the release process, and also for providing a wide range of follow-up and other services in the community.

CONCLUSION

Behavior modification approaches certainly are not the only ones in use. Nor can it be said that they are the only useful procedures. However, in the final analysis one could say that all methods of therapy are behavioral since the client's behavior—broadly defined to include the conceptual, emotional and motor expressions—is the only reality the therapist can deal with and modify. While many of the procedures discussed are not entirely new, what is fairly new are the developments in the experimental analysis of behavior, the controlled and experimental research through which such principles have been refined, and the systematic formulation of such findings into testable and scientific theory. Such research and related technological developments are designed to provide precise information which can be added to the body of scientific knowledge about human behavior. In the final analysis, the assessment of these and any other treatment approaches has to be made in the light of further experience, careful evaluation, and continued research to improve and further develop procedures which have scientific merit and demonstrated effectiveness.

REFERENCES

Bandura, A. and Walters, R. H.: *Social Learning and Personality Development.* New York, Holt, Rinehart & Winston, 1964.

Bandura, A.: Behavioral psychotherapy. *Scientific American,* March, 1967.

Burchard, J. and Tyler, V.: The modification of delinquent behavior through operant conditioning. *Behavior Research and Therapy,* 2:245-250, 1965.

Cohen, H. L., Filipczak, J. A. and Bis, J. S.: CASE Project: Contingencies Applicable to Special Education. Progress Report, August, 1965 (mimeo).

Cohen, H. L.: Educational Therapy. Paper presented at Third Conference on Research in Psychotherapy. Chicago, June, 1966.

Eysenck, H. J.: *Crime and Personality.* Boston, Houghton Mifflin, 1964.

Eysenck, H. J. (Ed.): *Experiments in Behavior Therapy.* Oxford, Pergamon Press, 1964.

Gilmore, C. P.: Omar Khayyam and his talking typewriter. *The Saturday Evening Post,* Nov. 20, 1965.

Goldiamond, I.: Justified and unjustified alarm over behavior control. In Milton, O. (Ed.): *Behavior Disorders: Perspectives and Trends.* Philadelphia, Lippincott, 1965.

Holland, J. G. and Skinner, B. F.: *The Analysis of Behavior.* New York, McGraw-Hill, 1961.

Krasner, L. and Ullmann, L. H. (Eds.): *Research in Behavior Modification.* New York, Holt, Rinehart & Winston, 1965.

McKee, J. H.: The Draper Experiment: a programmed learning project. In Ofiesh, G. D. and Meierhenry, W. C. (Eds.): *Trends in Programmed Instruction.* National Education Association, 1964.

Patterson, G. R. *et al.:* A behavior modification technique for the hyperactive child. *Behavior Research and Therapy, 2:*217-226, 1965.

Schwitzgebel, R. and Kolb, D. A.: Inducing change in adolescent delinquents. *Behavior Research and Therapy, 1:*297-304, 1964.

Schwitzgebel, R.: *Streetcorner Research.* Cambridge, Harvard University Press, 1964.

Shah, S. A.: Treatment of offenders: some behavioral concepts, principles and approaches. *Federal Probation,* June, 1966.

Shah, S. A.: Preparation for Release and Community Follow-up. Lectures given at the CASE Training Institute, National Training School for Boys, Washington, D.C. January, 1967 (mimeo).

Skinner, B. F.: *Science and Human Behavior.* New York, Macmillan, 1953.

Ullman, L. H. and Krasner, L. (Eds.): *Case Studies in Behavior Modification.* New York, Holt, Rinehart & Winston, 1965.

Wolpe, J.: *Psychotherapy by Reciprocal Inhibition.* Stanford, Calif., Stanford University Press, 1958.

Chapter 2

SHOULD AVERSION AND BEHAVIOUR THERAPY BE USED IN THE TREATMENT OF DELINQUENCY

H. M. HOLDEN

AFTER HEARING THE previous two speakers, many people will, I suspect, be feeling that there is really no ethical problem left to discuss. You will perhaps be saying that provided the motives of the therapist are all right, and provided one is reasonably human in dealing with one's patients, having respect for his dignity as a person, there is no problem left. I want to disagree with this view profoundly and try to demonstrate what seem to me to be very important problems indeed.

The trouble is that Mr. Gwynne Jones and Dr. Gelder are obviously such intelligent, reasonable and humane men that one could overlook certain aspects of the problem on the assumption that if *they* felt it was all right, then it must be all right. I find this rather disquieting; my fear is that their reasonableness and humanity have cloaked the real nature of the goods they are selling, and we do not appreciate how potentially dangerous these goods are. Perhaps our discussion so far has been a little too reasonable. I must warn you that I intend to hurl a few bricks.

I should like to bring several points to your notice about what has been said:

(1) Both the speakers skirted round the actual subject of the conference—namely, the treatment of delinquency. This was raised in the discussions later, but the topic as a whole has been by-passed.

Reprinted with permission from *British Journal of Criminology*, 5:377-387, 1965. (Institute For The Study And Treatment Of Delinquency.)

(2) Sexual deviations are *not* for the most part offences against the law. Transvestism and fetishism as such are not considered crimes, neither is homosexuality between women, and it may very well happen—if the Wolfenden Report is ever implemented—that homosexuality between men will not be either.

(3) The general assumption running through the whole conference so far is that the aim of medical psychiatric treatment is the modification of behaviour. I find this a highly questionable assumption.

(4) It has been *assumed* that delinquency and sexual deviation constitute an illness—like measles or typhoid—and that the treatment is therefore a medical responsibility. Again, I question this assumption.

(5) What is so interesting is that, having taken on this responsibility, we now find ourselves adopting the same old traditional methods of reward and punishment, albeit in a sophisticated form, as have been used for generations. We crept into this field under the banner of medical scientific objectivity and humanity; medicine was going to sweep away all the horrifying abuses of power and of the penal system. Psychiatrists have indeed come to be looked on as the priests of the twentieth century, the omniscient and omnipotent, with an answer to all legal and penal problems, and we have tended rather smugly and without counting the cost to accept this role—in the courts, for example. Yet what in fact do we come up with?—"aversion therapy." Whatever way you look at it, this is punishment—and in its extreme form a highly refined form of torture.

Undoubtedly delinquency causes suffering to others, and this is one of the main reasons why we feel we ought to do something about it. It is not, I suspect, the only reason. The idea of "punishment" of some kind is never very far from the idea of delinquency. I do not think there is any logical reason why delinquents should be punished, though there may be excellent psychological reasons. It may indeed be very "good" for them on occasions, but nevertheless I have the feeling that one of our main motives in punishing wrongdoers is a personal one—it is the thought that here are people who are not controlling their impulses to steal, destroy, etc., and are getting away with it. Why should they be allowed to? We have the same impulses ourselves, only during the course of our upbringing we have succeeded, often with great pain and difficulty, in controlling them. To see others clearly not controlling these same impulses is a great threat to our own stability; so we have to punish them to show them—*and ourselves*—that "you can't get away with it," that "crime doesn't pay," etc.

If I am right about these points, then we will have to tread very warily indeed. This really is an explosive topic, and none of us can be free of prejudice about it—certainly I myself am not; all I can claim is that I am to a limited extent aware of my own prejudices.

I, as a psychiatrist and doctor, am supposed to have some *psychiatric* experience in the "treatment" of offenders by medical means. I have no other special qualifications; I am not trained in the law, in moral philosophy, or in religious or spiritual matters, and I have no expert knowledge on these topics. I of course have views and prejudices on such matters which, I hope, guide my own personal life, but I am not going to discuss these views here; they are not a part of my expertise.

Now as I see it, my role as a doctor is quite clear: it is to attempt to relieve the suffering of my individual patients—*full stop*. Of course, as a doctor I have a duty to society as we all have, but in my view this is a duty which is secondary to my primary medical role, which is concerned with individuals. This is what I have been trained in, and in fact I do not think these roles are incompatible.

I should like to consider further some of the logical implications of our work as psychiatrists with delinquents. I should like to consider the logical justifications which we make use of as doctors for embarking on this kind of work at all. Inevitably anyone who thinks seriously about this subject has to come to terms with Lady Barbara Wootton, whose book *Social Science and Social Pathology* provides such a devastating attack on psychiatry and psychiatrists in this field. She has followed this up with another broadside, "The Law, The Deviant and The Doctor," published in the *British Medical Journal;* (1963). and as always she deserves to be taken extr.emely seriously. I personally have to agree with almost everything she says and with nearly every criticism she levels at us, and what I am going to say next is only an inferior re-hash of her ideas.

I think that most people would agree that the broad basis on which psychiatry rests at present (whether it be organically or analytically orientated) is the idea that there is such an entity as "mental illness" and that mentally disturbed individuals are "sick" in a similar sense to the way physically ill people are sick. The corollary to this is that there is such an entity as "mental health" towards which, presumably, we are all striving. The great difficulty about this concept, as Lady Wootton points out, is that mental health and mental illness are extraordinarily difficult to define, except in a circular way, and that very few of the enormous number of definitions in existence (Lady Wootton quotes page after page of them in her book) agree with each other. All of them also, either overtly or covertly, contain within themselves the value judgments of their authors, in spite of the attempt made to wrap them up in scientific-sounding language. Now I am sure that this is true. We all of us disapprove of, for instance, obsessional neurosis, or schizophrenia, because of their nuisance value. We may also feel very sorry for those who are suffering from these conditions, but we cannot be oblivious to the nuisance value.

When it comes to "mental health" we are in difficulties. Either we can define it as freedom from these conditions or else in some positive way as some ideal state. If we choose the latter, then all we are doing is to air our own particular prejudices—our own personal view of what a "healthy man" ought to be, and generally I think we succeed in creating our God in our own image. If we choose the former way, that is, the absence of pathological mental conditions, then we have to define for ourselves just where to draw the line between what we consider pathological and what we consider normal.

This is difficult in two ways. First of all, if like me, you believe that we are all more or less mad, then you have to decide at what point medical intervention should be regarded as advisable; secondly, you have to decide what kinds of deviation—either from the norm or from some ideal standard of your own—you are going to regard as "pathological," whatever that may mean, and as necessitating medical intervention rather than any other kind, say educational or penal. How are you going to make this decision? What criteria have you to go on?

Let us turn specifically to delinquency. Are we not all delinquent at times? Who has never broken the speed limit or fed a parking meter? What kinds of delinquency do you consider as justifying medical intervention—as constituting "illness" in a patient? Furthermore, the law may change; indeed, if the Wolfenden Report is ever implemented, homosexuality between consenting adults will no longer be considered delinquency. What criteria are we going to use to decide whether a given individual is ill or whether he is just plain wicked, whether he is well enough to receive punishment or ill enough to receive treatment? What a terrible moral responsibility we incur if we really do take it upon ourselves to decide such questions. As Lady Wootton says: "I have never found, either in the records of court proceedings or in literature, any convincing demonstration that an intelligible distinction between psychopathy and wickedness can be drawn in terms of any meaningful concept of moral or criminal responsibility."

The difficulty, Lady Wootton believes, arises from our belief that mental health is as clearly definable and scientific a concept as is physical health, and that mental illnesses are equivalent to physical illnesses; she shows, to my mind conclusively, that this is not the case. Homosexual activity is perhaps the best example: surely it is nonsense to believe that the presence or absence of "illness" can be controlled by Act of Parliament.

> In other words, when the medical profession embarks upon the treatment or rehabilitation of offenders, do we not need to ask ourselves what exactly is the disease to be treated and what is the hallmark of cure? It would be rash indeed to answer those questions by equating criminality with mental disorder and cure with willingness to

keep the law. But no pass from the ridiculous to the seriously controversial, what are we to say about homosexuality? Not only do many homosexuals absolutely refuse to regard themselves as sick (an opinion, moreover, which is shared by many of their sympathizers), but the view is also widely held that homosexual acts committed by consenting adults in private ought not to be criminal. We can hardly argue that a homosexual or any other offender qualifies as a medical case merely by virtue of the fact that he is liable to be convicted under the present law. Indeed, any attempt to identify criminality and illness is reduced to utter nonsense by the fact that the criminal law is not the same today as yesterday. It is constantly being chopped and changed about as Parliament in its wisdom may decide. Incest, for example, was not a crime until 1908, and attempted suicide has recently ceased to be criminal; but it would obviously be absurd to infer that in consequence of these legal changes the incestuous have passed into, and the would-be suicides out of, the category of sick persons. Definitions of illness can hardly be made to hang on the vagaries of the criminal law." (Wootton, *op. cit.*)

Now if indeed there is no such thing as mental illness and no such thing as mental health, then we ought surely to be aware of the fact and to consider very carefully, indeed precisely, what we do mean when we talk of "treatment," "therapy" or "cure" for "mental illness." And we ought to be particularly careful when we consider the application of our treatment to those sections of the community whose so-called "illness" consists of behavior which is offensive to the rest of us—either because we do not approve of it (e.g. homosexuality) or because of its nuisance value (e.g. stealing).

If as doctors we assume this responsibility, then we must be aware of the immensity of the step that we are taking—of the tremendous moral responsibility we are taking upon ourselves— and we must consider very carefully on what grounds we feel justified in taking it, because once taken it is likely to be irrevocable. We have to realize that we are making a moral judgment on our patients. Now this is something quite outside the normal role of a doctor. Indeed we have until now prided ourselves on being free from this kind of restraint; we are outside morals, not above or below them. "The doctor, therefore, who undertakes the psychiatric treatment of offenders is not quite like a doctor, or even a psychiatrist, elsewhere. His function is not just that of attending to the mental and physical illnesses of people who happen to be inside, in the same way as those same people would expect to be attended to outside. He has in effect become an agent of the State —part of the machinery of law enforcement. Such a change would perhaps have shocked Hippocrates. Certainly it is too profound a revolution to be allowed to slip by unnoticed. If the profession is to assume what are essentially corrective rather than therapeutic functions, it is surely important that this should be done openly, and not by any specious pretense that the two categories are indistinguishable" (Wootton, p. 200). If we make these moral judgments, then on what basis do we make them? Our own personal system of ethical values? or that of society as laid down by the law? If the former, then we do indeed lay ourselves wide open to attack. If the latter, then we are adopting the role of law enforcement officers, like policemen or prison officers. Do we want this role?

In my view a lot of the confusion arises because of our assumption that mental and physical disabilities are of necessity equivalent. Here I would go even further than Lady Wootton. Many people, if asked what doctors were for, would answer, "to cure illness"—just as everyone here seems to have assumed that our function as psychiatrists is to modify behavior. Now I do not believe either of these concepts is valid. There are in fact no such "things" as illnesses. There are only sick and suffering individuals. The concept of an "illness," a "disease," is a highly sophisticated abstraction. We have adopted it as perhaps the most valuable tool we have when dealing with organic physical illnesses. We can bring a certain amount of scientific objectivity into our work by doing so, and all the advances of modern medicine rest on this abstraction being a valid one. Nevertheless our role as doctors is not primarily to "cure illness"; it is to relieve the suffering of individuals.

Now there is no logical reason why this same intellectual abstraction (the concept of an illness) should apply to mental disturbance, and I think a lot of confusion has resulted from attempts to so apply it. Indeed the behaviorists have openly abandoned the concept. They say "there is no such thing as a neurosis; there are only symptoms due to faulty learning. Our job therefore is to modify their learning patterns to bring them into line" —but into line with what? With the law? With our own private system of ethics? What else?

I should like to go back to what I said a moment before. The task of a doctor is to relieve the suffering of individuals. If a habitual criminal complained to a surgeon of abdominal pain and was diagnosed as suffering from appendicitis, the surgeon would be justified in removing his appendix to relieve his pain. Would he be justified also in cutting off his hands to prevent him stealing as well—even if he *did* have the patient's consent to do so? Would this be the kind of responsibility that he would want to assume?

I am considerably disturbed by certain aspects of what I heard yesterday. It sounds only too like *1984* or *Brave New World*. Do we really have the right to assume control over our patient's "input" or will power by means of hypnosis? Do we think it is right to provide him with a pocket "do-it-yourself superego" in order to control his fantasies? It is only a very short step from this to the idea of "thought control," and perhaps "thought police" and "thought crime" as envisaged by George Orwell. I am far from happy when I hear that "only very co-operative patients" are suitable for this kind of treatment. What kind of a patient can he be that would be willing to abrogate the responsibility even for his own thoughts, to hand over this control to us? And what kind of people are we that we should want to assume this control over other people?

It is this assumption of omnipotence on our part that I find profoundly disquieting. I should like to take up with the behaviorist the question of his own counter-transference when administering shocks to his patients. I do not find the suggestion that it should be done by a machine at all satisfactory. It is *his* responsibility—*he* is doing this to his patient. If he feels it is wrong, then perhaps he should question himself as to whether the whole method is wrong, rather than hand over responsibility to an impersonal machine. The same problem arises when one considers capital punishment. I find it illogical that we should delegate to a professional hangman a job that we would not do ourselves because we would not like to sully our hands with such a dirty and degrading task. If it is wrong for *us* to do it then surely it is equally wrong for the hangman to do it, or for a machine to do it. The fact that a machine has taken over does not relieve us of the responsibility—we in fact *are* the hangmen. So, too, Modern behaviorists can ignore the sufferings of their animal subjects.

Now as a psychiatrist I have one tool to help me, in which I place all my faith. It is my ability to understand my patient's problems and my belief that if I can help my patient to understand his own problems he will then be in a better position to resolve his own difficulties and relieve his own suffering. Without this understanding I am useless.

Let us suppose now that I am approached by four patients who question me in the four ways which follow:

1. "Doctor, I am utterly miserable—my life is made hell by my mother-in-law; if only I could murder her I know I would be happy, but I lack the courage. Would you please help me to gain the courage to do it?"
2. "Doctor, I am a homosexual. I am perfectly contented to remain this way, indeed a change would be unthinkable, but recently I have become impotent; would you help me to recover my potency?"
3. "Doctor, I have an uncontrollable urge to steal—I know I shall soon be caught and sent to prison. Would you help me to overcome my impulse?"
4. "Doctor, I am terrified of going into the streets. I have a feeling of blind panic as soon as I go out of the front door. Could you help me to overcome this fear?"

My answer to all four—as a psychiatrist—is the same: "No, I won't —but let us see if together we can understand this problem better. You may find that if we can understand it, there may be a solution, not necessarily the one you think." Now I should be very interested to know what would be the approach of a behavior therapist to these four different patients. The last two would, I imagine, present no ethical problems, but what about the first two?

You will understand that I am not questioning the efficacy of the method; that is a separate problem altogether. Nor am I trying to examine the theoretical basis on which the concept of behavior therapy rests. I am concerned with the medical ethics, indeed the medical philosophy of the whole problem. Supposing that behavior therapy were 100 percent effective in every case; what would be the right thing to do with these two patients? I think the prospect is a rather terrifying one. As one of my homosexual patients said to me, "If they can do this to me, if they can force me against my conscious inclinations to change my sexual orientation from men to women, what is to prevent them changing it to cows?" I suggest this is a serious question and I should like to hear what the behaviorists have to say about it.

Now you may feel that provided the individual concerned asks for help himself, there can be no reason why he should not receive this kind of treatment. Why should one hold back behavior therapy from, for example, the compulsive thief, if it is indeed effective? If by applying the appropriate conditioning technique one can prevent him from stealing, surely this would be beneficial both to himself and to society. One could say that he would be "cured" of his tendency to steal.

I am not quite so happy about this. What about the first two men? Do we offer them the same kind of help, just because they ask for it? What then do we offer them? Do we say to the first: "Yes, I will help you regain your courage by conditioning techniques so that you may murder your mother-in-law?" Or do we alternatively try to impose our own moral standards on him with the aid of appropriate conditioning methods? If not, what do we do?

I suppose that the real reason for my disquiet is that conditioning and behavior therapy sound so familiar to me. Surely every parent or school teacher has practiced a crude kind of conditioning on her own children since time immemorial—the concepts of reward and punishment are as old as time. We are more sophisticated about it nowadays. We know where mother went wrong, and with the aid of our new expertise we could provide her with much more effective methods of training than the very crude techniques that she practiced on us. I am not opposed on principle to the idea of punishment; I am concerned only that we do not blind ourselves with science. If a homosexual is given a painful physical shock every time he experiences erotic feelings about another man, I call this punishment, however expertly and clinically and aseptically it may be administered and whatever scientific jargon may be used to describe it. It seems to me to make little difference if the individual concerned *asks* to be punished; this does not make it any less punishment. Indeed, anyone who has had any psychiatric experience at all learns to recognize the desire for punishment as a dangerous warning sign; after all, what can be more self-punishing than suicide? Personally I think that the fact that the patient asks for a particular kind of treatment, or at least gives his consent to it, cannot possibly be considered justification for carrying it out.

Agreed that we should be wrong in carrying out *any* treatment without the patient's consent, but it is *our* ethical responsibility that we are concerned with here, not his. This is *our* problem; we cannot shelve it by saying, "Oh, well, he asked me to do it to him." Patients make all kinds of peculiar demands and requests, which we do not necessarily carry out because we think it would be wrong to do so. In such cases we have no hesitation in saying that the patient's judgment may be at fault. Yet here, for some reason, we are prepared to shift all the responsibility onto him.

If I am right about this, then the behaviorist are asking us doctors and psychiatrists to add to our armamentarium of techniques that of "reward and punishment" in a highly sophisticated form. If we accept this tempting offer, we should do so with our eyes open. To me it is a highly dangerous gift and it adds to the already great medical responsibilities of a doctor a moral responsibility which I, for one, feel quite unfit to take up. To me the essence of being a medical man is that I do not have to exercise moral judgments on my patients except in very rare cases, such as for example, the certification of a patient against his own will on the ground that he may be a danger to others. If I am asked to reward or punish people, then who is it who makes the decisions as to who shall be rewarded and who punished? Until now it has been the lawyers and theologians who have made these decisions, and I am happy to leave them with this thankless task for which, after all, they are trained and I am not.

As a psychiatrist I do indeed feel that I have something to contribute on the subject of delinquency. On the theoretical side I think that we can sometimes throw light on the antecedents of antisocial behavior, while on the practical side I think that with individuals who themselves really want help, we can sometimes increase their own self-understanding so that they can find ways of dealing with their problems in a manner which is less destructive both to others and to themselves. However, I do not feel that there is anything in our psychiatric training which fits us to make moral judgments which are better than those made by anyone else; in recent years psychiatrists have been called upon more and more to make oracular pronouncements regarding all manner of subjects on which they really have no right to speak. It is terribly tempting, when called upon in this way, to rise to the bait and come out with some inane remark suitably disguised in technical jargon. We do ourselves no good in the long run by such pronouncements.

I find it very disturbing that so much power is being given to psychiatrists by the lay public—perhaps as a substitute for religion —and this is the real reason why I feel so disturbed by the rise of behavior therapy. In addition to being doctors, we are now asked to be moral arbiters and to mete out punishments and rewards as we think fit. You may say that it is not we who make these moral decisions; this is decided for us by the law. If this is so, then we are reduced to the level of law enforcement officers—which I find equally unsatisfactory. If punishment is indeed necessary for the protection of society, then let it be carried out by those whose job it is. If they wish to use the findings of behavior psychology to make their punishments more effective, then they are of course entitled to do so; but I do not see that this is a medical matter, and I personally am not prepared to call this therapy or to take any part in it.

REFERENCE

Wootton, Barbara: The law, the deviant, and the doctor. *British Medical Journal* (No. 5351), July 27, 1963, pp. 197-202.

Chapter 3

BEHAVIOR THERAPY AND THE BLACK DELINQUENT

SAMUEL L. KIMBLES

In another paper (Kimbles, 1971) I have stated that current psychotherapeutic conceptualizations tend to overlook lifestyles of blacks. Specifically, such failures to include the contributions of lifestyles to psychotherapeutic practice has led to a truncation or negation of the black client's experiences of himself and the world. The truncation of the experiences of the black client is, I feel, applicable by extension, to all other disadvantaged individuals as they enter psychotherapy. Moreover, since mental health institutions, correctional facilities and other such establishments are heavily populated with disadvantaged individuals, there is an urgent need to revamp our psychotherapeutic conceptualizations. The disproportionate number of black adolescents who populate correctional and mental institutions may be attributed to a multiplicity of contributing factors. The depressive reality of the daily lives of black individuals includes an entourage of poor housing, schools, reduced economic resources and political power, etc. Such factors lead to drug abuse, violence, and general antisocial behavior (Clark, 1965). The important fact is that for many black delinquents, antisocial behavior represents a desperate effort to avoid acquiescing to the overwhelming and oppressive reality of their lives in the ghetto. Unfortunately, however, the present response of the psychotherapeutic community to this psychosocial situation is to simply increase the application of existing, middle-class techniques and conceptualizations (unaltered) to the black individual. I feel that such unthinking application of techniques and conceptualizations does more harm than good.

This latter contention will be developed more fully with respect to behavior therapy which I consider an iatrogenic procedure.

The problems of the black individual in mental health and correctional institutions begin when he enters a system which has as its objective maximum control with the least amount of effort. In reality, this means that facilities are not concerned with life-styles, individual personalities, etc. It takes little reflection to recognize that such a lack of concern is common in the daily lives of the black individual. In addition, any treatment received by the black individual in institutions tends to be brief, less intense and with less sophisticated staff (Hollingshead and Redlich, 1958). In community settings, this same type of less intense, brief treatment is duplicated. Translated to the black delinquent, such a treatment program means something like: short, brief, ineffi-cient, too little-too late involvement. The assumption in institu-tional settings seems to be that anything is better than nothing; whereas, in community settings, the terms for such involvement are called (strangely enough) crisis intervention. The black in-dividual is likely to consider his whole life as one continuous crisis. For many black individuals, for instance, there is constant concern for the basic necessities of life (food, decent shelter, etc.). Hence, it is not surprising that many black delinquents adopt the manipulative, now-orientation of the hipster and hustler in order to obtain very basic life necessities. The official policies of insti-tutions is to control, as efficiently as possible, any and all delin-quents and criminals. Such goals as control and efficiency are shared by a group of psychotherapists who have a similar con-ceptualization about behavior—the behavior therapists.

Essentially, behavior therapy uses quasi-programmed tech-niques and procedures to effectuate changes in the individual's be-havior. Implicit within its methodology are the concepts of con-trol and manipulation. It is not my intention here to explore the scientific and logical validity of behavior therapy (Berger and McGaugh, 1965); rather, the focus will be upon the implication of how the implicit goals of control and manipulation run *counter* to the lifestyle of the black individual and thus do a great deal of harm.

The black delinquent is likely to enter psychotherapy or a correctional or mental health institution on an involuntary or probationary basis. The cultural context of his entrance into institutions has been stated above; the emotional context includes feelings of rejection and neglect in a world seen as a determined, hostile and angry place where people are controlled, manipulated and restricted by powerful others. He often feels, beneath the bravado, insignificant and worthless. He tends to be present-centered, externalized in orientation and motoric in his dealings with his world (Kimbles, 1971; Riessman, 1962). It seems to me that behavior therapy runs into difficulty when confronted with the lifestyle of the black delinquent. The deterministic stance of the behavior therapists fits in with the belief of the black delinquent that his life has been determined by a set of malevolent rules or bad luck. Within such a deterministic stance, both therapist and client are offered a convenient rationale for avoiding responsibility for their behavior. Ofman (1970, p. 8) summarizes responsibility this way:

> No feeling—love, fear, anxiety, depression, agitation—exists merely as a habit or of its own functional autonomy. It has no autonomy. It is a result, a consequence of a person's way of writing his biography. This fact most people choose not to face. They would rather believe their feelings are under complete external control. So they see behavior therapists who indeed affirm this fact: "You are right, your feelings are under my control, there is nothing significant inside of you, and I will lead you through a hierarchy of steps which will extinguish this pesky feeling." And the patient is all too willing to go along. After all, he wanted to believe he was the victim of external forces to begin with. Here both the therapist and the patient lock arms and reinforce each other's self-deception. Most assuredly, such procedures effect "cures." So do religious conversions, hypnosis, drugs and prefrontal lobotomies. It is crucial, however, to attend to the implications for man of what we are doing to man by following the dictates of such therapeutic positions.

The above discussion of responsibility is not meant to imply that the black delinquent is not subject to a hostile environment; rather, from the point of view of mental health, it is felt that a complete emphasis upon an externalized orientation promotes immaturity and lack of growth. Behavior therapy, when used indiscriminately, not only encourages its participants to take refuge in the illusory security of a deterministic world, but allows the therapist to stand back from full personal involvement with the patient or person. In so doing, he validates or affirms the black delinquent's feeling that he is an insignificant, worthless being, with whom no one wants to get involved. Further, there is validation of the black delinquent's feeling of the powerful other who stands back in the shadows and manipulates and controls his destiny (the absentee landlord of psychotherapy). The paradox of correctional and psychotherapeutic treatment of black delinquents is that despite their accurate reading of the callousness of the larger society, the thing that the delinquents need most (secondary to a vast sociocultural revamping) is a concrete experience of self-worth and value in the presence of caring others. Behavior therapy is least likely to communicate such caring.

Moreover, the therapeutic goals, however behaviorally stated, tend, in the absence of a complete analysis of the functional and adaptive value of the behavior for the youth's larger environment, to unwittingly foster generalized estrangement from friends and loved ones who exist in the real environment of the black delinquent. Many of the character traits and behavioral problems which bother many clinicians are simply ways which are developed by the black delinquent in order to survive in a hostile environment. Such traits as distrust, manipulation, hustling, disrespect for laws and generalized antisocial behavior are often the only ways by which the black individual can cushion himself from continuous hurt meted out by society through discrimination, racism and police brutality. Grier and Cobbs (1968, p. 179) state it this way:

> These and related traits are simply adaptive devices developed in response to a peculiar environment. They are no more pathological than the compulsive manner in which a diver checks his equipment before a dive or a pilot his parachute. They represent normal devices for "making it" in America, and clinicians who are interested in the psychological functioning of black people must get acquainted with this body of character traits which we call the Black Norm. It is a normal complement of psychological devices. . . . To regard the Black Norm as pathological and attempt to remove such traits by treatment

would be akin to analyzing away a hunter's cunning or a banker's prudence. This is a body of characteristics essential to life for Black men in America and woe be unto that therapist who does not recognize it.

Finally, I find objection to the shaping of behavior which "connotes a smaller number of behavioral choices in the repertoire of the client." (Carkhuff and Berenson, 1967). Creative and effective living requires instead a larger, more flexible bag of response possibilities.

REFERENCES

Berger, L. and McGaugh, J.L.: Critique and reformulation of "learning theory" approaches to psychotherapy and neuroses. *Psychological Bulletin, 63*:338-358, 1965.

Carkhuff, R.R. and Berenson, B.G.: *Beyond Counseling and Therapy.* New York, Holt, Rinehart and Winston, 1967.

Clark, K.B.: *Dark Ghetto.* New York, Harper and Row, 1965.

Grier, W.H. and Cobbs, P.M.: *Black Rage.* New York, Basic Books, 1968.

Hollingshead, A.B. and Redlich, F.C.: *Social Class and Mental Illness.* New York, John Wiley and Sons, 1958.

Kimbles, S.L.: The psychotherapeutic experience and the black client. Unpublished manuscript, University of Southern California School of Medicine, 1971.

Ofman, W.V.: *Psychotherapy as a humanistic existentialist encounter—key elements of the basis for practice.* Los Angeles, Psychological Affiliates Press, 1970.

Riessman, F.: *The Culturally Deprived Child.* New York, Harper and Row, 1962.

Chapter 4

SELF CONTROL IS LEARNED: EXTERNAL CONTROL PRECEDES INTERNAL CONTROL

BARBARA R. BISHOP

T HE IDEA OF ONE HUMAN BEING imposing any form of external control upon another seems to set most of our educated teeth on edge. It screams of *1984*—of Big Brother peering over an unsuspecting shoulder while we close our eyes, or at least our mouths, and speak of euphemistic "encouragements" and "interactions" rather than use the word "control." This is understandable if you are running for presidency of the local P.T.A., but is rather sophomoric in a professional milieu.

First, let us dispel the prime semantical taboo. Control is not necessarily equated with tyranny. Tyranny refers to a dictatorial relationship in which one party intends to somehow increase his own welfare at the expense of another person. Control, however, need not take on this meaning. It is simply a functional relationship between two variables. The variables may be "tyrannical" such as variable one, the fire burns and variable two, the trees are therefore consumed; the variables may be self-governing," such as a desire for money and yet denying yourself the act of burglary.

What, then, does it mean "to be in control"? It means two things: (a) to determine the contingencies for another's behavior, or (b) to determine them for your own behavior. The question raised in this chapter evolves from the second of these points— self-control. It asks how a person makes the transition from the "give me now!" infant stage to the "I can wait for pleasure" stage of the mature adult. As it happens, this second stage is totally dependent upon the initial stage, i.e. "contingencies by another" aspect of control.

Let us look at a young delinquent and build a hypothetical "schiz" for him. At the moment he is being held in the local juvenile hall for having stolen an automobile. Why is he here? Perhaps because he could not tell himself to wait and earn the money and then buy his own car. And why is it that he was unable to do this? The answer, of course, is a lack of control. The next question is why the lack? To answer this, let us view Spike at the age of two years.

Spike is standing in front of the cookie jar, hungry. He stands on a chair and reaches for a cookie; now mother enters. At this point she begins, though unaware of it, laying the groundwork for Spike's future attitude toward theft. She does this by choosing whether or not to impose *external* control on Spike. She can either tell him *no* and remove the cookies, or she can allow the pilfering to occur. There are, of course, two very different messages here for our potential delinquent. The one message says, "Sure, take what you want"; the other says, "Hold on, there is outside control here that won't allow this."

Ridiculous to say that this incident determined Spike's eventual career in car theft? Probably. But it is not ridiculous to say that this could have been the beginning of a total pattern. For Spike ever to acquire the self-control needed to remain outside of juvenile hall, he first needs the *external* message from another human being. Self-control does not just happen—it is a *learned* behavior.

This, of course, is a gross over-simplification. The development of self-control is an extremely complex occurrence and we are still in the very earliest of stages as far as its understanding. Let us leave Spike teetering between delinquency and social success and examine some of the positions held regarding the etiologies of the "self-control through stage" position.

Until quite recently, the predominant theory of the beginnings of conscience, morality, i.e. self-control, centered about the developmental concept—the idea that a child goes through certain stages roughly correlated with his chronological age. Freud suggested that this acquisition occurs through the incorporation of the standards of the parents by the child. This gives the child a *super-ego,* a secret voice deep inside which tells children what those things are of which the parents would and would not approve. This super-ego supplies resistance to temptation, shame for inadequacies and guilt or pride for his behaviors. In sum, the conscience is the residue from dependency and the oedipal situation, and it matures as the child progresses from the infant-id stage ("I want it now!") through the ego development stage ("I can wait!").

Piaget (1932) also sees several stages in the development of conscience with the addition of a strong cognitive component. From an analysis of childrens play, Piaget finds systematic changes in the understanding of rules. In stage one, the motor stage, the child regards rules as examples; in stage two these rules become sacred dogma emanating from adult authority; stage three is a cooperation stage in which the child seeks mutual consent in rules; and the final stage occurs as the child codifies the rules and sees them as principles of activity. These stages coordinate with the child's age.

Kohlberg (1963) sees the process with much similarity to Piaget. He divides the development of self-control into stages and views the process as a definite sequence of occurrence. The four-year-old, for example, judges the goodness or badness of an act according to the consequence meted out to the actor. As he reaches five or six, he begins to evaluate more, using moral labels and in terms of long-range rather than short-range reinforcement. By pre-adolescence the child is equipped to make "disinterested" impartial judgments based on the facts alone.

LEARNING THEORY

Learning theory speaks of the development of conscience as a function of response consequences. (Longstreth, 1968) External control must precede internal control and is learned through a series of parentally punished responses. A response occurs and is followed by a physical or psychological punishment; this punishment, by definition, includes the presence of anxiety (physiological arousal and cognition).

$$R \longrightarrow Punishment \longrightarrow Anxiety$$

This sequence allows for the classical conditioning of anxiety to the response, and thus allows for the eventual cessation of the external punishment per se. The child, therefore, learns to avoid making the response due to the anxiety it elicits rather than by the punishment it incurs. Learning theory further posits that any response that reduces this anxiety has a high probability of being repeated. Thus, the inhibition of the response is strengthened, as it is this which decreases the anxiety.

The crucial question is, If it is agreed that the child learns to experience anxiety about a certain response *while the parent is present,* what is true *in his absence?* Will not the child learn to discriminate, i.e. to inhibit the response in the presence of the relevant cue (mother)? The answer is *yes,* and thus to this point we have not really established any internalized control. The next step must then be to condition the anxiety to the response itself and not merely to the fear of detection, and this brings us to a most important discussion: the timing of punishment. We will return to Spike at the cookie jar. Perhaps he has completed the pilfer and is standing there with crumbs on his face. The parent could enter and now inflict a *delayed* punishment for the response. Two problems arise. First, is Spike totally aware of the *why* of the punishment? To help insure that he is, the parent can describe the act of cookie-snatching and explain its relationship to the spanking. This verbal re-creation may greatly help the conditioning process; however, too often the child is more concerned with experiencing the aversive event than he is in examining his crime.

The second problem is concerned with the anxiety. With delayed punishment, the aversive event occurs *after the fact* and thus is more closely associated with this end of the prohibited response than with its initiation. The sequence here is

Response begins $\longrightarrow$ R ends $\longrightarrow$ Punishment $\longrightarrow$ Anxiety

Here learning theory would tell us that the act closest to the punishment will be the act most intensely associated with the anxiety. Thus what we have is a child who continues to make the response but who feels miserable after he has finished!

The dilemma is even stickier. Punish early in the act and the

onset is then classically conditioned to the anxiety, but the termination of the act is relatively anxiety-free, thus presenting a child
who moralizes much before the "crime" but who feels just fine
afterward. The scales, however, seem to swing in favor of this
early punishment, as hopefully it will result in the cessation of the
response, the abortion, and thus preclude the necessity for conditioning anxiety to its end phases. The paradox remains, however. Early punishment does seem to result in an increased resistance to temptation yet also yields many fewer manifestations of
guilt or anxiety if the transgression does occur. Sticky indeed.

Is there not some more efficient method for helping a child
internalize an external agent of control? Perhaps the answer lies
less with the punishment of extant responses and more with the
prevention of their occurrence; this may sound utopian, yet it
seems plausible with a reasoning child. There will of course be
some early responses requiring a feedback of a type calling for a
physical punishment. The two-year-year-old trotting onto the
freeway is not asking for "reasoning" but is more in need of a
sharp feedback on his backside to transmit the message quickly
and effectively. The child slightly older, however, can be taught
to be aware of social consequences of behaviors. Thus, rather than
conditioning anxiety to the offending response, we would condition it to the child's *awareness* of consequences and how they
might be detrimental to himself or to other human beings. In this
model, self-control would develop along with the child's ability to
understand possible negative consequences.

Sadly however, knowledge is not enough. To truly develop a
morality, a child must experience the affective component. It is at
this junction that the learning theorist and the stage theorists
leave their parallelism and begin once again to coverage. It is here
that we need to wed two components necessary to self-control:
cognition *and* affect. It is here that the parental model becomes of
great importance. In a very insightful book on social learning,
Donna Gelfand (1969) cites a story reported by Dr. O. Hobart
Mowrer. There was a farmer who owned a parrot that absolutely
refused to talk. Night after night the farmer said "Say uncle,"
while the parrot steadfastly refused to open his beak. Finally, in

desperation the farmer picked up a stick, beating the parrot over the head and screaming, "Say uncle!" This, too, proved ineffective. In anger the farmer tossed the recalcitrant parrot into the chicken coop. Some days later he was passing the coop and heard a loud commotion. There stood the parrot ferociously beating a chicken over the head with a stick and screaming, "Say uncle! Say uncle!"

The point of this anecdote, of course, is to demonstrate two separate components in the acquisition of control. Not only must we be concerned with the classical conditioning of anxiety to a prohibitive response, but also our concern must be with the direct tutelage of said response. This modeling effect of the parent may indeed be even greater than the more direct training. The sage who commented "Do as I say, not as I do," was perhaps wiser than he knew. How often do we see the well-meaning parent slapping a child while remonstrating with him not to hit his little sister!

The modeling effect must, then, play an important role in the development of an internalized mode of responding. It is here that a child begins to change the parents "Thou shalt not" to his own "I shall not." It starts with, depending on your schooling, identification or imitation. For practical purposes we shall use the terms synonymously. The literature carries numerous theories in explanation of this phenomenon. Freud speaks of the anaclitic identification occurring when the child, fearing a withdrawal of the nurturing parent, *incorporates* the parents characteristics—becomes *like* the parent. Whiting proposes a "status-envy theory" which postulates the child's envy of the adult's consumption of life's goodies. The theory bearing the most empirical substantiation, however, is the "power theory" in which the child envies and subsequently identifies with not the consumer but the *controller* of reinforcements. Albert Bandura and his associates (1962, 1963, 1965) have completed voluminous works on this treatise. One extremely important finding is that although punishing a model tends to inhibit the performance of the prohibited act, it in no way inhibits the *learning* of said act. A second important ingredient lies in the consequences to the model. Children rewarded for performing the act earlier punished in the model can and do carry it through in detail.

TRANSITION

The acquisition and maintenance of self-control then, is no different than the controlling of *another's* behavior—you manipulate variables. Consider the transition which occurs between (a) total control by another and (b) total self-control. We speak of "screwing up courage," "talking ourselves into a good mood," "counting to 10," and so on. We tell ourselves, "I'll get out of this warm bed when I count to three." Thus, we appear to go through a mediational process. First the control of another maintains a child's behavior; later on the child talks to himself, e.g. "You shouldn't take the cookies," and finally the "talking" is totally covert and internalized. Often we see young children discipline themselves as if they were the adult as well as the child; the four-year-old who spanks his own hand as he reaches for the forbidden toy; the six-year-old who says, "Your father will yell at you if you get this dress dirty!"

Meichenbaum and Goodman (1971) actually *trained* the impulsive child to talk to himself. They went through a progression of steps in which (a) the experimenter performed the task, describing it aloud; (b) the child performed as the experimental described it; (c) the child then performed and described it out loud; (d) the child then whispered it, and (e) he finally performed the task without overt lip movement. In this manner, the child both instructed himself verbally, and reinforced or corrected his attempts. These authors concluded that "The impulsive children were taught to use their private speech for orienting, organizing, regulating, and self-rewarding functions with the consequences of greater self-control."

The road to self-control, then, may be peopled by first mother, then an articulate homunculus and finally by a more covert silent "conscience." All successful control is accomplished only when there is a system of immediate feedback. The young child depends upon the monitoring adult for this feedback; with increased maturity he monitors his own behavior, speaking with his lips the words of the mother; gradually, mother's voice dims and the child acquires an internal standard of behavior.

Meanwhile back at the cookie jar. . . Spike remains teetering. At this point we know several methods of handling his temptation. We can punish the early intention; we could punish the terminal act, verbally recreating the scene for him; or now we could introduce a model. How should the ideal model perform? Again the literature is replete with model-observer characteristics and interactions. We will concern ourselves with only a few here.

In most theories of identification, analytical or learning, the role of nurturance is emphasized. The warm, affectionate parent assumes a positive image for the child and becomes a source for behavior through imitation. There is empirical support for this assumption in that children who experience a nurturant model display more imitative responses than do children exposed to a nonrewarding adult. This is in agreement with the idea that the child tends to identify with the rewarding, powerful adult rather than with the weak, ineffective one.

A second empirical finding was in discord with the stage theories of moral development. Rather than going through the predetermined stages of objective and subjective morality, Bandura *et al.* found that the provision of models could effectively alter the children's moral judgments. They also found that immediate-gratification children would increase their preference for delayed-gratification rewards when exposed to a high-delay model (a most important concept when dealing with low-delay delinquent children). Stumphauzer (see Chapter 9) did carry out such a study by increasing delay of gratification in young prison inmates through the imitation of high-delay peer models. Let us return to the issue of punishment as a means for beginning the road from external to internal control and examine it in light of a social model. First, we know that the warm, nurturant model has the best chance of producing a nondelinquent child. This type of parent is one who depends less on physical punishment and more on the temporary withdrawal of love. Anxiety about *social consequences prior* to the forbidden response can be most easily conditioned by the adult model who (a) behaves as he wishes the child to behave and (b) is seen by the child as a nurturant, yet powerful person. In this manner the anxiety is connected even to an *intention* to respond antisocially, i.e. unlike the preferred model, and there is no need for after-the-fact response suppression by punishment. A control may then be said to be internalized if it can reliably be actualized *in the absence* of the adult model.

What have we then that we can apply to our teetering delinquent? To be the most assured that Spike will not pilfer from the cookie jar and later possibly transfer this activity to stealing cars, we must provide him with several aids. These must reach him in a threefold manner: through his cognition, his affect and the consequences of his behaviors. The most effective agent of all three is in the person of a warm, affectionate, "powerful" parent-figure. This parent should not only verbalize correct behavior for Spike, but must also *behave himself* as he wishes Spike to behave. This modeling can be done in a multitude of ways—actually or symbolically. The choice and sharing of books, movies, and TV programs is a way of saying, "Be like this, be like these models of which I approve." The consequences to the models are important, but keep in mind that the antisocial behavior is still being learned. The car thief is imprisoned—but he did exhibit "good car-stealing behavior" before he was caught! The same applies to violence. Exposing the child to violence, either through the parents' behavior or through symbolic representation, is exposing him to a way of life. Whether he ever performs as such himself is dependent on numerous variables, including response consequences to the model and his own subjective motivation.

Through this model, then, Spike is experiencing both a cognitive and an affective pattern possible in his own life. A continued exposure can be given through the early consequences to intended and completed undesirable behaviors. This is accomplished both through the classical conditioning of anxiety to responses or response-tendencies and by the operant consequences of a completed action. Here the problem earlier cited in using actual punishment must be kept in mind, i.e. anxiety only at the onset, or feelings of guilt only after the fact.

In sum, Spike needs a model who is (a) warm and nurturant

(b) powerful in the sense of being in control of the "goods and bads" of life and (c) a consistent dispenser of rewards and punishments. Physical punishment (or psychological) is a desired act only with the very young or incompetent child who cannot yet utilize a rational understanding of response consequences. In general, a temporary withdrawal of a parent's approval is *far more effective* than a corporal punishment, as it tends to produce a much more adjusted, internally controlled child (Sears, Maccoby and Levin, 1957). The child brought up on external control alone will never grow into an adult capable of self-control but will continue to be dependent upon these externals.

You are probably saying to yourself, "O.K., that may work with a very young child, but let's consider that Spike hasn't had all this and is *already* behaving as a delinquent. Then what?" It is a rougher problem and one with which our extant penal institutions have been attempting to deal for hundreds of years. And they are failing miserably. Perhaps we are now on the way to understanding why. What *is* their approach to the offender, child or adult? The offender is immediately deprived of all of his sources for obtaining rewards; he is given only models who, like himself, or perhaps worse than himself, have been and are behaving in an antisocial manner; he is removed from any source of warmth and nurturance; in sum he is physically and psychologically punished. To make matters worse, the punishment is delivered *long* after the "criminal" response, thus conditioning the anxiety only to "after the fact." What we are in effect doing, and doing exceedingly well, is to produce someone far more capable and likely to behave in a socially *un*acceptable way once we remove the prison walls! All of the ingredients are there—the models who succeed in expertly performing antisocial acts; the removal of acceptable modes of gaining rewards; delayed punishment which results only in a temporary suppression of the behavior; peer-model approval not for social responses but for *anti*social responses. Had we deliberately set out to create a world for inculcating criminal behavior we could hardly have done better!

The importance of a social modeling effect seems to be totally disregarded by our extant institutions. If it is true that peer influences are generally stronger for a delinquent population than are authority models, then these institutions are setting up the ideal situation for reinforcing delinquent behaviors! Buehler, Patterson and Furniss (1966) performed a series of studies considering this very point. They concluded that such institutions are "teaching machines" which program and maintain "deviant behavior rather than. . .retraining the child to more socially adaptive behavior." They also noted that whereas the peer groups *consistently* rewarded deviant responses, the adult group was extremely inconsistent in punishing these behaviors, thus severely reducing the staff effectiveness.

The better way? Perhaps it is to switch the message; to provide models to the young offender, models who behave and are successful in our society; to provide rewards for making or even approximating socially approved responses; and to eliminate the continued emphasis on external control of the offender. This is *not* to say that external control is not necessary. It *is*. It *always* precedes internal control. But the experineces must be so structured as to foster a gradual identification, imitation, and internalization of these external controls until they become the foundation of a mature self-control.

REFERENCES

Bandura, A.: Social learning through imitation. In Jones, M.R. (Ed.): *Nebraska Symposium on Motivation*. Lincoln, Univ. of Nebraska Press, 1962.

Bandura, A.: Influence of model's reinforcement contingencies on the acquisition of imitative responses. *Journal of Personality and Social Psychology*, *1*:589-595, 1965.

Bandura, A. and Walters, H.R.: *Social Learning and Personality Development*. New York, Holt Rinhart and Winston, 1963.

Beuhler, R. E.: The reinforcement of behavior in institutional settings. *Behavior Research and Therapy*, *4*:157-167, 1966.

Gelfand, Donna M.: *Social Learning in Childhood*. California, Brooks/Cole Publishing Co., 1969.

Kohlberg, L.: The development of children's orientations toward a moral order: 1. Sequence in the development of moral thought. *Vita Humana*, *6*:11-33, 1963.

Longstreth, L. E.: *Psychological Development of the Child*. New York, The Ronald Press, 1968.

Meichenbaum, D.H. and Goodman, J.: Training impulsive children to talk to themselves: a means of developing self-control. *Journal of Abnormal Psychology*, 77 (No. 2):115-126, 1971.

Mussen, P. H., Conger, J.J. and Kagan, J.: *Child Development and Personality*. New York, Harper and Row, 1956.

Piaget, J.: *The Moral Judgment of the Child*. London, Routledge and Kegan, Paul, 1932.

Sears, R.R., Maccoby, Eleanor E., and Levin, H.: *Patterns of Child Rearing*. Evanston, Illinois, Row, Peterson, 1957.

Chapter 5

BEHAVIOR MODIFICATION WITH DELINQUENTS: SOME UNFORSEEN CONTINGENCIES

JOHN D. BURCHARD

In RECENT YEARS there has been a remarkable increase in the application of learning principles to the broad areas of education, treatment and rehabilitation. (Bandura, 1969; Bradfield, 1970; Franks, 1969; Ulrich, 1966) This has been particularily true in the area of crime and delinquency where programs variously labeled "behavior modification," "behavior therapy," "operant conditioning" and "reinforcement therapy" have been developed in prisons, training schools, institutions, halfway houses and community-based prevention programs.

Although behavior modification programs differ markedly in terms of the specific procedures they utilize, each one is usually based on the general assumption that there is a functional relationship between antisocial behavior and the environment in which it occurs. Granted this assumption, then it becomes clear that one way to change delinquent behavior is to change the environment. This then is probably the basic difference between the behavior modification approach and some of the more traditional psychological and psychiatric methods of rehabilitating criminals and delinquents. Instead of trying to change the person through some type of periodic, psychotherapeutic or verbal medication, the focus is on changing the environment so that appropriate behaviors are strengthened or weakened. In general, the environment is arranged so that adaptive behavior is strengthened

Paper read at the American Orthopsychiatry Association meeting in New York, April 1971. Reprinted with permission of the author.

through rewarding consequences and maladaptive or antisocial behavior is weakened through non-rewarding and/or punishing consequences.

There seems to be little question but that the behavior modification approach has been productive and that much of the present enthusiasm is warranted. Let me describe briefly four different programs which give rise to such optimism, two of which relate to prevention and two of which relate to rehabilitation.

One of the preventive programs was developed by Tharp, Wetzel and their associates (Tharp, 1969) in Arizona while the second is presently being conducted by Wolf, Phillips and others (Bailey, 1970; Phillips, 1968) at the University of Kansas. In both instances the population being served consisted of adolescent boys who displayed a high frequency of antisocial behavior but had not been adjudicated delinquent. Also in both instances the basic procedure was to arrange the environment so that rewards were contingent upon small, successive approximations of adaptive behavior in a variety of situations. The main difference was that the Arizona project was conducted in the natural environment with boys residing at home while the Kansas project was conducted within a home-style, residential setting (achievement place). While it is still too early to properly assess the effects of either program, preliminary studies have been quite impressive. Through the systematic manipulation of reinforcement contingencies, high frequencies of intolerable, disruptive behavior have been replaced by behavior which is much more adaptive and related to community survival.

Both of the rehabilitation programs I will briefly describe took place within correctional facilities. One was developed by Cohen and his associates (Cohen, 1968; Cohen, 1968) at the National Training School when it was in Washington D.C. and the other by McKee and his associates (Clements, 1968) at Draper Prison in Alabama. In both programs the environment was arranged so that aversive consequences were minimized and inmates did not have to do anything to obtain the basic necessities of penal life. However, for those who wanted to improve their lifestyle points or marks could be earned through small units of academic achievement and cashed in for more interesting food, special privileges, opportunities to spend time in a recreation lounge, and occasional trips away from the institution. As a result of these systems, the attitudes of the inmates greatly improved; on a voluntary basis they began to spend long hours on their school work and related behavior problems were greatly decreased.

As mentioned above, the results of these programs are impressive and the enthusiasm of their proponents seems warranted. However, the entire picture regarding the future of behavior modification does not consist of unqualified optimism. It sees clear that the behavior modification approach will not be the final phase in the rehabilitation of delinquents and criminals; at least not at the state at which behavior modification is today. There is considerable historical evidence that new treatment approaches, if they are to survive at all, are initially met with overwhelming attention and enthusiasm, are hailed as the solution to all problems and are included in the treatment armament of most respectable institutions and agencies. However, once the initial dust has settled, the really significant issues begin to arise. Due to the objective, empirical nature of many behavior modification programs, the question of whether or not behavior can really be modified has already received an affirmative answer, at least with respect to many different, overt behaviors. However, there are other issues which currently plague the development and possibly even the survival of the behavior modification approach.

Basically, the issues I am referring to relate to what constitutes behavior modification, the manner in which it should be applied (especially with criminals and delinquents) and the need to go beyond the repeated demonstration of the law of effect (Thorndike, 1932) and focus on the more important problem of generalization or the transition from the artificial or controlled environment to the natural environment. Without further emphasis and investigation on these issues, it is likely that behavior modification will go the way of many fads.

Much of what I have to say with respect to these issues stems from my own personal experience over the past five years in developing a behavior modification program for delinquent retardates at Murdoch Center, in North Carolina (Burchard, 1967). Since we did not anticipate these issues, I have referred to them as unforeseen contingencies. However, on the basis of what I have seen, heard and read about other behavior modification programs, I am convinced that these issues relate to the general status of behavior modification. I will try to describe each one as concisely as possible.

First, there appears to be considerable confusion with respect to what constitutes behavior modification (Birnbrauer, 1970). While it is generally agreed that the techniques are derived from or consistent with the principles of learning, i.e. shaping, prompting, fading, reinforcement, extinction, punishment, there is considerable variation in the manner in which those techniques are applied. For example, in many situations behavior modification merely connotes the administration of certain procedures. Predetermined behaviors are rewarded, ignored or punished through contingency management. However, there is no systematic data collection or analysis to provide empirical verification of the effects of those procedures. Procedures selected and maintained on an a priori basis ("They were shown to be effective in someone else's program") or on the basis of "good common sense" ("TV is reinforcing for most kids"). Unfortunately, good common sense or knowing what works with others is not good enough; especially in working with delinquents and criminals. It would seem that if the solution were that simple, the problems would have been solved a long time ago.

One of the major assets of the behavior modification approach is that it is amenable to continuous, empirical verification. Procedures can be selected, maintained and modified on the basis of their effects on behavior and not on the basis of common sense, subjective impression or guesswork. This emphasis on the dynamic aspect of behavior modification, the interaction between procedure and effect, has resulted in the process being relabeled *applied behavior analysis* (Baer, 1968). My main point then, is that systematic empirical analysis of the effects of specific behavior modification procedures should be an intergral part of every behavior modification program. Without carefully defining and monitoring the behaviors to be modified, the value of a behavior modification is extremely limited.

The second issue pertains to the manner in which behavior modification programs should be applied, especially with delinquents and criminals. There is little question regarding the power of contingency management. If the consequences are of sufficient magnitude, whether positive or negative, it is relatively easy to produce at least a temporary change in behavior. But are there any negative side effects associated with that change in behavior? It is a question which warrants further consideration.

Much has been written regarding the possible negative side effects of aversive control. While punishment or the threat of punishment frequently results in an immediate change in behavior, it weakens the relationship (or, in behavioral terms, the reinforcement contingency) between the person who administers, and the person who receives the punishment. Also, although punishment may produce a persistent effect in the presence of the punishing agent, there is the question of the effect in the absence of the punishing agent. At least in some situations punished behavior occurs more frequently in the absence of the punishing agent.

Negative side effects may not occur only in the context of punishment. There is some evidence that for some individuals the process of managing reinforcement contingencies, even where the contingencies are primarily positive, produces undesirable side effects. The negative side effect is that after the contingency is removed the behavior which was previously required to get a particular consequence occurs less frequently than it did before the contingency was applied. For example, and adolescent is told that in order to be able to watch TV at night he must clean his room. Because TV is a powerful reinforcer for this particular individual, he cleans his room while the contingency is in effect. However, after the contingency is removed, he cleans his room less often than he did before the contingency was applied. Is this because he wants the contingency to be reinstated? Or is it because he does not think you feel it is important that he cleans his room anymore? Or is it because of something else? The reaction is similar to what some social psychologists refer to as "reactance," a motivational opposition to a decrease in freedom (Brehm, 1966). Certainly one's freedom is limited in a contingency management program, especially one in which the consequences one previously enjoyed on a non-contingent basis are suddenly made contingent upon some difficult or undesirable behavior.

The point I am trying to make is that in administering a behavior modification program, the guiding principle should not be to utilize the procedure which produces the greatest and most immediate change in behavior. Depending upon the procedure and how it is administered, it is possible that there will be negative side effects which will be incompatible with long-range goals. This is particularly true with punishment and may even be true in programs in which the contingency management involves gross or unsubtle limits of "choice" or "freedom." On numerous occasions I have been asked why the old training school and reformatory point systems proved to be so ineffective when they appeared to involve contingency management. It appears to me that the contingency management used in those programs were based almost entirely upon aversive control. Either one "behaved" or he lost something desirable. Possible it is reinforcing not to engage in such behavior in the absence of such control, call it reactance or whatever.

The *final issue* pertains to the problem of generalization. As mentioned above there is little question regarding the power of behavior modification techniques. In most instances it has been found that a behavior can be modified in a desirable direction if the consequences (especially the immediate consequences) can be manipulated or controlled. However, in the process of controlling a consequence, an artificial contingency is introduced. And while the artificial contingency may produce successful behavior modification, there is still the question of how to bring the modified behavior under the control of natural contingencies. To illustrate the problem, it may be possible to get a delinquent youth to display good manners by paying him tokens for successive approximations of appropriate behavior at meal time. Depending upon the severity of the problem, establishing good table manners could be an impressive and worthy achievement even though accomplished through artificial contingencies. However, if the rehabilitation (or habilitation) is to be complete, it is necessary to eventually bring the good table manners under the control of natural contingencies. There are few places in society where a person will get paid for displaying good manners.

Due to the zeal of many behaviorists for empirical verification, the magnitude of the problem is demonstrated repeatedly. That is, in order to demonstrate that a particular technique has produced a significant change in behavior, the behavior modifier will frequently switch from the treatment conditions, i.e. the artificial contingency, to a no-treatment condition (which frequently represents the natural contingency). This is the typical ABA experimental design. And what the behavior modifier typically finds is that once the treatment conditions (the artificial contingencies) are removed, the behavior quickly reverts back to its pre-treatment level or frequency. To use an example with table manners, once good table manners were established, the token might be removed (or administered non-contingently) to see if it was the contingent administration of token that produced the good table manners. And under such conditions one is likely to find that the level or frequency of good table manners will decline.

While it is necessary to perform manipulations such as those involved in the ABA design, it is important not to stop with the demonstration of a causal relationship between a behavior and a particular consequence. The fact that the behavior deteriorates when the contingency is changed or removed points out the problem of generalization. It is time for those involved in behavior modification programs to move beyond the repeated demonstration of the law of effect and to focus more on building increased resistance to those effects. Although there have been some efforts in this direction, much additional research is needed.

To summarize, I began this paper by pointing out the increasing appeal of the use of behavior modification with criminals and delinquents and gave several examples of sound programs in the area of prevention and rehabilitation. At the same time I have tried to point out that in my opinion the behavior modification approach has not solved all of the problems and that, in fact, there are several issues which presently plague its effectiveness. In general these issues relate the need to establish behavior modification programs on an empirical or analytic basis, the need to focus on possible side effects which are incompatible with long-range goals and finally the need to go beyond a demonstration of the power of behavior modification techniques and focus on problems of generalization. In the process of making such a lengthy presentation I hope I have provided some clarification of the present status of behavior modification with delinquents together with some implications for its future.

REFERENCES

Baer, D.M., Wolf, M., and Risley, T.R.: Some current dimensions of applied behavior analysis. *Journal of Applied Behavior Analysis, 1*:91-97, 1968.

Bailey, J.S., Wolf, M.M., and Phillips, E.L.: Home-based reinforcement and the modification of pre-delinquents' classroom behavior. *Journal of Applied Behavior Analysis, 3*:223-233, 1970.

Bandura, Albert: *Principles of Behavior Modification.* New York, Holt, Rinehart and Winston, 1969.

Birnbrauer, J.S., Burchard, J.D. and Burchard, Sara N.: Wanted: behavior analysts. In R.H. Bradfield (Ed.): *Behavior Modification: The Human Effort.* San Rafael, California, Dimensions Publishing Co., 1970.

Bradfield, Robert H. (Ed.): *Behavior Modification: The Human Effort.* San Rafael, California, Dimensions Publishing Co., 1970.

Brehm, J.W.: *A Theory of Psychological Reactance.* New York, Academic Press, 1966.

Burchard, J.D.: Systematic socialization: a programmed environment for the habilitation of antisocial retardates. *Psychological Record, 11*:461-476, 1967.

Clements, C.B. and McKee, J.M.: Programmed instruction for institutionalized offenders: contingency management and performance contracts. *Psychological Report, 22*:957-964, 1968.

Cohen, J.L.: Educational therapy; the design of learning environments. In J.M. Shlien (Ed.): *Research in Psychotherapy.* Washington, D.C.: American Psychological Association, 1968, pp. 21-53.

Cohen, H.L., Filipaczak, J., Bis, J., Cohen, J., Goldiamond, I., and Larkin, P.: Case II—Model: A Contingency-oriented 24-hour Learning Environment in a Juvenile Correctional Institution. Silver Spring, Maryland, Educational Facility Press, 1968.

Franks, Cyril M. (Ed.): *Behavior Therapy: Appraisal and Status.* New York, McGraw-Hill Book Company, 1969.

Phillips, E.L.: Achievement Place: token reinforcement procedures in a home-style rehabilitation setting for "pre-delinquent" boys. *Journal of Applied Behavior Analysis, 1:*213-223, 1968.

Tharp, R.G. and Wetzel, R.J.: *Behavior Modification in the Natural Environment.* New York, Academic Press, 1969.

Thorndike, E.L.: Reward and punishment in animal learning. *Comparative Psychological Monographs,* No. 8, Whole No. 39, 1932.

Ulrich, Roger, Stachnik, Thomas, and Mabry, John (Eds.): *Control of Human Behavior,* vols. I, II. Glenview, Illinois, Scott, Foresman and Company, 1966.

PART
TWO

Basic Research in Behavior Therapy
With Delinquents

INTRODUCTION

JEROME S. STUMPHAUZER

Behavior therapy is defined as the systematic application of psychological principles of learning in modifying human deviant behavior. The term behavior therapy is usually restricted to *applied* behavior modification, i.e. to an actual treatment program. There is, however, a substantial literature of more basic research, which, while it may have obvious and very important implications for treatment, is not actually a therapy per se. In this section a sampling of such papers, dealing with basic research in behavior therapy with delinquents, is presented in the hope that they will both stimulate further research in the important variables involved, and provide information useful in developing new applied treatment programs. Paul (1969, p. 60) suggests, "Before embarking upon controlled research in the clinical context, laboratory-based designs may serve the major purposes of developing techniques of changing behavior and explanatory principles, and the determination of parameters of influence from which new therapeutic techniques may be derived."

It is being suggested here that there is a very orderly set of events in the development of a behavior therapy program, and that applied treatment programs do necessarily rely heavily on previous, more basic research. For example, a particular variable relating to positive reinforcement may have first been studied in an animal laboratory. Next those results may have been replicated and extended to a human laboratory, and finally these results used in an applied treatment program. This implies science with a definite direction as explored by Baron (1971) in his discussion of the relevancy of experimental psychology. Accepting that kind of progression, there is an obvious need for continuing and even expanding basic research in behavior therapy with delinquents.

It should be the goal of all behavior therapy to be experimental, and one of the strong points should be that it is continually self-evaluating and provisions should be made for self-correction. There should be objective measurement of causal events. If the variables being manipulated are affecting the behavior under surveillance it should be obvious; likewise if they are not. But even while well-designed behavior therapy programs are by nature experimental, they are also by nature based on previous controlled study. This will be more obvious when the papers in this and remaining sections are read and their reference lists reviewed.

It has long been thought that detention homes, boys industrial schools and other institutions for youthful offenders actually represent a place to learn delinquent behaviors rather than a place to learn socially acceptable modes of response. These specialized "learning programs" are under the direction of other prisoners who represent powerful models to be imitated and who shape antisocial behavior through reward (social approval and extrinsic goods) and punishment (physical punitiveness and withdrawal of approval). In Chapter 6, Buehler, Patterson and Furniss present a series of basic research studies convincingly showing that, as in the National Council on Crime and Delinquency's picture, "Prison isn't a waste of time, a lot of kids come out learning a trade." The findings of these studies are that the delinquents' peers in these (and perhaps other) institutions for delinquents tended to reward delinquent or antisocial behavior and to punish moves toward socially acceptable behavior. On the other hand, the institutional staff were more *in*consistent and alternately positively reinforced and punished the delinquents for the same behaviors. The peer group seemed to be running their own behavior therapy program, and indeed in a more sophisticated and efficient manner than the staff! It appeared, then, that delinquent behavior was being taught *in* these institutions. This research is basic and important in that the information provided here needs to be considered when one is planning and developing a behavior therapy program in institutions (see Part Three). First, the influence of peers must be evaluated and then either be minimized, controlled, or used to promote *pro*social behavior—as done by Stumphauzer (Ch. 9).

Secondly, and as Buehler *et al.* suggest, an effective behavioral approach would include systematic observation and tailor-made consistent schedules of reward and punishment (a token economy).

In Chapter 7, Horton provides a well-controlled study of aggression in delinquent boys. In this study she also sheds some light on one of the concerns listed by Burchard in Chapter 5—that of generalization. This study makes use of the *principle of positive reinforcement.* The experimental design is a baseline or experimental analysis of behavior design in which control over aggression in a card game was demonstrated by (a) measuring the frequency of the aggression *before* any experimental intervention (baseline) and (b) then by alternating series of sessions when aggression meets with positive reinforcement with sessions in which nonaggressive behavior is rewarded. A second game was played after the card games, and although aggression was measured, reinforcement was not used (this being the generalization measure). Aggressive behavior did generalize from the first situation to the second. Since aggression is such an important component of delinquent behavior, close qualitative or quantitative control over it is imperative in any comprehensive behavior therapy program with delinquents. Basic research such as that of Horton is needed to help in developing such programs.

In Chapter 8, Stumphauzer demonstrates close control over delay choices in youthful offenders by systematic use of the *principle of social reinforcement.* A baseline design is utilized in exploring one method of controlling delaying behavior—a class of behaviors especially important for many delinquents in that they are impulsive, hedonistic, and do not delay gratification.

Albert Bandura and his colleagues at Stanford University have carried out with normal subjects three lines of basic research which seem to have particular relevance in modifying delinquent behavior. Through his extensive research and writing, Bandura has been the key figure in exploring the variables controlling the *principle of modeling and imitative learning* (Bandura, 1962; Bandura and Walters, 1964; Bandura, 1965; Bandura, 1970). In one study having relevance for delinquency, Bandura, Ross, and Ross (1963) demonstrated the acquisition of certain aggressive behaviors in young children by exposure to aggressive models. Hartman (1969) demonstrated similar observational learning in an experiment with delinquent subjects. In a second line of research, Bandura and McDonald (1963) showed change in the moral judgments of children through imitation. A similar demonstration of imitative learning of moral judgments, but with delinquents, was made by Prentice (1970). A third line of relevant research is on delay of gratification. In a first study, Bandura and Mischel (1965) modified self-imposed delay of reward in fourth and fifth graders using adult models. Using older, prestigious prisoner peers as models, Stumphauzer (Ch. 9) increased delay of gratification in younger inmates using a pretest post-test control group design. Further, the delaying behavior on the measure modeled did generalize to another measure which was not specifically modeled in the study and the effect was maintained at a one-month follow-up.

These lines of research demonstrate the acquisition of three important types of behaviors in delinquents using imitative learning (aggression, moral judgments, and delay of gratification), but they are not treatment programs. While imitative learning has been shown to be a powerful method for changing the behavior of delinquents, very little treatment or behavior therapy has yet been carried out using this mode of learning. Sarason's (1968) project in Seattle, Washington, is the notable exception. He worked with groups of delinquents about to leave an institution. College graduate students served as models who demonstrated first a poor way of handling a situation (e.g. applying for a job or a confrontation with police), and then they modeled a more appropriate way of behaving in such situations. The delinquents then were each asked to imitate the models' preferred way of handling each situation. Improvements were seen as a result of these modeling experiences, but they were only indirect measures of whatever learning took place. For example, rather than seeing whether delinquents improved in their *actual* job-interviewing behavior or in their behavior when talking with police (behavior they supposedly learned through observation), results were based instead on changes in ratings and psychological test results. Also, it is suggested here that older, prestigious peers might make better (more effective) models for delinquents than college students. Studies of the relative effectiveness of various models for delinquents are needed. Buehler *et al.* did show how influential the delinquent peer group can be, and Stumphauzer showed that prestigious peers could influence the behavior of youthful offenders in a prosocial direction just through modeling. Imitative learning seems potentially a very fruitful approach for behavior therapy with delinquents; its potentials are just beginning to be realized in behavior therapy in general. As early as 1965, Bandura was questioning why we make such extensive use of imitative learning in training counselors and therapists and yet fail to use this powerful mode of learning in our treatment programs. Mowrer (1966) has underscored this point further.

REFERENCES

Bandura, A.: Social learning through imitation. In M. R. Jones (Ed): *Nebraska Symposium on Motivation:* University of Nebraska Press, Lincoln, 1962, pp. 211-269.

Bandura, A.: Behavioral modifications through modeling procedures. In Krasner, L., and Ullman, L. P. (Eds.): *Research in Behavior Modification.* New York, Holt, Rinehart and Winston, 1965, pp. 310-340.

Bandura, A.: Behavioral psychotherapy. *Scientific American, 216:*2-8, 1967.

Bandura, A.: *Principles of behavior modification.* New York, Holt, Rinehart and Winston, 1970.

Bandura, A., and McDonald, F. J.: Influence of social reinforcement and the behavior of models in shaping children's moral judgments. *Journal of Abnormal and Social Psychology, 67:*274-281, 1963.

Bandura, A., and Mischel, W.: Modification of self-imposed delay of reward through exposure to live and symbolic models. *Journal of Personality and Social Psychology, 2:*298-705, 1965.

Bandura, A., Ross, D., and Ross, A.: Imitation of film-mediated aggressive models. *Journal of Abnormal and Social Psychology, 66:*3-11, 1963.

Bandura, A., and Walters, R. H.: *Social learning and personality development.* New York, Holt, Rinehart and Winston, 1964.

Baron, J.: Is experimental psychology relevant? *American Psychologist, 26:* 713-716, 1971.

Paul, G. L.: Behavior modification research: design and tactics. In Franks, C. M. (Ed.): *Behavior Therapy: Appraisal and Status.* New York, McGraw-Hill, 1969, pp. 29-62.

Hartman, D. P.: Influence of symbolically modeled instrumental aggression and pain cues on aggressive behavior. *Journal of Personality and Social Psychology, 11:*280-288, 1969.

Mowrer, O. H.: The behavior therapies, with special reference to modeling and imitation. *American Journal of Psychotherapy, 20:*439-461, 1966.

Prentice, N. M.: Influence of actual and symbolic modeling in argumenting moral development of adolescent delinquents. Paper read at the Southwestern Psychological Association meetings, St. Louis, April 23, 1970.

Sarason, I. G.: Verbal learning, modeling, and juvenile delinquency. *American Psychologist, 23:*254-266, 1968.

Chapter 6

THE REINFORCEMENT OF BEHAVIOR
IN INSTITUTIONAL SETTINGS

R. E. BUEHLER, G. R. PATTERSON and J. M. FURNISS

T HE IMPORTANCE of the peer group in shaping and controlling behavior has been stressed by both sociocultural and psychological theorists. The present report summarizes a series of pilot studies which identify some of the behavioral processes associated with shaping and controlling behavior within a peer group of delinquent adolescents.

The assumptions implicit in these studies are derived from recent literature on social learning and interpersonal communications behavior. Specifically, it is assumed that the interpersonal communication transactions within a peer group function as reinforcers. When put in terms of a reinforcement paradigm, this means that in the peer-group situation, behavior operates upon the social environment. The nature of the environmental response (s) (which often is not a single act but multifarious movements on the part of several persons) influences the future probabilities of the recurrence of the behavior. If the environmental response is rewarding to the actor, the act will tend to be repeated. If the response is aversive and act tends not to recur. Within this general framework, outlined initially by Skinner (1953), we are suggesting that the delinquent peer group provides massive schedules of positive reinforcement for deviant behavior and negative reinforcement or punishment for socially conforming behavior. If these hypotheses are correct, it would appear that settings which provide prolonged interpersonal transactions among

Reprinted with permission from *Behavior Research and Therapy*, 4:157-167, 1966. (Pergamon Press)

delinquent adolescents might be expected to provide an excellent opportunity for maintaining existing deviant behavior, and for the "novice" an opportunity to acquire new sets of deviant behavior. We would hypothesize too that within the institutional setting, the majority of social reinforcers are provided by the peer group rather than by the staff. The institutional setting thus would be seen as a "teaching machine" programmed for the maintenance and acquisition of deviant behavior rather than for retraining the child to more socially adaptive behavior.

STUDY NUMBER ONE

A pilot study by Patterson (1963) provided a preliminary test for these hypotheses. Fifteen two-hour observations were made in a detention home for delinquent children. The observer sampled most of her observations from a small group of delinquent girls. After observing for a period of time, the observer would withdraw and write a descriptive account of each episode in which either a delinquent response or a response which was obviously conforming to social norms occurred. Each behavioral description also outlined the consequences of these responses, e.g. *Roberta:* "She is sickening" (referring to the housemother); *Steve:* "Not very smart either." Karen laughs. This direct criticism of an adult authority figure is reinforced immediately by two different members of the peer group. The various delinquent responses were classified into responses reflexing delinquent value systems, i.e. deviant sex behaviors, breaking rules, any form of rejection of adult authority, aggressive talk and expressing ideas consistent with delinquent behavior. The other major category of responses consisted of behavior corresponding to societal norms, such as talking of going to college, admission of feelings of guilt and regret for having indulged in delinquent acts, expressions of expectations regarding avoidance of delinquent behavior, saying they liked someone on the staff, and expression of cooperation with the treatment program.

The consequences of this behavior were classified into two general categories: "positive reinforcement" and "punishment." Under the heading of positive reinforcement were included such peer reactions as approval, agreement, interest, attention, laughing, smiling, imitating the speaker, etc. Under the heading of punishment were categorized such behaviors as disagreeing, threatening, frowning, ignoring, sneering, etc.

The data were clear in showing overwhelming positive reinforcement (70 percent) for such behavior as rule breaking, criticisms of adults and adult rules, aggressive behavior, and "kicks." In keeping with the hypotheses, the peer group was most likely to disapprove when the behavior in question deviated from the delinquent norms. These data, of course, represented a limited sample obtained by one observer from one group in a single institutional setting. Although the results obtained were in keeping with the general predictions made, it was necessary to carry out an extensive replication before placing any confidence in the conclusions. Such a replication was carried out in study number two which is reported in more detail below.

STUDY NUMBER TWO

The methodology in a study conducted by Furniss (1964) was derived from the social reinforcement model utilized by Patterson and an interpersonal communications behavior analysis method developed by Buehler and Richmond (1963). These two methodologies were combined because it appeared to the writers that each set of procedure would contribute something unique to our understanding of delinquent behavior. Social learning research has tended to simply classify communication behavior as verbal or nonverbal, without identifying the specific communication behavior which is utilized by members of particular subgroups of the population. Since sociocultural studies have long indicated that there are wide variations among people in the use of interpersonal communication behavior, it follows that there are no standard reinforcement contingencies which cross all age, sex, and cultural subgroups. As a means for obtaining more precise measures of peer group social reinforcement behavior in an institutional setting, Furniss combined the interpersonal communication behavior analysis method and the social reinforcement method utilized previously by Patterson.

The interpersonal communication analysis method is for observing and measuring interpersonal communication behavior in terms of four postulated levels of communication (Richmond and Buehler, 1962; Buehler and Richmond, 1963 a and b). This method, developed within a transactional rather than a self-action or interactional frame of reference (Dewey and Bentley, 1949) is based upon the postulate that all interpersonal behavior is communication and that this behavior occurs on four primary levels. These levels are (a) biochemical, (b) motor movement, (c) speech and (d) technology. Each of the four levels or categories has subcategories which are defined operationally in terms of observable movement on the part of a person during interpersonal transactional episodes. The unit of measure is a time interval of 2.5 sec. All behavior which occurs in any category is scored once in each interval. Meaning, intent, effects, etc. are rigorously excluded from scoring system as these are seen as observer's subjective interpretations of the observed behavior and should be derived, if necessary, from analyses of the sequences of ongoing behavior rather than imputed to the behavior by the observer.

It was predicted that the combination of these two methods and their implicit coding systems would result in a more powerful instrument for measuring the specific reinforcement processes within a peer group. Furniss' study was done in a state institution for girls who had been committed by juvenile courts for a variety of socially maladaptive behaviors.

Methods

Observations were made during students' leisure time hours on the cottages. The observer would note all interaction episodes on the part of the subject or subjects being observed at the time and immediately after write a detailed list of all behavior which she observed. These lists were later coded independently by two judges for level of communication on which each observed act occurred; whether the act was in accordance with delinquent or socially appropriate norms; and the peer response (s) (reinforcements). Responses were categorized as positive reinforcements if there was an indication of attention or approval given the subject by a peer or peers, and as punishments if the peer response was disinterest or disapproval. The criteria used in classifying behavior as delinquent or nondelinguent were derived from the girl's handbook of the institution which listed the institution's expectations regarding inmate behavior. The congruence between the social norms expressed in the handbook and those operant in the culture of the communities from which the girls came has never been validated empirically, but was accepted tentatively for purposes of the study.

First, it was hypothesized that the peer group would provide more social approval than disapproval for delinquent behavior. It was also hypothesized that the schedule of rewards for delinquent behavior and the amount of delinquent behavior would not vary as a function of the differences in the social living situations (cottages) within the institution. Third, it was hypothesized that the reinforcing behavior would be significantly more frequent on the nonverbal than verbal levels of communication.*

Six subjects were randomly selected in each of two "open" (less restricted, presumably less delinquent girls) and two "closed" (more restricted, presumably more delinquent girls) cottages, for a total of twenty-four subjects. The subjects' age range was 13.5 to 18 years. Length of institutionalization varied from 2 to 30 months. Prior institutionalization was not checked. On each of the four cottages, the groups were heterogenous with respect to age, length of residence in the institution, and behavior which led to commitment by the courts.

Each subject's interpersonal transactions with peers were observed for a total of 50 minutes, composed of two 25-minute periods on two different days. The order of subject observations was random on each cottage and observations were distributed equally, over time, on all cottages.

Results

Analysis of the data yielded the following results:

1. In peer reinforcement of delinquent behavior, the non-

---

*This hypothesis was not stated in Miss Furniss' original research design but was added by Buehler and Patterson in analyzing her data.

verbal levels of communications were used in 82 percent of the reinforcing responses, while verbal reinforcement was used in only 18 percent of the responses, on all sample cottages.

2. In peer reinforcement of socially conforming behavior, 36 percent of the reinforcers occurred on the level of speech and 64 percent occurred on the nonverbal levels.

3. The frequency of delinquent responses did not differ with respect to "open" versus "closed" cottages. Consequently, "open" as compared to "closed" cottage status did not signify any significant difference in the frequency of delinquent behavior within the peer group.

4. Delinquent behavior was rewarded by the peer group on the open cottages as frequently as it was rewarded on the closed cottages.

5. On all sample cottages (four of the institution's eight) the reinforcement of delinquent responses by peers occurred significantly more often $(P<.001)$ than the punishment of delinquent responses.

6. On all sample cottages the peer group punished socially conforming behavior more frequently $(P<.01)$ than they rewarded such behavior.

These results are extremely suggestive as to what learning takes place within the inmate social system in an institution and what is involved in altering behavior in treatment institutions. In the main, delinquent behavior on the part of the peer group and its members occurs and is reinforced on the nonverbal level of behavior. In other words, the bulk of the teaching among the girls is nonverbal. This corresponds with well-known postulates regarding communication behavior as articulated by Mead (1934), Hall (1959) and others.

In terms of treatment processes, it becomes obvious that the continuous peer group reinforcement of behavior by nonverbal communications must be taken into account and dealt with. It is clear that verbal behavior among peers does not alone accurately represent the teaching process which actually takes place within peer groups. Furthermore the data from the closed cottages suggest that institutional criteria for "improved behavior" may be related simply to "security" (more or less locked doors) and other maintenance variables rather than to changed social attitudes and behavior. In actual ratio of punishment versus reward for delinquent or nondelinquent behavior, Furniss' data agree essentially with those previously obtained (in a smaller institution) by Patterson, namely, in 132 responses to delinquent behavior, 116 (88 percent) were rewarding and 16 (12 percent) were punishing. Thus, regardless of institution size, the peer group communication transactions tend to maintain the very attitudes and behavior which led to institutionalization.

STUDY NUMBER THREE

The next in this series of pilot studies consisted of efforts to test some methods for developing a specific behavioral analysis for each individual member of a delinquent peer group in an institution, to refine the methods of determining the peer group reinforcement contingencies, and to develop procedures for determining schedules of reinforcement to be administered initially by the staff and eventually by the peer group itself.

The two previous pilot studies, while focusing for empirical purposes only upon the peer group, did nevertheless lead to the definite impression that staff members in both settings tended to reward and punish indiscriminately. The focus of attention in the third study was upon the peer group behavior and the reinforcement contingencies dispensed by the immediate staff members.

The assumption in this study was borrowed directly from current social reinforcement literature. This assumption involves both the interpersonal communication and the social reinforcement paradigms discussed previously. An analysis of current literature indicates that first, the behavior which needs to be either reinforced or extinguished must be identified specifically and second, the environmental response (reinforcing agent) must be on the same level of communication as the act which is to be reinforced. There are exceptions to this, of course, but this is assumed to be a general rule, e.g. smiling or frowning is a more spontaneous response to a smile than is a verbal statement such as "I am glad to see you smile" or "Stop your smiling." In an official communication system such as presented by a school, a verbal punishment or reward may be used by the teacher in response to a nonverbal act on the part of the student, but within the peer group itself, as Furniss' data indicated, there is a high level of congruence between the level of communication utilized by the actor and the peer group respondents. We would speculate that this congruence in levels of communication through which reinforcements are continuously dispensed in ongoing peer group transactions may be one reason why the peer group is so effective in shaping and controlling behavior.

These considerations, among others, suggested to Buehler and Patterson that the field of investigation should be enlarged to include the reinforcing behavior operant in the total social system of one residential cottage in the institution for delinquent girls which was utilized in Furniss' study. This involved refining the methods for identifying the schedules of reinforcement within the peer group of girls and the reinforcing behavior of the staff members with reference to the girls' behavior.

Methods

Behavioral observations were made by an observer equipped with a small portable dictation machine with a microphone inserted in a rubber mask which covered the observer's mouth. As a means for obtaining a maximum amount of data on individual girls, a sample of six subjects was selected randomly for daily observations. The observer went on the cottage at 4:00 P.M., five days a week and remained until the girls' bedtime at 9:00 P.M. The observations included two one-hour group meetings each week, which were conducted by the senior author. Two cottage supervisors (housemothers) and a staff social worker attended the group meetings along with the twenty-four resident girls.

The observer focused her attention on the interpersonal transactions on the part of the six subjects, including their transactions with staff members. The tapes were transcribed each day and separate sheets were extracted for each of the six subjects and each staff member. These individual behavioral protocols were coded in terms of communication and reinforcement categories.

Behavioral Diagnoses

The behavioral protocols obtained in the manner described above were utilized along with behavioral data in the subject's case folder in developing a specific behavioral diagnosis for each subject. The following data presents in some detail a sample of a behavioral diagnosis and a reinforcement prescription for one subject.

Personal history. I.Q. 124. Father inconsistent in his reinforcing behavior, ranging from over-indulgence to physical cruelty. Mother indulged in frequent outbursts of anger and unreasonable accusations. The unreasonable demands made upon the subject by her parents led to a cruelty petition against the home by the Juvenile Court. Subject was committed to the institution after several unsatisfactory foster home placements. Intake information indicated that the subject defied family authority, had few friends, considerable heterosexual activity with a variety of partners, AWOL from foster homes. She alternated between affectionate and hostile behavior with reference to adults. When she felt rejected, she became immature and demanding. Adults generally found her annoying and troublesome and rejected her. Her response to adult rejection was to act out as described above. She had one illegitimate child and refused to give it up. The child was being cared for by the subject's mother and this led to constant friction between the subject and her mother. Subject wanted to live away from her family and care for her child.

The institutional staff reported of the same ambivalent pattern toward adults. The subject appeared to the staff to be eager to please, demanded much attention, manipulated adults and peers, refused to obey rules, tended to be loud, noisy, disruptive and coercive. The staff saw her as acting in a superior manner toward her peers, attempting to boss them, and as being generally rejected by her peers.

The subject's interpersonal transactional behavior was observed at intervals over a period of five days. The kind of reinforcements she was being given by her peer group and by the staff and her responses are presented in Table I.

These behavioral data indicate that the peer group punished the subject for identifying with social norms in a ratio of almost three to one, while the staff rewarded her in a ratio of nine to one. However, the frequency of the reinforcements that were dis-

Behavior Therapy With Delinquents

pensed by the peers greatly outnumbered those dispensed by the staff. Furthermore, when she was hostile toward her peers, they rewarded her in a greater than two to one ratio and when she was hostile toward adults, the adults punished her more or less consistently. She tended to punish her peers when they made social gestures toward her, although she rewarded adults for doing the same thing. The peer group's persistent punishment when the subject verbalized identifications with social norms is very clear. She expressed thirty-seven such identifications and the peer group

TABLE 6-I

Behavior	Reward for Subject's Behavior				Subject's Reward to Others			
	From Peers		From Adults		To Peers		To Adults	
	No. Observed	Reinforcement	No. Observed	Reinforcement	No. Observed	Reinforcement	No. Observed	Reinforcement
Social	29	12+ / 17—	23	16+ / 7—	8	3+ / 5—	5	5+ / 0—
Hostility	19	13+ / 6—	5	0+ / 5—	2	0+ / 2—	0	
Coercive	9	1+ / 8—	3	0+ / 3—	5	1+ / 4—	1	0+ / 1—
Identification with delinquency	1	0+ / 1—	1	1+ / 0—	0		0	
Identification with social norms	37	10+ / 27—	20	18+ / 2—	2	1+ / 1—	0	

+positive reward.
—punishment.

punished her twenty-seven times and rewarded her ten times. The staff, on the other hand, rewarded her eighteen out of twenty times that she identified with social norms in their presence.

These observations indicate that the reinforcement system for the subject tended to be very inconsistent. Her peers tended to reward her for being a delinquent and to punish her whenever she made moves toward socially appropriate behavior, while the staff would alternately reward her and punish her for the same acts.

In the group sessions the subject behaved as would be predicted from the reports and observations shown above. She would verbally identify herself with social norms (getting a job and taking care of her child, staying out of further trouble with Juvenile

Court, etc.) and was persistently punished by her peers for these identifications. She would retaliate and some of her peers would counter-retaliate. This intragroup conflict would rise in intensity as long as the group discussion leader played a nondirective role. When the leader's role shifted to identifying the group's behavior (e.g. "S is trying to say that she wants to leave this institution, get a job, etc. and some of you girls are punishing her for wanting to do these things"), the girls who silently approved S's behavior would begin to reward her.

It was noticeable in the group meetings that the more aggressive, dominating and coercive girls tended to punish those girls who attempted to show some socially conforming attitudes, expectations and behavior. This was particularly true of another subject who was the leader of an informal subgroup of girls on the cottage. This girl saw the group meetings as a distinct threat to her control over her domineering "gang." A previous group leader had given in to the two rival informal groups on the cottage and was meeting separately with each of them. Under the former leader's nondirective leadership the two rival gangs remained intact and in daily conflict for control of the communal life on the cottage. When this gang behavior was pointed up in meetings of all the girls and the staff, the two gang leaders would aggressively punish every girl who in one way or another supported the discussion leader's efforts to elicit cooperation in seeking solutions to the intra-cottage problems. This behavior strengthened the authors' assumption that if schedules of reinforcement within the peer group are to be changed in the direction of socially appropriate behavior, something other than "nondirective" evocative therapy is required.

The behavioral analyses described above suggested that the initial treatment prescription for the subject may be as follows:

Reward
1. Every socially appropriate approach to an adult.
2. All of the subject's references to her maternal role and her maternal role responsibilities.
3. Give the subject much attention and praise when she engages in social responsible acts toward her peers.

4. Reward the subject's peers when they reward her socially appropriate acts.
5. Reward the subject's peers when they resist being coerced by the subject.

Punishment
1. Ignore the subject's loud, boisterous, coercive and bossy behavior.
2. Confront and in any other appropriate way punish the subject's peers when they punish her for her efforts to conform to socially appropriate norms.

Each of the six subjects' behavior was observed and analyzed in the manner described above. The specific behavioral categories for each girl varied, however. Such categories as isolation from peers, passive resistance, or physical aggression were also used in order to tailor-make the descriptive system for each girl. One subject in particular, a very attractive girl who was a strong leader among her peers, showed thirteen coercive acts towards her peers for which she was rewarded nine times and punished only four times. She also showed fourteen coercive acts towards adults and was rewarded seven times and punished seven times by adults. She showed hostility towards adults in the presence of her peers a total of twenty-six times and was rewarded by her peers twelve times and punished fourteen times. For the same behavior she was rewarded three times and punished twenty-three times by adults. This suggested how she was being taught by her peer group to be an aggressive, coercive leader and to continue to be hostile and defiant toward adults.

The observed transactions between the staff and the girls were not as frequent as were the transactions among the peers because the adult staff members showed a tendency to remain in their offices or to sit on the periphery of the social group. However, the observed adult behavior of six staff members who at one time or the other were on the cottage over a period of a week, is summarized in Table II.

These data support the impression obtained in the preceding studies, namely, that staff members tended to reinforce and to punish indiscriminately. Such vacillating schedules of reinforcement we assume, would tend to reduce severely the effectiveness of the staff in influencing inmate behavior in any direction. In the two classes of behavior with the greatest frequency, social and coercive, the staff response was approximately equal in punishment and in reward. It is interesting to note too that the girls reinforced and punished the staff in an equally inconsistent manner. The peer group's response to coping behavior on the part of the staff is particulary interesting in view of the traditions of staff

TABLE 6-II

BEHAVIOR OF SIX STAFF MEMBERS IN THE COTTAGE, ONE WEEK OF OBSERVATION

Behavior	Reinforcement Given to Girls		Reinforcement Received from Girls	
	No. Observed	Ratio	No. Observed	Ratio
Social	18	11+ 7—	19	10+ 9—
Coercive	20	11+ 9—	14	11+ 3—
Hostile	1	1+ 0—	16	8+ 8—
Information giving	3	1+ 2—	4	3+ 1—
Information asked	5	3+ 2—		
Usurping role of student	5	3+ 2—		
Coping with problems			4	1+ 3—
Not coping			12	3+ 9—
Decision making:				
Self			15	10+ 5—
Refer decision to girl			7	4+ 3—
Refer decision to group			7	1+ 6—
Refer decision to administrator			11	3+ 8—

authority and responsibility in penal institutions. When the staff failed to cope with problems they were punished in a three to one ratio. When staff referred problems back to the group for group action and/or decision, the staff was punished by the peer group in a ratio of six to one. Also, when staff referred problems to the administration the peer group punished them consistently (8:3). The implications of these data for further research and theory construction with reference to therapeutic and/or educational social systems are challenging indeed.

DISCUSSION

The persistence of delinquent behavior in institutions where the official aim is to "correct" such behavior has been documented repeatedly in long and melancholy "recidivism" lists. Of equal note is the fact frequently mentioned in the literature, that during the process of institutionalization, many cases of adolescent deviation (e.g. truancy, running away from home,) are converted into severe criminal offenders. The "peer group culture" has been blamed for these reversals of official intentions, but *how* the peer group achieves these effects has not been identified or described in *behavioral* terms. Nor has the staff behavior which contributes to these effects been documented. The data in the three studies reviewed above identify two separate behavioral systems within a single peer group and the other is operated by the staff. While no data were obtained in these pilot studies on the relative effects of the two behavioral systems, other data on peer group phenomena (Patterson, 1963; Schrag, 1961; and others) permit us to hypothesize that it is the peer group behavioral system which has the predominating effects. In fact, it is reasonable to hypothesize that the inmate behavioral system not only shapes and controls its own members, but also it shapes and controls the behavior of the staff.

The problem, as we see it, is to identify and to establish controls over the behavior occurring in peer groups which keeps the group resistant to institutional treatment objectives. We emphasize the term "treatment objective" because these data suggest that while the objective of the institutions in which the data were obtained was to "correct" the delinquency, the behavioral operations of the staff tended to reward or punish delinquent behavior indiscriminately. There is ample evidence in social reinforcement research that when reinforcements are inconsistent the reinforcing agent has no effect.

These data suggest that a social reinforcement approach to behavioral diagnosis and treatment planning and operations is feasible. The impressive data on behavior modification which has been summarized in part by Krasner and Ullmann (1965) and by Bandura and Walters (1963), as well as in a wide range of scientific journals, suggest that this may be a promising approach to treatment operations in a "correctional" setting.

As an initial step to modifying delinquent schedules of reinforcement within a peer group, we assume that a rigorous behavioral approach needs to be adopted by the staff. It was noted by the authors in informal conversations with staff members that they had a marked tendency to attach moral labels to the inmates and would respond to the label rather than to specific behavior of the labeled girl (e.g. Mary is "good," therefore she will be rewarded persistently regardless of her behavior, Susie is "bad," therefore she will be punished persistently regardless of whatever moves she makes toward socially conforming behavior). Once a behavioral frame of reference is adopted, the next step in this paradigm would be to adopt a rigorous observational system for identifying the specific behaviors and reinforcing contingencies within the inmate peer groups. The method of observing the behavior as described above is simple, requires no instruments and can be adopted easily by relatively untrained persons (the research assistant in Study No. 3 was a college sophomore). The final steps would be to tailor-make a schedule of reinforcement to fit each separate inmate and the group as a whole, and to teach the staff how to use their own interpersonal communication behavior as a source of reinforcement.

REFERENCES

Bandura, A. and Walters, R. H.: *Social Learning and Personality Development*. New York, Holt, Rinehart and Winston, 1963.

Buehler, R. E. and Richmond, J. F.: Interpersonal communication behavior analysis; a research method. *J Commun, XIII*(No. 3), 1963a.

Buehler, R. E. and Richmond, J. F.: Pilot study on interpersonal communication behavior analysis method. Research report, Board of Control, Salem, Oregon, 1963b.

Dewey, J. and Bentley, A. F.: *Knowing and the Known*. Boston, Beacon Press, 1949.

Furniss, Jean: Peer Reinforcement of Behavior in an Institution for Delinquent Girls. Unpublished master's thesis, Oregon State University, 1964.

Hall, E. T.: *The Silent Language*. New York, Doubleday, 1959.

Krasner, L. and Ulmann, L.P.: *Case Studies in Behavior Modification*. New York, Holt, Rinehart and Winston, 1965.

Mead, G. H.: *Mind, Self and Society*. Chicago, University of Chicago Press, 1934.

Patterson, G. R.: The Peer Group as Delinquency Reinforcement Agent. Unpublished research report, Child Research Laboratory: Eugene, Oregon, University of Oregon, 1963.

Richmond, J. F. and Buehler, R. E.: Interpersonal communication: a theoretical formation. *J Commun, XII*(No. 1), 1962.

Schrag, C.: Some foundations for a theory of corrections. In Cressey, *The Prison*. New York, Holt, Rinehart and Winston, 1961.

Skinner, B. F.: *Science and Human Behavior*. New York, Macmillan, 1953.

Chapter 7

GENERALIZATION OF AGGRESSIVE BEHAVIOR IN ADOLESCENT DELINQUENT BOYS

LOIS E. HORTON

Recent experimental evidence (Bandura and Walters, 1963; Bandura, Ross, and Ross, 1963; Brown and Elliott, 1965; Burchard and Tyler, 1965) has shown learning theory to be a fruitful approach to the study of aggressive behavior and its control. Within a learning framework, aggressive responses may be seen as instrumental responses, operating on the environment to produce reinforcement for the individual.

The definition of aggressive behavior has proven difficult. The labeling of a response as aggressive frequently involves social judgments concerning intentionality (Dollard, Doob, Miller, Mowrer, and Sears, 1939) and intensity (Walters and Brown, 1963) of responses. Most theorists, however, consider aggressive behavior as that which produces or is potentially capable of producing harm or pain (Bandura and Walters, 1963).

Aggressive responses, when viewed as learned responses capable of being manipulated by operant conditioning procedures,

Reprinted with permission from *Journal of Applied Behavior Analysis, 3*:205-211, 1970. (University of Kansas, Department of Human Development)

This paper is based on a thesis submitted to the Graduate School of the University of Hawaii in partial fulfillment of the requirements for the Master of Arts degree. The author expresses appreciation to Dr. Karl A. Minke for his support and encouragement throughout this research project. Gratitude is expressed to the administration and staff of the Salvation Army Facilities for Children, Honolulu, Hawaii, whose cooperation made this research possible and to Mr. Charles Figley and Mr. Ramon Tanaka, students at the University of Hawaii, for their assistance in the conduct of this study.

may, according to the principles of learning theory, also generalize to similar situations. The extent of this generalization and the conditions under which it will occur are questions as yet not fully answered. Of particular interest is the possibility of the generalization of aggressive or nonaggressive responses from the controlled experimental setting to another setting that is not under experimental control.

Walters and Brown (1963) reported that high-intensity aggressive response did generalize and that subjects trained to make high-intensity aggressive and nonaggressive responses emitted more responses rated as aggressive in a generalization situation than did subjects trained to make low-intensity responses (Walters and Brown, 1964). Wahler (1969), using behavior therapy techniques with parents and children in the home situation, found no generalization to the children's behavior in school.

With social learning theory and research findings on the conditioning and generalization of aggressive behavior as a referent, this experiment was undertaken with delinquent adolescent boys. Several authors (Cohen, 1955; Kvaraceus and Miller, 1959; Cloward and Ohlin, 1960) have indicated that the treatment of aggressive and/or delinquent behavior with this population is particularly difficult because a boy's peer group pressures are frequently stronger than an adult therapist's influence and usually serve to maintain delinquent, aggressive behavior. In other words, behavior modification with delinquent adolescent boys may be difficult because the reinforcers manipulated by the peer group are frequently stronger than those manipulated by the therapist and are usually contingent upon the deviant behaviors that are to be changed. For this reason, procedures were employed to assure that the peer group's reinforcement contingencies would be congruent with those imposed by the experimenter.

It was hypothesized that the frequency of aggressive responses would increase if reinforced in a particular situation, and conversely, that if only nonaggressive responses were reinforced in the situation, aggressive responses would decrease. It was further hypothesized that the behavior reinforced in a situation would generalize to a different situation in which no reinforcement was given, provided that the two situations had a sufficient number of stimuli in common.

METHOD

Subjects

Six males, ranging in age from 11 years, 5 months to 15 years, 10 months, with a mean age of 12 years, 10 months, were resident at a home for delinquent, emotionally disturbed children, to which they had been referred either by a social welfare organization or by the family court. Three of the six subjects had juvenile court records at the time of the experiment and the psychiatric diagnosis for all subjects was "adjustment reaction to childhood." Three of the six subjects were characterized by an administrator of the home as having consistently aggressive patterns of responding; three were described as being not overtly aggressive. The length of stay in the home for the subjects ranged from two months to 2 years, 10 months, with a mean of 1 year, 4 months.

Setting

The experiment, which was conducted in the living-dining area of the cottage in which five of the six subjects resided, lasted for seven weeks, with approximately 20 minute sessions on four consecutive evenings each week. With the exception of three vacation days, which will be discussed in more detail later, the experimental sessions followed the subjects' dinner hour and preceded their study hour.

Procedures

Subjects engaged in two game situations during each experimental session, the games being conducted by two student assistants. On the first day, subjects were told that the same two games would be played for each session of the experiment in order "to see how you like them and to see how long you will like to play them." They were then given specific instructions for playing the games and were told that after about one week they would be able to earn money while playing the first game. Subjects were informed that no money would ever be given for the second game.

They were also told that weekly payments would be given and that these payments would also be contingent upon winnings in the first game only.

For the first experimental game, each of three pairs of subjects engaged in the card game "War" (situation A). For each of the three card games played per session, a deck of playing cards and 52 poker chips were divided evenly between the two players. Each subject's poker chips were placed in a paper cup to preclude their loss, and an empty paper cup was placed between the players. A trial consisted of the playing of one card by each member of the pair, the player of the card of the highest value being the winner of that trial. Suits were given a relative value so that no tie would occur when each player played a card of the same numerical value. Two response options were open to the winner of a trial. He could either slap the hand of the loser or he could instruct the loser to forfeit one poker chip, placing it in the paper cup between the players. Any hand-slap in this game was counted as an aggressive response. Instructing the loser to forfeit a poker chip was defined as a nonaggressive response. The subjects were specifically told that the poker chips themselves had no value but that their use constituted "part of the rules of the game."

The three pairs of subjects played this game in succession, making a total at 78 trials for each session. All aggressive response for the three card games were totaled, giving a single measure of aggressive responding for each session. Although each session had 78 clearly defined trials, aggressive responses could exceed 78 per session, if on a given trial both the winner and the loser emitted a hand-slap response or if either emitted more than one slap on a trial.

At the beginning of the experiment, each subject was paired with another subject for the first game situation. Pairings were changed for each of five consecutive sessions so that each subject was paired with every other subject during that time. After five sessions the original pairs were used. Pair rotations continued in the same order throughout the experiment regardless of the length of each experimental period.

To maintain participation in the experimental situation, particularly during the baseline period, money was given to each subject at the end of each week of the experiment, with payment being made after the training situation. The amount of money was based upon the number of cards won during the week and therefore was dependent upon chance. For the baseline period, payments were given according to rank order of the subjects' winnings and were $3.00, $2.50, $2.00, $1.50, $1.00, and $0.50 respectively. Weekly payment for the baseline period was given for the total cards won over five sessions; after the baseline period, payment was given for the total cards won in the four sessions conducted per week. For each week after the baseline period, weekly payments based upon the subjects' winnings were $2.00, $1.00, $0.75, $0.50, $0.10, and $0.05 respectively.

After the baseline period, immediate reinforcement contingent upon aggressive responses was instituted in the card games. A small open cardboard box was placed on the table between the players and the following instructions were given to all subjects by the experimenter.

> Beginning today, you will be able to earn anywhere from 0 to 47 cents a day. Everyone will get the same amount for each day.
>
> Once in a while during each card game, I'll drop a bean in this box. At the end of all three card games, the beans will be counted and you will get money according to how many beans there are in the box.

Only the first response on each trial was reinforced and immediate reinforcement was given only once per trial. Aggressive or nonaggressive responses were alternately reinforced over four experimental periods, beginning with the reinforcement of aggressive responses in the first period. Throughout the experimental sessions, backup reinforcers were given immediately after the card games at a ratio of 5:3. That is, for every five beans in the box, three cents were given to each subject.

The baseline period was in effect for six sessions, experimental period I for five sessions, experimental period II for nine sessions, experiment period III for four sessions, and experimental period IV for four sessions, making a total of 28 sessions or seven weeks for the entire experiment.

Following the card games each day, all subjects engaged in a game of "Steal the Bacon" (situation B), for which two teams of three members each were formed. Team members were rotated so that by the end of 10 sessions each subject had been paired with all possible combinations of two other subjects and had played against all possible combinations of three other subjects. At the end of 10 sessions, the original groupings were used with team rotations continuing in the same order throughout the experiment. During this game, each player had a large handkerchief inserted in his belt or pocket in such a way that it was readily visible and easily removed without need of physical contact. At the beginning of this game for each session, each member of a team was assigned a number from one to three. Each team was seated on a couch at opposite sides of the game area, which was approximately 20 by 20 feet. A hand towel was placed on the floor in the center of the game area and an experimenter called out a number. Members of opposing teams identified by that number proceeded to the center of the game area. The first player to pick up the towel and to reach his seat on the couch without having his handkerchief taken by his opponent made a point for his team. The duration of this game was 8 minutes, during which time instances of physical contact, regardless of intensity, were tabulated to give a single measure of aggressive responding per session. In this situation, physical contact included punching, slapping, kicking, and pushing or pulling. Any time a subject's body came into contact with another subject, or with an experimenter, it was counted as an instance of aggression. Pushing or pulling with two hands, for example, was counted as two aggressive responses. Hitting another subject with an object was also counted as an aggressive response. At the conclusion of this game for each session, the subjects were simply told which team had scored the greatest number of points; no monetary reinforcement was ever delivered.

RESULTS

In the card game the hitting response was readily manipulated through the reinforcement of aggressive or nonaggressive responses as shown in Figure 7-1. In the generalization game, the level of aggressive responses was usually related to the card game

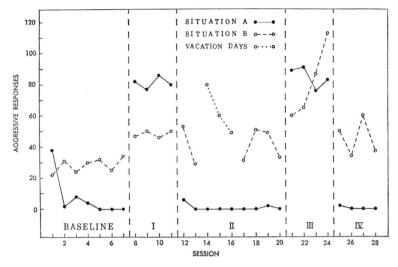

Figure 7-1. Aggressive responses per session.

contingencies, although no reinforcement was scheduled during this situation.

Training Situation

For the first session during the baseline period, approximately one-half of the total responses were aggressive. Thereafter, aggressive responses rapidly declined. By the fifth session and continuing through the seventh session, there were no aggressive responses. The mean number of aggressive responses per session for the card games during the baseline period was seven.

Aggressive responses were reinforced during the first experimental period. For the first session of this period there were no aggressive responses and thus no additional reinforcers were given. Since the generalization of a conditioned behavior was of primary interest in this experiment, and there was no opportunity for reinforcement during this first session, data from this session were added to the baseline period for graphic presentation and for the computation of means. In the second session, an aggressive response was emitted on the first trial and immediate reinforcement was given. Following this reinforcement, acquisition of the conditioned response was rapid. During the second session, the first pair of players did not emit any response on three trials. No non-aggressive responses were emitted during the remainder of this experimental period. The number of aggressive responses for three of four sessions in this period was more than one per trial, even though reinforcement was given for only one response per trial. During one session there were eight trials on which multiple aggressive responses occurred, either in the form of hits by both the winner and the loser or more than one hit per trial by the winner. The mean number of aggressive responses per session for the card games during this period was 81.

On the first trial of the second experimental period, an aggressive response was emitted. When no reinforcement was given, a nonaggressive response was emitted. There were six aggressive responses made during the first session under this nonaggressive contingency. By the third game of the first session under this contingency, aggressive responses had been eliminated. The mean number of aggressive responses during the entire period was 0.9.

A nonaggressive response was emitted for the first response during the third experimental period and was not reinforced. Acquisition of the aggressive response was rapid; aggressive responses were frequently recorded at more than one per trial. For two sessions during this period, 11 and 13 multiple hits were recorded. Our casual observations indicated that there may have been other effects of this condition. For example, during the third session, a player and a bystander became involved in a fist fight, with one subject jumping from a table to attack the other, and it was necessary in our opinion to restrain them. Furthermore, by the fourth session, aggressive behavior in the form of slapping, punching, and verbal aggression directed toward the experimenters was frequently observed. However, only game hand-slaps were counted in the measure of aggressive responding. The mean number of aggressive responses per session for the card games during this period was 85.

A nonaggressive response was emitted on the first trial during the last experimental period and immediate reinforcement was given. Aggressive responding was eliminated by the second session and no further aggressive responding was recorded for this period. The mean number of aggressive responses during this period was 0.5 in the card games.

Generalization Situation

In the generalization situation, an aggressive response was defined as an instance of physical contact, as described above. During the second experimental period, an observer reliability index was obtained by comparing the count of aggressive responses taken by the experimenter and that taken by an experimental assistant who was unaware of the numerical value of the previous counts. Comparisons were made by use of the formula *smaller/larger × 100*. An observer reliability index of 97 percent was attained. A check of observer reliability four sessions later yielded an index of 94 percent.

During the baseline period (Fig. 7-1), a fairly stable amount of aggressive behavior was noted. Much aggressive behavior in the form of punching and slapping occurred between teammates during this period. The mean number of aggressive responses per session was 29.

When immediate reinforcement for aggressive behavior was received in the card games during the first experimental period, an immediate and substantial rise in aggressive behavior was noted in the generalization game. Aggressive responses stabilized at this new level over four sessions. Aggression not only increased in frequency during this period, but our subjective observations indicated a rise in the intensity of aggressive behavior. In our opinion, it became necessary at one point during this period to discourage one subject from throwing a four-foot-long bolster from a couch at the members of the opposing team. The mean number of aggressive responses per session in this situation during the first experimental period was 48.

During the first session of the second experimental period, the number of aggressive responses continued to rise. During the second session under the nonaggression contingency, aggressive responses declined to a level within the baseline range. On the following three days of the experiment, the subjects were scheduled to go on vacation outings immediately after the experimental sessions. During those days, we observed a rise in aggressive responding. For the first of these vacation days, which were plotted separately in Figure 1, aggressive responding in this game reached a level surpassing that of the previous period of conditioning aggressive responses in the card game. Over the next two sessions, aggression showed a gradual decline to the level of the previous conditioning period. Aggressive responses became fairly stable during the last four sessions of this period when the special outings were no longer scheduled. By the end of this period, aggressive responding had decreased to a level lower than that of the previous period. Patterns of aggressive behavior were very similar to those under the previous experimental conditions, except that little aggression was directed toward teammates. One subject directed some physical aggression toward the experimenters and this was included in the count of aggressive behavior. The mean number of aggressive responses for the generalization situation, including sessions preceding vacation outings, was 48. The mean number per session not including vacation outing sessions was 41.

During the third experimental period an immediate rise in aggressive behavior was noted. By the fourth session, aggressive behavior was so frequent that it became difficult to conduct the game. It seemed as if almost every call of a number resulted in a fist fight or a wrestling match between subjects. The mean number of aggressive responses per session for this period was 81. For the first time, aggressive responses in the generalization game exceeded the number in the card game.

An immediate and pronounced reduction in aggressive responses was noted during the first session of the last experimental period. The mean number of aggressive responses per session for this game during the last experimental period was 45.

An overall increase in aggressive responding occurred in the generalization game when aggressive responses were reinforced in the card games. The second time that aggressive responses were reinforced, an increase of 68 percent in aggressive responding was noted over the mean number of aggressive responses obtained during the first aggressive contingency. A comparison of the two periods of reinforcing nonaggressive responses in the card games shows that the mean number of aggressive responses in the generalization situation decreased slightly, by six percent, the second time. However, if the data from vacation days are omitted, aggressive responding in the generalization situation shows a slight increase across periods of reinforcing nonaggressive responses in the card games.

A general increase in aggressive responding over the baseline measurement was seen for the entire experiment. That is, the mean number of aggressive responses in the generalization situation never decreased to the mean number obtained during the baseline period. There was, however, a corresponding reversal of the trend of aggressive responses in the generalization game for each reversal of reinforcement contingencies in the card games.

DISCUSSION

The present results support the view that aggressive responding can be a learned behavior that can be modified by operant conditioning procedures. Further, the results indicate that a group's aggressive behavior reinforced in one experimental situation will generalize to a different situation in which explicit reinforcement for such behavior is not provided.

The group reinforcement contingencies used in this experiment seemed to be effective with the delinquent adolescent population. Our informal observations indicated that the peer group's reinforcement contingences were compatible with the experimental contingencies. Some subjects frequently seemed to persuade others to emit responses in the card game that were compatible with the contingencies in effect at that time. Thus, in the card games, peer reinforcement may have helped to produce the immediate and significant change in responding for each reversal of experimental contingencies.

There were also indications that these peer reinforcement contingencies generalized. Often during periods of reinforcing nonaggressive responses, subjects appeared to attempt to dissuade a few particularly aggressive subjects from aggressive responding in the generalization game. A marked difference in the type of aggressive responding was also informally noted for different experimental periods. More tackling and fighting or wrestling between three or more subjects at one time seemed to occur during aggressive contingencies than appeared to occur during nonaggressive contingencies. Conversely, during the nonaggressive contingencies, subjects seemed more often to attempt to prevent opponents' making points by taking their handkerchiefs, which could be done with no physical contact, than by using sheer physical force.

These informal observations suggest that the generalization of the peer group's reinforcement contingencies may have been a major reason for the generalization of responses that did occur.

Concerning the relative efficacy of aggressive and nonaggressive reinforcement contingencies in the generalization situation, it was noted that the generalization of nonaggressive responses was slower, more variable and less pronuonced than was the generalization of aggressive responses, with no decrease below the baseline measure during nonaggressive contingencies.

Although the means for periods of reinforcing nonaggressive responses did not indicate a decrease to baseline level, response trends for each period indicate that such differences might have been observed had these periods been extended. Time limitations, however, made extension of these periods impossible.

Since the reversal of the trend of aggressive behavior from each experimental period to the next in the generalization situation may be assumed to be due to the change in reinforcement contingencies, these reversals give support to the hypothesis that conditioned nonaggressive responses and conditioned aggressive responses will generalize to another situation where reinforcement is not scheduled. Of particular interest is the fact that the reversal in trend occurred even when aggressive responses were at a very high and rapidly rising rate before the reversal of reinforcement.

REFERENCES

Bandura, A., Ross, D., and Ross, S.: Imitation of film-mediated aggressive models. *Journal of Abnormal Social Psychology, 66:*3-11, 1963.

Bandura, A. and Walters, R. H.: *Social Learning and Personality Development.* New York, Holt, Rinehart and Winston, 1963.

Brown, P. and Elliott, R.: Control of aggression in a nursery-school class. *Journal of Experimental Child Psychology,* 2:103-107, 1965.

Burchard, J. and Tyler, V., Jr.: The modification of delinquent behavior through operant conditioning. *Behavior Research and Therapy,* 2:245-250, 1965.

Cloward, R. A. and Ohlin, L. E.: *Delinquency and Opportunity.* Glencoe, Ill., The Free Press, 1960.

Cohen, A. K.: *Delinquent Boys: the Culture of the Gang.* Glencoe, Ill., The Free Press, 1955.

Dollard, J., Doob, L. W., Miller, N. E., Mowrer, O. H., and Sears, R. R.: *Frustration and Aggression.* New Haven, Conn., Yale University Press, 1939.

Kvaraceus, W. C. and Miller, W. B.: *Delinquent Behavior, Culture and the Individual.* Washington, D.C., National Educational Association of the United States, 1959.

Wahler, R. G.: Setting generality: some specific and general effects of child behavior therapy. *Journal of Applied Behavior Analysis,* 2:239-246, 1969.

Walters, R. H. and Brown, M. Studies of reinforcement of aggresison. Part II: transfer of responses to an interpersonal situation. *Child Development,* 1963, vol. 34, 563-572.

Walters, R. H. and Brown, M.: A test of the high-magnitude theory of aggression. *Journal of Experimental Child Psychology,* 1:376-387, 1964.

Chapter 8

MODIFICATION OF DELAY CHOICES IN INSTITUTIONALIZED YOUTHFUL OFFENDERS THROUGH SOCIAL REINFORCEMENT

JEROME S. STUMPHAUZER

T HE ABILITY TO WORK and wait for larger rewards, later in time, is stressed in virtually all discussions of normal child development. To learn to delay immediate gratification in favor of later, more valuable reward is an important part of the socialization process. Many juvenile delinquents and adult criminals represent a failure of this socialization. Empirical support for this contention is given by Mischel (1961). Very simply, he offered children a series of choices between something they could have immediately and something more valuable for which they would have to wait. It was found that the delinquents in the sample showed a preference for immediate, smaller rewards. Bandura and Mischel (1965) were able to modify delay of self-reward in fourth- and fifth-grade children by exposure to adult models who displayed the opposite delay orientations. In a preliminary study, Stumphauzer (in press) replicated and extended these findings by increasing the percentage of delay choices in four youthful offenders through exposure to peer models who displayed high-delay orientations. That study is currently being expanded to include more subjects, a control group, and measures of generalization.

Social reinforcement, the response-contingent attention and/or

Reprinted with permission from *Psychonomic Science, 18:*222-223, 1970. (Psychonomic Journals, Inc.) Based in part on a paper given at Florida Psychological Association, Orlando, May 3, 1969.

approval of another person, has been the topic of a good deal of recent experimental research and behavioral psychotherapy. Gewirtz and Baer (1958), for example, found that simple utterances like "Good" and "Mm-hmm" could control the frequency of a behavior in children. In a behavior-modification program, Stumphauzer (1969) was able to control eating behavior and cooperation in a 23-year-old hospitalized anorexic patient with the contingent social attention of an uncle. The present study attempted to control delay of self-reward through response-contingent social reinforcement. Since the experimenter was a staff psychologist at the institution, it seemed particularly relevant to determine if the behavior of inmates could be controlled or modified by his contingent approval.

METHOD

Four 19-year-old inmates of the Federal Correctional Institution for Youthful Offenders in Tallahasse, Florida, served as Subjects. This medium-security institution of 500 inmates serves the southeastern section of the country.

A list of 100 choices between something they could have immediately and something more valuable for which they would have to wait was developed for this population, with the examples provided by Mischel (personal communication). Half of the choices were monetary (e.g. "Would you rather have 25 cents today or 50 cents in 3 weeks?"), and half were between small articles (e.g.) "Would you rather have one pack of cigarettes today or two packs in 3 weeks?"). Subjects seen individually, were told that they would be given a series of choices and to choose carefully and realistically because they would actually receive four of their choices, although they would not know which until the very end. The 100 choices, on index cards, were administered in a random order to each subject. During the baseline phase, or first 25 choices, the choices of the subject were simply recorded. For the second 25 choices, delay choices met with approval from the experimenter—either "Good" or "Mm-hmm." In the third, or reversal, phase of 25 choices, social reinforcement was contingent on immediate or "today" choices. For the final 25 choices, delay

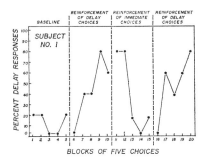

Figure 8-1. Percent delay responses as a function of phases of the experiment for the first subject.

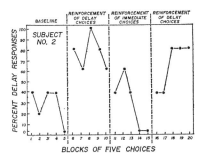

Figure 8-2. Percent delay responses as a function of phases of the experiment for the second subject.

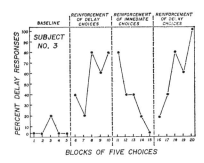

Figure 8-3. Percent delay responses as a function of phases of the experiment for the third subject.

choices were again reinforced. At the end of the sessions, Subjects were given four of the choices they had made.

RESULTS

During the baseline phase, all four Subjects demonstrated an immediate-gratification orientation, with delay choices varying from 0 to 40 percent (see figures). In phase 2, reinforcement of delay choices, delay choices were seen to increase from 60 to 100 percent in each Subject. In phase 3, or reversal phase, reinforcement of immediate choices, delay choices decreased to 0 percent in all Subjects by the last block of five choices. Finally, reinstatement of high-delay behavior was achieved in phase 4 with delay responses reaching 80 to 100 percent in all four Subjects.

DISCUSSION

Control of delay behavior, in this case percent delayed self-reward choices, was achieved with contingent social reinforcement. This adds further evidence in support of contingent application of social approval for behavior change. The general class of behavior, delay of gratification, is seen as an important and socially relevant behavior for this population as they typically show hedonistic, immediate-gratification orientations. The approval of a psychologist did seem to be an effective reinforcer for this behavior change. Subjects did not indicate any knowledge of the contingencies operating in this experiment. However, no claim for "learning without awareness" is made since no detailed postconditioning interview (e.g. Speilberger, 1962) was conducted.

Thus far, two behavior modification regimes have resulted in control of delaying behavior in these inmates: (a) exposure to high-delay peer models (Stumphauzer, in press) and (b) the present study using social reinforcement. It is suggested that a behavior-modification program aimed at increased delay of gratification in delinquents and youthful offender would require repeated modeling of high-delay behavior by several models in a number of different situations. Further, social reinforcement, other more extrinsic reinforcers, and scheduling variables might be manipulated to achieve the generalized delay of gratification.

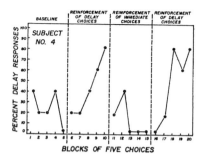

Figure 8-4. Percent delay responses as a function of phases of the experiment for the fourth subject.

REFERENCES

Bandura, A. and Mischel, W.: Modification of self-imposed delay of reward through exposure to live and symbolic models. *Journal of Personality and Social Psychology, 2:298-705, 1965.*

Gewirtz, J.L. and Baer, D.M.: The effect of brief social deprivation on behaviors for a social reinforcer. *Journal of Abnormal and Social Psychology, 56:49-56, 1958.*

Mischel, W.: Preference for delayed reinforcement and social responsibility. *Journal of Abnormal and Social Psychology, 62:1-7, 1961.*

Spielberger, C.D.: The role of awareness in verbal conditioning. In Eriksen, C.W. (Ed.): *Behavior and Awareness.* Durham, Duke University Press, 1962, pp. 73-101.

Stumphauzer, J.S.: Application of reinforcement contingencies with a 23-year-old anorexic patient. *Psychological Reports, 24:109-110, 1969.*

Stumphauzer, J.S.: Increased delay of gratification in four youthful offenders through exposure to a model. *Crime and Delinquency Abstracts* (in press).

Chapter 9

INCREASED DELAY OF GRATIFICATION IN YOUNG PRISON INMATES THROUGH IMITATION OF HIGH-DELAY PEER MODELS

JEROME S. STUMPHAUZER

T HE ABILITY TO WORK and wait for larger rewards, later in time, is stressed in virtually all discussions of normal personality development (e.g. Bijou and Baer, 1961; Freud, 1946; Mischel, 1966; Singer, 1955). To learn to delay immediate gratification in favor of later, more valuable reward is an important part of the socialization process. The criminal or psychopathic personality may best represent a failure in this development. Shapiro (1965) suggested that "the psychopath is the very model of the impulsive style . . . his aim is the quick concrete gain [p. 157]." Often, juvenile delinquents are also characterized by this inability to delay gratification. McCord and McCord (1964) consider the delinquent "like an infant, absorbed in his own needs, vehemently de-

Reprinted with permission from the *Journal of Personality and Social Psychology,* 21:10-17, 1972. (American Psychological Association)

This paper is based on a dissertation submitted to the faculty of the College of Arts and Sciences of Florida State University, in partial fulfillment of the requirements for the PhD degree. An earlier abbreviated version of this paper was read at the April 1969 meeting of the Florida Psychological Association, Orlando. These findings have been published in a private circulated technical bulletin series of the Federal Correctional Institution, Tallahassee, Florida: *FCI Research Reports,* 1969, *1*(6):1-67. The author wishes to express his appreciation to Wallace A. Kennedy for his guidance throughout all phases of this research; to A. Cooper Price for his support and cooperation at the Federal Correctional Institution; and to Albert Bandura and Walter Mischel for their encouragement, helpful suggestions, and modeling. This study was supported in part by Grant NL-135 from the National Institute of Law Enforcement and Crimnal Justice. This does not necessarily indicate the concurrence of the institute in the statement or conclusions contained herein.

manding satiation [p. 9]." Empirical support for the view that delinquents are immediate gratifiers is offered by Mischel (1961a). Very simply, he offered children a series of real choices between something they could have immediately or something more valuable for which they would have to wait. He found that delinquents showed a preference for smaller but immediate rewards. Similarly, Rosenquist and Megargee (1969) asked delinquents and nondelinquents what they would do with various sums of money (25¢, $2, $20, and $200). As expected, nondelinquents were more likely to say they would save their money, while delinquents were more likely to say they would spend it immediately on pleasurable items.

Delay of gratification, measured by series of choices, has received a good deal of research attention from Mischel and his colleagues (Bandura and Mischel, 1965; Mischel, 1958, 1961a, 1961b, 1966; Mischel and Gilligan, 1964; Mischel and Grusec, 1966; Mischel and Metzner, 1962; Mischel and Staub, 1965). Stumphauzer (1970b) systematically altered the percentage of delay choices in young prison inmates through the use of contingent social approval. The present study is an extension of the Bandura and Mischel (1965) findings. Using the series of choices measure, Bandura and Mischel selected two groups of children, one showing a tendency to choose immediate rewards and the other a tendency to choose delays rewards. Subjects from each group were exposed to live models, symbolic models, or no models (control group). Adult models, also in a series of choices, displayed delay orientations opposite to those of the subject. For example, subjects originally showing preference for immediate rewards observed a model who preferred delayed, more valuable rewards. Both live and symbolic modeling were effective in modifying delay orientations, although changes induced by the live model were somewhat more stable over time.

The Bandura and Mischel study shows the modification of delay orientations using modeling techniques. Since delinquents and youthful offenders tend to show immediate gratification orientations, as demonstrated by both Mischel (1961a) and Rosenquist and Megargee (1969), it was the plan of the present study to systematically replicate and extend the Bandura-Mischel findings with a youthful offender population. Live models were used with young prison inmates indicating an immediate gratification orientation. An additional measure of delay orientation, other than that displayed by the models, was needed to examine response generalization. A measure similar to that of Rosenquist and Megargee was developed for use as an additional measure of delaying behavior. Thus, examinations of both generalization over time, provided by a follow-up measure, and generalization to another but similar response were made.

While a number of studies demonstrate control of delinquent behavior by reinforcement variables (Stumphauzer, 1970a), some support for the use of modeling techniques for the modification of delinquent behavior is available as well. In a "token economy" for delinquents, Cohen, Filipszak, Bis, and Cohen (1966) found unexpectedly that delinquents began to imitate the experimenters. The subjects went so far as to "spend" some of their points to acquire clothing similar to that of the staff. Unfortunately, the acquisition of these imitative behaviors was simply noted, and the imitative behavior received no systematic investigation. Truax, Shapiro, and Wargo (1968) exposed delinquents about to begin group therapy to tape recordings of other ongoing groups in the hope that they would vicariously learn what was expected of them in the group. Results, in the form of changes in self-concept for Minnesota Multiphasic Personality Inventory profiles, suggest that the vicarious experiences of group therapy did not have positive effects. No mention was made of behaviors observed in the tapes and subsequently performed by the delinquents. Similarly, Sarason (1968) demonstrated the effects of modeling experiences in groups of institutionalized delinquents, but his dependent measures were only indirectly related to the modeling. Hartmann (1969) did show the acquisition of aggressive behavior (ostensibly delivering shocks to another person) in delinquents through imitation. In the present study it was necessary to consider who would make a particularly good (efficient) model for delinquents or young prison inmates to imitate. In reviewing the literature, Bandura (1962, 1969) has found effective models to be attractive, rewarding, prestigeful, competent, powerful, and to have high status. Schwitzgebel (1964) suggested using only those who are somewhat older than the delinquents and who are employed in some trade feasible for the delinquent to enter and thus provide a role model and a source of new patterns of behavior. Bandura (personal communication, April, 1968) further suggested that delinquents themselves might be used as models. Delinquents who have nearly completed the program in an institution, and who are relatively near the time of release, may be effective models for more newly admitted inmates. Such "successful" inmates may well appear competent, prestigeful, and to have high status. The use of peer models is further supported by those many discussions (Longstreth, 1968) of the important influence of peers in the socialization process.

METHOD

Subjects

The 40 subjects in this study were inmates of the Federal Correctional Institution for Youthful Offenders in Tallahassee, Florida. This is a medium security institution with a total of approximately 500 inmates, who reside in four dormitories and range in age from 18 to 26. The subjects were (a) newly admitted inmates, (b) from 18 to 20 years of age, (c) Caucasian males, and (d) they had a sentence of at least three months duration. With the use of the choice-list, the 40 subjects were selected from groups of newly admitted inmates as preferring immediate gratification (more than 70% immediate reward choices). Of the 40 subjects, 20 were exposed to a model, and 20 were assigned to a control group with no exposure to a model.

Models

In the light of the model characteristics and suggestions discussed earlier, two older, somewhat prestigious inmates were selected as models for this study. They were confederates and told what behavior to display for subjects to observe. In each case, relative to the subject, the model was older (ages 21 and 23), had been at the institution longer (several months), were relatively near the time of discharge, and had a prestigious work assigment (institutional photographer and x-ray technician). New inmates were assigned initially to a low-prestige detail such as custodian or food-service worker. Each model had one "professional" contact with each subject, either taking his identification photograph or chest x-ray on admission to the institution. To guard against contamination of the experiment by extensive contact of models and subjects, no model was paired with a subject who resided in the same dormitory as the model. Also, subjects were exposed to each model at a rate of no more than one subject per week. Since there were two models, each served as model for 10 of the 20 model-exposed subjects.

Choice List

The four choice-lists (A, B, C, and D) were developed for this particular population. Money is available to these inmates only in their institutional accounts. Inmates are permitted to spend this money in the commissary on certain hours during the week. Examples of items available are cigarettes, cigars, various candy and food snacks, magazines, and personal grooming needs. Since most of these items are sought after by inmates, they represent a ready list of realistic rewards for this population. Money may be used as a reward by adding it to the inmate's account. A pool of choices between immediate or delayed but more valuable rewards was developed. As in previous research, half of the choices were monetary (e.g. 35¢ now or 50¢ in 1 week), and half were between small articles (e.g. small candy bar now or large one in 1 week). The item lists used by Mischel (personal communication, May 21, 1968) were used as a model as far as the ratio of quantity of reward for given delay periods and the length of delay periods. For each of four lists, seven monetary and seven small-article choices were selected randomly from the pool of 100 choices. The resulting four choice-lists, consisting of 14 choice items each, were administered in a random order to 30 newly admitted inmates as a preliminary study of the scales themselves. Cross-correlations of percentage delay choices on the four choice-lists, ranging from .87 to .94, were found to be highly statistically significant (P < .001).

For each subject, list A, B, or C served as the initial measure of delay orientation or base rate. List D was used for the model's choices which 20 of the subjects observed. List A, B, or C was used to measure the subject's delay orientation immediately after exposure to the model. Finally, list A, B, or C was used as the follow-up or temporal generalization measure one month later. Approximately one-sixth of the subjects in each group received Lists A, B, and C in the following orders across the three phases of the study: ABC, ACB, BCA, CAB, and CBA.

Money-Saving Measures

The Rosenquist and Megargee (1969) measure of delay orientation, simply asking subjects what they would do with certain amounts of money, was developed into a forced-choice measure rather than an open-ended measure. By providing subjects with five choices— (a) spend all of it, (b) spend most (75%) of it, (c) spend half and save half of it, (d) save most (75%) of it, and (e) save all of it—a numerical index of delay orientation could quickly be determined and be available for later statistical analysis. Since inmates could spend no more than $20 a month, the $200-item used by Rosenquist and Megargee seemed unrealistic for this population and was not included. Therefore, three questions made up the money-saving measure for this study: (a) If 25 cents were added to your account, what would you do with it? (b) If two dollars were added to your account, what would you do with it? and (c) If $20 were added to your account, what would you do with it? Thus, a choice list and the money-saving measure were given at each of the three phases of the study to all 40 subjects.

Reinforcement

To make choices on the choice-lists realistic, the subjects were actually given one of their 14 choices each time a list was administered to them (after Bandura and Mischel, 1965). Since they received either an immediate or delayed reward, this could be considered a differential reinforcement of that particular type of responding. To determine any effect of this reinforcement, half (10) of the model exposed and half (10) of the no-model group received only delayed rewards. The other half of each group received only immediate rewards. Each time, of course, the subjects did receive one of the items that they had actually chosen. Since each subject responded to three choice lists, each received a total of three rewards.

Procedure

The procedure closely followed that of Bandura and Mischel (1965) with the notable exceptions that (a) only live models were used, (b) only with inmate subjects who had immediate gratification orientations, (c) another measure of delay orientation was added to examine response generalization, and (d) the same experimenter conducted all three phases of the study.

The first phase of the experiment (premeasure) consisted of the selection of subjects. One of the choice lists was administered to newly admitted, 18- to 20-year-old Caucasian inmates. These inmates were called in individually, and the experimenter read instructions similar to those of Bandura and Mischel:

> I am interested in finding out how people choose when they are offered different kinds of choices. I will be asking you to make some choices: the choices will be between two things both of which you want, but if you choose one you can't have the other. Answer each question to show what you would really take. This is not a test, there are no right or wrong answers. For example, the choice might be 50 cents now or 75 cents next week. If you took the 50 cents now you could not have the 75 cents next week and if you wait for the 75 cents next week you could not have the 50 cents now. I will offer you 14 such choices. Choose very carefully and realistically because in one of the choices you will really get what you choose. You won't know which one of your 14 choices you'll actually get until the very end, so choose very carefully each time.

The 14 items of a choice-list were then displayed on a desk for the subject, and his choices were recorded. In an earlier study, Stumphauzer (1970) found that social reinforcement ("good" or "mm-hmm") could control the percentage of delay choices in this population. Therefore, care was taken in the present study to simply record the data matter-of-factly. Next, the money-saving measure was given. If the subject was indeed to receive an immediate reward, he was given one of his immediate choices at that time. If he was to receive a delayed reward, he was given one of his delay choices after the specific time period. All subjects received a reward within four weeks, with four weeks being the longest delay period. Number of delayed reward choices for each subject were tabulated, and only those subjects choosing less than 30 percent delay choices (four choices or less) continued as subjects in the study. Forty subjects were selected in this manner, 20 were assigned to the modeling and 20 to the control group. Subjects in the two groups were matched with regard to number of delay choices on this first measure.

Approximately four weeks after the premeasure, control subjects were administered another choice list and money-saving measure, and again they received one of their choices within the next four weeks. Subjects in the modeling condition individually observed a model who showed the opposite delay orientation; that is, the model consistenly made delay of self-reward choices to choice-list D. The subject was led to believe that the model was also a subject. Both model and subject were called in at the same time. In order to make the difference between model and subject explicit to the subject, a short point interview was conducted by asking such questions as "How old are you? How long have you been at F.C.I. [Federal Correctional Institute], how many months? What is your work detail here?" Next, the experimenter read the instructions and turned to the model saying, "Let's start with you." The choices of choice-list D were displayed for the model (while the subject was observing) and the model's responses recorded. Rather than summarize his delayed orientation rationale, as in the Bandura-Mischel (1965) study, it seemed more natural in this setting to have the models make two side comments while they were making their choices. For one monetary item they said, "That's pretty good interest, I'll take the ____ in ____ weeks." For one of the other choices, the model said, "I can wait for that." Next, the model was given the money-saving measure on a clipboard and in such a way that the subject could not observe the model's responses to this measure. The model was then excused under the pretext, "You can go now, you probably have things to do." The items of another choice list were then dis-

played for the subject and his choice recorded. Again, he responded to the money-saving measure, and he received one of his
choices, depending on whether he was in the immediate or delayed reinforcement half of his group, within four weeks. The results of this choice-list provided the postexposure to model measure of delay orientation and indicated any immediate modeling
effect. The response to this second money-saving measure indicated any immediate response generalization effect.

Four weeks later, for the final (follow-up) phase of the study,
each of the 40 subjects was administered a third choice-list and
the money-saving measure. For the 20 experimental subjects, the
results of this choice list determined the stability of any modeling
effect, over this period of time. If there was a modeling effect, the
money-saving measure provided an index of response generalization to a second measure of delay behavior *not* observed directly
in the model. For the control group, results of the three choice-
lists and the three money-saving measures indicated any change
in delay behavior just as a function of differential reinforcements
and time and not as a function of exposure to high-delay peer
models.

RESULTS

A repeated-measures analysis of variance was computed on the
percentage of delay choices across the three phases of the experiment (see Fig. 9-1), and the modeling effect was found to be
highly statistically significant ($F = 108.29$, $df = 1/36$, $p < .001$).
Further comparisons of the pairs of means across experimental
phases show that both groups that were exposed to a high-delay
model significantly increased their delay of gratification regardless of whether they actually received delayed ($t = 8.21$, $df = 9$,
$p < .001$) or immediate ($t = 5.13$, $df = 9$, $p < .001$) reinforcements. Furthermore, this modeling effect was maintained to a
significant degree four weeks after exposure to the high-delay peer
models for both the delayed ($t = 6.72$, $df = 9$, $p < .001$) and the
immediate ($t = 3.46$, $df = 9$, $p < .01$) reinforcement groups. No
significant change in percentage of delay choices was found in the
groups which were not exposed to a model.

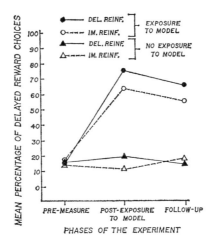

Figure 9-1. Mean percentage of delayed reward choices as a function of modeling condition, reinforcement condition, and phases of the experiment.

As a measure of response generalization, that is, generalization to a second measure of delay gratification which was not directly observed in the model, a series of three hypothetical money-saving measures was administered to all subjects at all three phases of the study. Three amounts of money were used: 25 cents, two dollars and 20 dollars. The percentage that subjects would save was tabulated at 0, 25, 50, 75, or 100 percent due to the forced-choice nature of the measure. Figure 9-2 shows the mean percentage the subjects would save of 25 cents as a function of experimental phases. A repeated-measures analysis of variance was computed and, as in the delay choice measure, the modeling effect was found to be highly significant ($F = 31.71$, $df = 1/36$, $p < .001$). No other source of variance was found to reach the .05 level of significance. Further compaisons by the t test of pairs of means across phases revealed that both groups exposed to models increased the percentage they would save: delayed reinforcement group ($t = 2.90$, $df = 9$, $p < .05$) and immediate reinforcement group ($t = 3.75$, $df = 9$, $p < .01$). The modeling effect was maintained four weeks later in both the delayed ($t = 2.94$, $df = 9$, $p < .05$) and immediate ($t = 2.28$, $df = 9$, $p < .05$) reinforcement groups. Again, no significant changes were found in the no-model group.

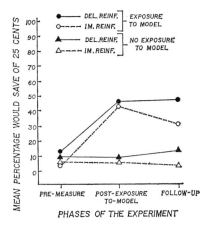

Figure 9-2. Mean percentage that subjects would save of 25 cents as a function of modeling condition, reinforcement condition, and phases of the experiment.

Mean percentage that subjects would save of two dollars as a function of experimental phases is presented in Figure 9-3. What appeared to be substantial differences between groups at the pre-

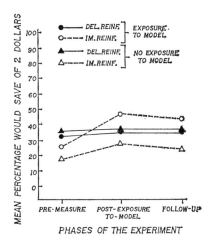

Figure 9-3. Mean percentage that subject would save of two dollars as a function of modeling condition, reinforcement condition, and phases of the experiment.

measure phase were noted. However, a simple analysis of variance was computed on these values, and the *F* ratio did not reach a statistically significant level. A repeated-measures analysis of variance was computed and revealed a significant *modeling × phases* interaction effect ($F = 3.91$, $df = 2/72$, $p < .05$). No other F value reached the .05 level of significance in this analysis. In an attempt to further identify the sources of variance, two sets of *t* tests between means were computed: between pairs of means across phases and between the groups at each of the three phases. Results revealed that no *t* value reached significance. Thus, modeling, reinforcement, and phases were found to have no statistically significant effect by themselves. In combination, however, modeling and phases did have a significant interaction effect on this two-dollar measure.

Finally, Figure 9-4 shows the mean percentage that subjects would save of 20 dollars as a function of experimental phases. In no case did an *F* value reach the .05 level of statistical significance in a repeated-measures analysis of variance. Thus, no modeling, reinforcement, phases, or interaction effects were found for the 20-dollar measure of response generalization.

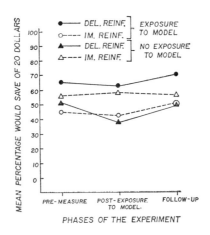

Figure 9-4. Mean percentage that subjects would save of $20 as a function of modeling condition, reinforcement condition, and phases of the experiment.

DISCUSSION

In this study it was found that not only did exposure to high-delay peer models immediately increase percentage of delay choices, but that this effect was maintained one month later as well. Further, this change in delay of gratification through imitation did generalize to two hypothetical money-saving measures (25¢ and $2). No effect on the 20-dollar measure was found. The 20-dollar measure may have been unrealistic in the population since, as noted earlier, inmates can spend a maximum of only 20 dollars each month. Actually, very few have this large an amount in their accounts. Rosenquist and Megargee (1969) also found the larger amounts of money unrealistic in their delinquent populations. Since models displayed delay responses only to choices between items ranging in values less than one dollar, there would be less reason to expect generalization to a measure so different in value as 20 dollars. Indeed, with regard to generalization, the data do order themselves on a similarily dimension, the effects becoming increasingly weaker as similarity decreased. The value of the objects chosen by models varied from about 25 cents to one dollar. A strong modeling effect was found for similar choices of objects. Of the generalization measures, the "save 25 cents" was the most similar in value, and a strong effect was found. For the "save two dollars" measure a weaker effect was found, and no effect on the least similar measure, "save 20 dollars," was found.

Since the same experimenter conducted all three phases of the study, it might be questioned what effect his repeated association with the phases might have had. A stronger case for a modeling effect may have been made if different experimenters had been used for the modeling and follow-up phases of the study. Bandura and Mischel (1965) did use such controls and did find a strong modeling effect. Care was taken in the present study to avoid any social reinforcement effect (Stumphauzer, 1970). One "message" definitely given by the experimenter, which might be taken as a cue as to what he wanted, was his differential reinforcement of either delayed or immediate reinforcement choices. The data suggest no such reinforcement effect. More precisely, when initially low-delay subjects (Fig. 1) were on the one hand reinforced for immediate reward choices but on the other hand exposed to a high-delay model, only an *increase* in delay choices was found, suggesting only a strong modeling effect.

It is the psychoanalytic view (e.g. Freud, 1946; Singer, 1955) that the beginnings of the delaying mechanism signal the emergence of the reality principle, and further that determinants of the "mechanism" are sought in hypothetical internal events—ego organizations and energy systems. In contrast, both the Bandura-Mischel findings and the present study support the social learning view that self-controlling behavior is determined by *external, social* stimulus events. Another alternative theory of the development of self-control is offered by Bijou and Baer (1961). Their view is that self-control is learned as are all other operant responses, through reinforcement. The findings of the present study do not support such a view since differential reinforcement was found to have no effect on delay behavior. This is not to imply that delay behavior cannot be controlled by manipulation of reinforcement variables. Indeed, Stumphauzer (1970) was able to systematically change the percentage of delay choices through the use of social reinforcement. The point is that in the present study, extrinsic reinforcement was not a necessary condition to achieve the change in delay orientation. As Bandura (1962) suggested in his formulation of imitative learning, a behavior may be acquired simply through observation. Reinforcement variables *may* then play a role in subsequent performance of the learned responses.

Gewirtz and Stingle (1968) have made a strong case for the learning of generalized imitation as the basis for identification. Baer and Sherman (1964) see the key to understanding imitative learning in the closer examination of generalized imitation. The present study did find generalization of imitation to a second series of responses within the larger response class, delay of gratification. Low-delay inmates who were exposed to high-delay models not only increased their percentage of delay choices, but also their hypothetical money-saving activity on a measure not directly observed in the model. This generalization of imitation effect, especially when considered in its extreme (identification), is very important when looking forward to the use of imitation in behavior therapy programs. If the imitation were only of the specific response displayed by the model, and there were no hope of generalization to other somewhat similar responses, then imitative learning would probably have little future use as a behavior modification regime. The present study did find the generalization, and the effect was maintained one month later. It is suggested, within the social-learning view supported here, that generalized delay of gratification is achieved in normal personality development through repeated modeling of delaying behavior by several models (parents and peers) and in many different situations. Further, it is likely that imitation of delay behavior then meets with social approval and extrinsic reinforcement. In certain delinquents and adult criminal offenders, these particular socialization agents may not have been present or, indeed, the opposite may have been the case—there may have been modeling and reinforcement of impulsive, hedonistic, and antisocial behavior. In keeping with the above discussion, it is suggested that a behavior modification program aimed at an increased delay of gratification in delinquents and youthful offenders would require repeated modeling of high-delay behavior by several models in diverse situations. Furthermore, reinforcement variables would have to be manipulated to achieve more generalized delay of gratification (see Stumphauzer, in press).

REFERENCES

Baer, D. M. and Sherman, J. A.: Reinforcement control of generalized imitation in young children. *Journal of Experimental Child Psychology, 1:*37-49, 1964.

Bandura, A.: Social learning through imitation. *Nebraska Symposium on Motivation, 10:*211-269, 1962.

Bandura, A.: *Principles of Behavior Modification.* New York, Holt, Rinehart and Winston, 1969.

Bandura, A., and Mischel, W.: Modification of self-imposed delay of reward through exposure to live and symbolic models. *Journal of Personality and Social Psychology, 2:*698-705, 1965.

Bijou, S. W. and Baer, D. M.: *Child Development I: A Systematic and Empirical Theory.* New York, Appleton-Century-Crafts, 1961.

Cohen, H. L., Filipczak, J. A., Bis, J. S. and Cohen, J. E.: CASE project: Contingencies applicable for special education. In Weber, R. E. (Ed.):

A Book on Education and Delinquency. Washington, D. C., Office of Juvenile Delinquency and Youth Development, United States Department of Health, Education, and Welfare, 1966.

Freud, S.: Formulations regarding the two principles in mental functioning. In *Collected Papers*, vol. 4, London, Hogarth Press, 1946.

Gewirtz, J. L. and Stingle, K. G.: Learning of generalized imitation as the basis for identification. *Psychological Review, 75:*374-397, 1968.

Hartmann, D. P.: Influence of symbolically modeled instrumental aggression and pain cues on aggressive behavior. *Journal of Personality and Social Psychology, 11:*280-288, 1969.

Longstreth, L. E.: *Psychological Development of the Child*. New York, Ronald Press, 1968.

McCord, W. and McCord, J.: *The Psychopath: An Essay on the Criminal Mind*. New York, Van Nostrand, 1964.

Mischel, W.: Preference for delayed reinforcement: An experimental study of a cultural observation. *Journal of Abnormal and Social Psychology, 56:*57-61, 1958.

Mischel, W.: Preference for delayed reinforcement and social responsibility. *Journal of Abnormal and Social Psychology, 62:*1-7, 1961a.

Mischel, W.: Delay of gratification, need for achievement, and acquiescence in another culture. *Journal of Abnormal and Social Psychology, 62:*543-552, 1961b.

Mischel, W.: Research and theory on delay of gratification. In Maher, B. A. (Ed.): *Progress in Experimental Personality Research*, vol. 2, New York, Academic Press, 1966.

Mischel, W. and Gilligan, C.: Delay of gratification, motivation for the prohibited gratification, and responses to temptation. *Journal of Abnormal and Social Psychology, 69:*411-417, 1964.

Mischel, W. and Grusec, J.: Determinants of the rehearsal and transmission of neutral and aversive behaviors. *Journal of Personality and Social Psychology, 3:*197-205, 1966.

Mischel, W. and Metzner, R.: Preference for delayed reward as a function of age, intelligence, and length of delay interval. *Journal of Abnormal and Social Psychology, 64:*425-431, 1962.

Mischel, W. and Staub, E.: Effects of expectancy on working and waiting for larger rewards. *Journal of Personality and Social Psychology, 2:*625-633, 1965.

Rosenquist, C. M., and Megargee, E. I.: *Delinquency in Three Cultures*. Austin, University of Texas Press, 1969.

Sarason, I. G.: Verbal learning, modeling, and juvenile delinquency. *American Psychologist, 23:*254-266, 1968.

Schwitzgebel, R. K.: *Street-corner Research: An Experimental Approach to the Juvenile Delinquent*. Cambridge, Harvard University Press, 1964.

Shapiro, D.: *Neurotic Styles.* New York, Basic Books, 1965.

Singer, J. L.: Delayed gratification and ego development: Implications for clinical and experimental research. *Journal of Consulting Psychology, 19:* 259-266, 1955.

Stumphauzer, J. S.: Behavior modification with juvenile delinquents. A critical review. *FCI Technical and Treatment Notes, 1*(2):1-22, 1970a.

Stumphauzer, J. S.: Modification of delay choices in institutionalized youthful offenders through social reinforcement. *Psychonomic Science, 18:*222-223, 1970b.

Stumphauzer, J. S.: *Behavior Therapy with Delinquents.* Springfield, Thomas (in press).

Truax, C. B., Shapiro, J. G., and Wargo, D. G.: The Effects of alternate sessions and vicarious therapy pretraining on group psychotherapy. *International Journal of Group Psychotherapy, 18:*186-198, 1968.

PART
THREE

Modification of Delinquent Behavior in Institutions

INTRODUCTION

JEROME S. STUMPHAUZER

T HE UNITED STATES has a great many institutions for young criminals—federal correctional institutions for youthful offenders; state schools for boys; local juvenile halls and detention homes. By every indication, our society will continue to incarcerate juvenile criminals. In this section, programs implimenting behavior therapy inside such institutions are presented.

Punishment, whether in the form of incarceration or infliction of physical pain, is surely the most commonly used "treatment" for delinquents. There is, however, a noteworthy lack of controlled study of the effects of punishment on delinquent behavior. Historically, as Burchard (1967) suggests, punishment has been used for revenge, deterrence, and/or for social protection. Yet efficacy of its use with delinquents remains largely an open question.

Within the psychological principles of learning, punishment may be defined as a response consequent that decreases the future probability of that response (Azrin and Holtz, 1966). Punishment may take two major forms: (a) aversive stimulation (physical pain, reprimand, disapproval, etc.) and (b) time-out from positive reinforcement, a response contingent loss of opportunity for reinforcement, e.g. brief social isolation following "acting-up" behavior (Michael and Myerson, 1966). In Chapter 10, Levinson, Ingram and Azcarate makes use of the first type of punishment—aversive stimulation. In Chapter 11, Tyler and Brown use time-out from positive reinforcement.

One punishment often used in delinquent and youthful offender institutions is confinement to a "segregation" or "lock-

137

up" unit which amounts to going to jail inside a prison. This confinement often follows some form of misconduct, and duration of confinement varies from a day to several weeks. This form of punishment seems particularly ineffective for a sizeable number of inmates in each institution in that they are chronic visitors to the segregation unit. It might be questioned why segregation does *not* represent a good application of the *principle of punishment,* or more specifically, time-out from positive reinforcement. While this topic needs controlled study itself, it may be suggested here, and through the editor's experience working in such institutions, that (a) its use is not consistent; (b) this "punishment" is often delayed and is not immediate; (c) the time-out period is probably too long; (d) the contingencies are not usually explained to the inmates; and (e) there is usually no way for the inmate to stop the confinement with appropriate behavior (see *principle of negative reinforcement*) .

In Chapter 10, Levinson, Ingram and Azcarate report a novel approach for controlling the rule-infracting behavior of inmates who were subject to the segregation unit at the former National Training School for Boys in Washington, D.C.—they used group therapy as punishment, i.e. aversive stimulation. Levinson *et al.* selected inmates who were chronic visitors to the segregation unit and this group of inmates seemed to have particularly negative feelings toward group therapy; they found it aversive. Group therapy was made mandatory for them, but they could avoid the "therapy" sessions by completing three successive months without going to segregation. Further rule infractions resulted in continued punishment. The investigators did find a 43 percent average decrease in misconduct reports. Some of the inmates did admit that they stayed out of segregation "to get out of this damn group!" This was a very limited study and only used seventeen inmates in a case study design, but Levinson *et al.* did demonstrate how one form of punishment may be used with institutionalized delinquents in a behavior therapy program. A true experimental design could have been effected by random assignment to this group and a control group which would have received the usual "treatment." A comparison of rule infractions between the two groups would then show the effectiveness of this program.

The use of the second form of punishment, time-out from positive reinforcement, has been examined in a number of studies (Burchard and Tyler, 1965; Burchard, 1967). Tyler and Brown (Ch. 11) set out to eliminate the acting-up of 15 institutionalized delinquents around a pool table in a training school cottage. Misbehavior during pool-playing sessions resulted in either (a) confinement in an isolation room for fifteen minutes, or (b) verbal reprimand, which Tyler and Brown unfortunately term the "No Punishment" condition. Actually, the two major forms of punishment, aversive stimulation (here, verbal reprimand) and time-out from positive reinforcement (here, isolation), are being compared. Time-out was found to be much more successful than verbal reprimand. The experimental design used here falls short of being an experimental analysis design, in that there was no baseline or base-rate measure of rule infracting *before* starting the program; the authors themselves go into other methodological problems. Tyler and Brown further discuss the problems of resistance to extinction and generalization to other situations. They conclude, somewhat pessimistically, that they were not yet even turning out good law-abiding pool players. A study by Bishop and Stumphauzer (unpublished) may shed some light on Tyler and Burchard's concern over time-out and generalization. In that study, two time-out conditions were explored: in the first condition, the contingencies were clearly spelled out to the child (awareness condition); in the second condition, the contingencies were not explained to the children (without awareness condition). In the awareness condition, there was both more rapid conditioning *and* greater generalization of the conditioning effects. One inference might be, then, that behaviors that would meet with time-out should be fully discussed with delinquents before a time-out program is implemented. For example, *"Every* time you start a fight, you will be put in isolation for fifteen minutes."

One of the greatest contributions of behavior modification and behavior therapy over the past few years has been in the field of education (see Birnbrauer, Wolf, Kidder, and Tague, 1965; Wolf, Giles, and Hall, 1968; Clark, Lachowicz, and Wolf, 1968; Thomas, Becker, and Armstrong, 1968; Madsen, Becker, and Thomas, 1968). Motivation of students and classroom management are often especially difficult with delinquents in institutions and in the community as well. The incentives and behavioral control provided by behavior therapy programs are particularly well-suited for institutional schools. Brown's (1970) manual for classroom management, may be particularly useful, while Fargo, Behrns, and Nolen (1970) provide a source book of behavior therapy in education. In Chapter 12, Meichenbaum, Bowers, and Ross, provide an exemplary project of such work with institutionalized delinquent girls. Utilizing a baseline, or experimental analysis design, and money as a generalized reinforcer, Meichenbaum *et al.* effectively show control over the appropriate classroom behavior of delinquent girls. Bednar, Zelhart, Greathouse and Weinberg (1970) provide a study of behavior therapy in the education of delinquent boys; as does Tyler (1965, 1967) and Tyler and Brown (1967).

Behavior therapy techniques have been extended globally to whole groups of institutionalized patients, and these systems have been called token economies. This work was pioneered with wards of schizophrenic patients at Anna State Hospital, Illinois, by Ayllon, Azrin and their collegues (Ayllon and Michael, 1959; Ayllon and Sommer, 1960; Ayllon and Haughton, 1962; Ayllon and Azrin, 1964; Ayllon and Azrin, 1965). Through consistent use of generalized reinforcers (tokens, money, social approval), they have dramatically modified the behavior of these patients in the direction of more socially acceptable and adaptable behaviors. In their book, *The Token Economy,* Ayllon and Azrin (1968) provide an excellent example and guide for those interested in setting up such a program.

A well-executed extension of this token economy concept was made by Burchard (1967), who worked with delinquent retardates. Burchard cogently described the usual treatment programs for these retarded youths; they either received *indiscriminate* punishment (imprisonment and isolation), or *indiscrimi-*

nate reinforcement (love and acceptance). Neither regime has demonstrated efficiency in teaching these individuals social adaptiveness. Twelve mildly retarded delinquents took part in the program. Token rewards and punishment (a combination of loss of tokens and brief social isolation) were used. Both rewards and punishments were administered immediately in contrast to most institutional programs of delayed reward and delayed punishment. A first experiment focused on the effectiveness of token reward on two behaviors—sitting at a desk during workshop or sitting at a desk in school. The effects of contingent and noncontingent reward were examined. High frequencies of the behaviors were found under the contingent condition, while preformance immediately decreased in the noncontingent condition. In the second experiment, Burchard examined effect of contingent and noncontingent punishment on such antisocial behaviors as stealing, lying, cheating, fighting, property damage, and verbal assault. In general, these responses increased during noncontingent punishment, but some overlap between condition was found. Burchard, too, discusses the problem of returning the "programmed" inmate to society. Like Tyler and Brown, he talks of "phasing the residents out" into the community. One suggestion for this problem is a "quarterway" house where token reward would depend on job performance and only gradually would residents be introduced to a halfway house and then the natural contingencies of the larger society. Burchard shows systematic modification of specific behaviors in a controlled environment and pointedly discusses the problems of returning delinquents to the less well-controlled real world.

A large-scale token economy at the National Training School for Boys, in Washington, D.C., was reported by Cohen, Filipczak, Bis, Cohen, and Larkin (1968). They converted an old cottage into a "24-hour learning environment" for 41 teenage delinquents from the institution population. Eighty-five percent of the subjects were school dropouts. Generalized reinforcements, in the form of points (later converted to money), were used to motivate them. Dependent measures were hours of school work, achievement in programmed courses, and grade-level progress. These delinquents, with their, "What's in it for me?" orientation, soon found there was something in it for them. Over the year that they had participated in the project, significant increases were found in academic progress and a significant mean gain of 12.5 IQ points on the Revised Beta was found as well. In addition, social and attitudinal changes were found. There was a new pride of ownership in personal belongings and in living quarters. Discipline became no more than a minor problem; officers were even removed during the weekly day-shift. The authors stress their philosophy as being of major importance. Rather than the usual penal code, "Do what we say, or be punished," they applied a positive reinforcing approach, which did not force the inmates to do anything. While claims of diversion of a "large amount of aggression" to productive learning are made by Cohen *et al.,* there is no direct observable evidence that this, in particular, was the case. Further, a subsequent follow-up would have been needed to examine the long-term effects of this program.

One concern of administrative staffs of institutions and certainly of taxpayers, is the cost of such a model program, especially since trained personnel are required and delinquents do indeed receive monetary rewards. Cohen *et al.* concluded that once established, such token economy could maintain its operations at a cost per inmate that would be equivalent to that of a traditional training school.

In January, 1969, a major step in behavior therapy with delinquents was made—the Robert F. Kennedy Youth Center opened in Morgantown, West Virginia, to replace the old National Training School for Boys. Its program is largely a token economy and the previous findings of Cohen *et al.* were influential in its design. In Chapter 13, Karacki and Levinson describe the program in detail and discuss some of the initial experiences in beginning such a large-scale project. While no definitive results are provided yet, Karacki and Levinson are optimistic of the program and its wide-scale applicability. Another exemplary, large-scale token economy is being evaluated by the California Youth Authority (Jesness, 1970). Youth are being randomly assigned to two large institutions for delinquent boys. In one, the program is behavior therapy and in the other, transactional analysis. In Chapter 14, Jesness and DeRisi present their contingency management programs from the institution using behavior therapy and their findings are quite encouraging. The results and full evaluation of both the Kennedy Youth Center and the California Youth Authority projects should be especially important for the future treatment of youth in institutions.

REFERENCES

Ayllon, T., and Azrin, N. H.: Reinforcement and instructions with mental patients. *The Journal of the Experimental Analysis of Behavior, 7:*327-331, 1964.

Ayllon, T., and Azrin, N. H.: The measurement and reinforcement of behavior of psychotics. *Journal of the Experimental Analysis of Behavior,* 2:357-383, 1965.

Ayllon, T., and Azrin, N. H.: *The Token Economy: A Motivational System for Therapy and Rehabilitation.* New York, Appleton-Century-Crofts, 1968.

Ayllon, T., and Haughton, E.: Control of the behavior of schizophrenic patients by food. *Journal of the Experimental Analysis of Behavior, 5:*343-352, 1962.

Ayllon, T., and Michael, J.: The psychiatric nurse as a behavioral engineer. *Journal of the Experimental Analysis of Behavior, 2:*323-334, 1959.

Ayllon, T., and Sommer, R. A.: A directive or a permissive approach. *Mental Hospitals, 11:*45-48, 1960.

Azrin, N. H., and Holtz, W. E.: Punishment. In Honig, W. K. (Ed.): *Operant Behavior: Areas of Research and Application.* New York, Appleton, 1966, 380-447.

Bishop, B. R., and Stumphauzer, J. S.: Control of thumbsucking by withdrawal and representation of television cartoons. Florida State University, unpublished manuscript.

Bednar, R. L., Zelhart, P. F., Greathouse, L., and Weinberg, S.: Operant-conditioning principles in the treatment of learning and behavior problems with delinquent boys. *Journal of Counseling Psychology, 17:*492-497, 1970.

Birnbrauer, J. S., Wolf, M. M., Kidder, J. D., and Tague, C. E.: Classroom behavior of retarded pupils with token reinforcement. *Journal of Experimental Child Psychology, 2:*219-236, 1965.

Brown, D.: *Changing Student Behavior: A New Approach to Discipline.* Dubuque, Iowa, William C. Brown, 1971.

Burchard, J. D.: Systematic socialization: A programmed environment for the habilitation of antisocial retardates. *Psychological Record, 17:*461-476, 1967.

Burchard, J. D., and Tyler, V. O.: The modification of delinquent behavior through operant conditioning. *Behavior Research and Therapy,* 2:245-250, 1965.

Clark, M., Lachowicz, J., and Wolf, M. M.: A pilot basic education program for school dropouts incorporating a token reinforcement system. *Behavior Research and Therapy,* 6:183-188, 1968.

Cohen, H. L., Filipczak, J., Bis, J., Cohen, J. E. and Larkin, P.: *Contingencies Applicable to Special Education-motivationally Oriented Design for an Ecology of Learning.* Department of Health, Education and Welfare, 1968.

Fargo, G. A., Behrns, C., and Nolen, P.: *Behavior Modification in the Classroom.* Belmont, California, Wadsworth, 1970.

Jesness, C. F.: The youth center research project: Differential treatment of delinquents in institutions (third annual progress report). California Department of the Youth Authority, 1970.

Madsen, C. H., Becker, W. C. and Thomas, D. R.: Rules, praise, and ignoring: Elements of elementary classroom control. *Journal of Applied Behavior Analysis, 1:*139-150, 1968.

Michael, J., and Meyerson, L.: A behavioral approach to human control. In Ulrich, R., Stachnik, T., and Mabry, J. (Eds.): *Control of Human Behavior.* Glenview Illinois, Scott, Foresman, 1966, pp. 23-31.

Thomas, D. R., Becker, W. C., and Armstrong, M.: Production and elimination of disruptive classroom behavior by systematically varying teacher's behavior. *Journal of Applied Behavior Analysis, 1:*35-45, 1968.

Tyler, V. O.: Exploring the use of operant techniques in the rehabilitation of delinquent boys. Paper read at American Psychological Association Meeting, Chicago, September, 1965.

Tyler, V. O.: Application of operant token reinforcement to academic performance of an institutionalized delinquent. *Psychological Reports, 21:*249-260, 1967.

Tyler, V. O., and Brown, G. D.: Token reinforcement of academic performance with institutionalized delinquent boys. Paper read at the Western Psychological Association, San Francisco, May, 1967.

Wolf, M. M., Giles, D. J., and Hall, R. B.: Experiments with token reinforcement in a remedial classroom. *Behavior Research and Therapy, 6:*51-64, 1968.

Chapter 10

THE USE OF SWIFT, BRIEF ISOLATION AS A GROUP CONTROL DEVICE FOR INSTITUTIONALIZED DELINQUENTS

VERNON O. TYLER, JR. *and* G. DUANE BROWN

Operant techniques are proving effective in the treatment of mental hospital patients (Ayllon and Michael, 1950; Ayllon, 1960, 1963; Ayllon and Haughton, 1962; Ayllon and Azrin, 1964, 1965; Ayllon *et al.,* 1965) , autistic children (e.g. Wolf *et al.,* 1964) , and retardates (e.g. Birnbrauer *et al.,* 1965) . Work has also been done with adolescent delinquents (Slack, 1960, a,b; Schwitzgebel, 1960, 1963, 1964; Schwitzgebel and Kolb, 1964; Burchard and Tyler, 1965; Tyler, 1965) .

However, work with delinquents, especially in a training school setting, poses many problems. In a school for delinquents, the size of living units, the limited number of staff, the large number of youngsters, and the numerous responsibilities of the staff member make it difficult to set up individualized programs with-

Reprinted with permission from *Behavior Research and Therapy,* 5:1-9, 1967. (Pergamon Press)

Acknowledgements—Grateful appreciation is due to GUS LINDQUIST, Superintendent, and ROBERT H. KOSCHNICK, Assistant Superintendent, for their support and encouragement of this study; cottage supervisors RUDOLPHA BUSE and ALLEN HODGE, and cottage staff EDITH SMITH, LEW STREIT, RALPH GIGER, ROBERT BARNES, and ROBERT HINTON for their work with Ss and collection of data; JOHN D. BURCHARD and DON R. SHUPE for suggestions and assistance; ROY BUEHLER for his valuable critical comments on this paper; and GEORGE EASTMAN, SARA BURCHARD, DOREEN BEAZLEY, JERRY SIMPSON, PATRICIA SOAPES, and MARY WAGNER who collected and compiled data.

Portions of this paper were originally presented at the American Psychological Association, Chicago, September, 1965.

out extra staff to record data and administer contingencies with precision. Ayllon and his co-workers (Ayllon and Haughton, 1962; Ayllon and Azrin, 1964, 1965) have shown that general procedures applied to a group of mental hospital patients can be effective in modifying their behavior. However, these procedures may not prove effective with delinquent behavior which so often is under close peer control (e.g. Buehler *et al.,* 1966).

In addition, staff motivation and previous training create problems. Traditionally, training schools tend to be thought of as quite punitive and regimented. However, the school in which this study took place has a tradition of kindly handling of children, good food and clothing, good schooling, and numerous recreational and coeducational activities. Roughly speaking, the theory of treatment here is that if the needs of these children are met, the need for delinquent behavior will decline. "Fairness" is also an important concept used by staff in handling of youngsters. The use of operant techniques in a setting such as this may well be as difficult as their use in a more punitive, regimented setting. In the present setting, at times, the staff may develop the feeling that researchers are "playing games," but not really "helping kids." And, in addition, research efforts are seen as making work harder for staff rather than easier.

The six cottage staff-members who are responsible for around-the-clock care of twenty or more youths in the experimental cottage at Fort Worden, however, became involved in thinking about the use of operant techniques. Several previous attempts had been made to set up contingency programs for individual youngsters (e.g. Burchard and Tyler, 1965; Tyler, 1965). This chapter reports an exploratory effort to apply a general operant procedure to a group of institutionalized youngsters.

After a period of discussions with the staff, several forms of misbehavior which might prove susceptible to manipulation by operant techniques were selected and a plan developed. This plan (a) attacked a problem which was important to staff and (b) involved the use of a general rule which could be applied to all of the children in the living unit. The problem concerned the way boys behaved around the pool table in the day room. Boys were not following the formal rules of the game and were misbehaving in other ways. This behavior was rarely so serious as to warrant severe sanctions such as placing the offender in the isolation unit. Staff usually warned offenders; sometimes they banned use of the pool table for an hour or so. Individuals who were especially troublesome were restricted from playing for a day or two.

PROCEDURE

The subjects in this study were fifteen boys age 13 to 15, committed by the courts of the State of Washington for auto theft, assault, "incorrigibility," sex offenses, etc. In order to carry out this project, a simple 4×8 ft "time-out" room was constructed in one corner of the cottage. This facilitated placing youngsters in isolation and removing them without the delays involved in using more distant isolation units. This study took place in three phases:

Phase I, Punishment, 26 June 1964 to 13 August 1964 (7 weeks)

Phase II, No Punishment, 14 August 1964 to 16 November 1964 ($13\frac{1}{2}$ weeks)

Phase III, Punishment, 17 November 1964 to 31 March 1965 (20 weeks)

Prior to Phase I, the cottage staff agreed on what constituted undesirable behavior around the pool table: breaking the rules of the game, throwing or hitting with the pool cue, scuffling around the table, "bothering" other players, bouncing the balls onto the floor, touching moving balls, excessive kibitzing, arguing, etc. Because of staff concern about this misbehavior, no waiting period to establish a baseline or operant level of misbehavior was possible. The program began immediately with the punishment condition, Phase I. Every time a subject misbehaved in any of the above-mentioned ways, he was immediately placed in the time-out room for 15 minutes. There were to be no warnings, no discussions, no arguments and no second chances. When a subject misbehaved, he was simply taken in a very matter-of-fact way to the time-out room. Staff might explain to the point of saying, "You fouled up," but no more. At the same time the staff noted the subject's name and offense on a record sheet.

After a time, a no punishment condition (Phase II) was instituted to observe the effects on behavior. The time-out room was locked. When a subject misbehaved, the staff member would mildly reprimand him with a statement such as "Now cut it out," "I'm warning you," "Don't let that happen again," etc. After the no punishment condition had been underway for a brief time, the staff once again expressed serious concern about the problem of misbehavior at the pool table and requested experimenters to reinstate the punishment procedure. As a consequence, the punishment condition was resumed (Phase III) before a stabilized operant level of misbehavior was established. Unfortunately, subjects were moving into and out of the cottage prior to and during this study. Although all subjects in the cottage were subjected to the conditions of the study, data are only reported here on subjects who were in residence during at least two phases of the study.

RESULTS

Cumulative records of offenses compiled on a weekly basis may be seen in Figure 10-1. The clear trend in the data was that as subjects were punished for their misbehavior, this behavior declined in rate; when punishment was not administered, the behavior increased in rate. All fifteen subjects showed this pattern.

Subjects 7, 9, 11, 12, 13, 14, and 15 showed a markedly rapid decline in response rate following the onset of Phase III.

The subjects fell into two distinct groups on the basis of rate of offending. Subjects 1, 2, 3, 4, 9, 10, 11, and 12 fell in a high-rate group and the remaining subjects in a low-rate group. Although all subjects misbehaved at a lower rate under the punishment condition, the clear difference between the two groups was maintained under both punishment and no punishment conditions.

In a brief search for factors which might account for these differences in offense rate, five cottage staff-members who were acquainted with the subjects were asked to rate them on three dichotomous dimensions: frequency of pool playing, sociability, and severity of delinquency. Rater agreement ranged from 50 to

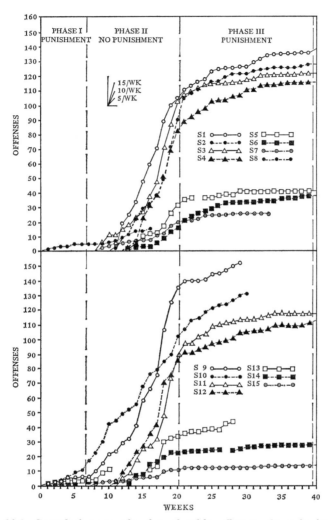

Figure 10-1. Cumulative records of pool table offenses. Gaps in individual records indicate subject was absent from cottage 7 or more days.

100 percent depending on the subject rated; some raters could not recall certain subjects well enough to rate them. In spite of the shortcomings of these data, the modal rating for each subject was used as a basis for comparing ratings with frequency of offense in 2 × 2 contingency tables which may be found in Table 10-I.

TABLE 10-I
RATE OF POOL TABLE OFFENSES VS. MODAL RATINGS OF FREQUENCE
OF PLAYING, SOCIABILITY, AND SEVERITY OF DELINQUENCY

| | Frequency of Playing | | Sociability | | Delinquency | |
	Seldom	Frequent	Isolate	Sociable	Mild	Severe
Offense rate						
High	3	5	2	6	5	3
Low	5	1	4	1	3	4
	No. $= 14$*		No. $= 13$*		No. $= 15$	
	P $= .121$†		P $= .084$		P $= .344$	

*Ss removed. In each case one rater failed to rate and remaining ratings were tied.
†Fisher's exact probability test.

Probabilities of the obtained or more extreme values by Fisher's exact test (Siegel, 1956) are included. Since it was predicted that high frequency of pool playing, high sociability and severe delinquency would all be associated with high offense rates, one-tailed tests were used. The predictions concerning frequency of pool playing and sociability were supported (albeit at low levels of significance), while the trend with regard to severity of delinquency was not. The data suggest that rate of offending correlated with frequency of playing pool and sociability.

DISCUSSION

Methodological Problems

A number of methodological limitations were present which Might be expected in a situation in which experimenters have limited control of the cottage unit and limited staff for collecting relevant data.

1. The data do not take into account the opportunities for making offenses which depend on frequency of pool playing. The opportunities available for playing pool depend on the day of the week (the pool table is available more often on weekends), whether school is in session and whether it is the season of the year when most subjects are outdoors. Also the data do not take into account the rate at which subjects chose to use the pool table although the data of Table 10-I suggest that rate of playing is related to rate of offending.

2. The data do not take into account changing standards or criteria for determining whether a subject has misbehaved. During the course

of this study, staff were still becoming acquainted with the definitions of misbehavior and staff turnover aggravated this problem. Staff working on different shifts had varying degrees of familiarity with the procedures. For example, people working the night shift had practically no contact with pool table behavior; when they transferred to afternoon work they had maximal contact. Almost every time the experimenters talked to staff about the definitions of misbehavior the number of recorded offenses noticeably increased. Apparently staff were more alert to observe and record behavior following these discussions. Finally, the staff who recorded data also administered the punishment, thus possibly biasing record keeping.

3. As much as possible subjects were on a continuous punishment schedule, that is, every time they offended they were to be placed in the time-out room. Since staff could not observe them at all times, undoubtedly numerous offenses were neither recorded nor punished. The magnitude of this problem and its consequences are unknown.

4. The number of subjects in the cottage increased from a low of approximately fourteen to a high of twenty-three during the course of the experiment. There were more subjects for the staff to watch thereby taking time from their observation of pool table behavior. More children in the cottage meant each subject had less opportunity to play at the pool table which may have reduced the measured rate of offending.

5. Probably most important of all, the data do not include measures of peer group social reinforcement (attention, approval, sympathy, etc.) of pool table misbehavior.

A number of factors, then, were probably affecting the records, some tending to increase the rates of offending and some tending to lower them in unknown ways and magnitudes.

The Findings

Clearly, under punishment conditions there was a decline in the rate of offending and under non-punishment conditions an increase in rate of offending. It was also clear to the cottage staff on a casual observation basis that this was true.

As indicated above, circumstances did not permit collection of data on peer reactions following each pool table offense. However, institutional experience and an extensive literature (e.g. Cohen, 1955; Shulman, 1961; Redl and Wineman, 1951, 1952; Patterson and Anderson, 1964) strongly suggest that peer reactions exert considerable control over a youngster's behavior, probably more than does staff handling. In a closed living group of inmates one would expect group controls to be at a maximum (Schrag, 1961). Considering the probable power of the group in the present situation, it is rather surprising that the simple staff intervention employed had any systematic effect at all on offense rates. One might reasonably have predicted the peer group influence would completely overshadow the staff influence.

Why was this punishment procedure effective? In the first place, it is speculated that the very mildness of the punishment made the contingency moderately immune to peer group involvement. For example, by the end of the study, many a subject had come to the point that when he committed an offense at the pool table, he automatically laid down his pool cue and walked to the time-out room without staff direction; frequently boys were placed in the room without locking the door. The boys rather perfunctorily accepted the consequence of being placed in the time-out room. Apparently, it was not a severe disgrace in the eyes of the group nor was it grounds for group expression of sympathy. Either group disapproval or sympathy might have produced considerably different results. Brief confinement immediately following misbehavior apparently provided little stimulation for strong peer reactions. A closely related observation has to do with the manner of staff handling of youngsters. The cottage staff became quite skilled in confining youngsters in a perfunctory non-emotional way which probably minimized the possibility of the group "rallying" and "making a martyr" of the offending subject. It is speculated that the mild punishment made it less likely that the staff would evidence feelings of guilt or revenge. In addition, the fact that staff generally manifest a benevolent, concerned attitude toward youngsters and attempt to "meet their needs" may be associated with the youngsters accepting punishment from them. It would be interesting to compare the effect of this contingency in a more authoritarian, punitive institutional context.

Further research that includes measures of the effects of peer group reactions and staff reactions to misbehavior on misbehavior rates and contrasts punitive with less punitive milieux is needed.

A related social process, vicarious conditioning (e.g. Bandura *et al.,* 1964) , may also have been involved in this study but no provision was made to assess it. This is another question requiring investigation.

It is a little unclear as to why the offense rate at the beginnings of Phase III leveled off so quickly for some subjects (7, 9, 11, 12, 13, 14, and 15) . Some of these subjects who had previously experienced this punishment apparently "caught on" rather quickly when Phase III began. Also, it had become part of the lore of the cottage that a boy goes to the time-out room if he commits offenses. The boys were never clear in stating that they were aware of the onset of Phase II, however. If they had verbalized on this matter, they might have spoken of "getting away" with misbehavior more often than previously, a pattern often observed in delinquents. Rules are set up by adults and then not consistently enforced and the youngsters quickly distinguish between what adults say and what they do. Thus verbal discriminations and group factors may have served to heighten the boys' awareness of the contingency when it was reestablished in Phase III. The first few punishments at the beginning of Phase III may have served as discriminative stimuli indicating the punishment procedure had once again been "turned on."

The rapid decline in response rate after reestablishment of punishment at the beginning of Phase III may relate to the common observation that delinquents are skillful at discriminating what they can and cannot get away with. If the delinquents are able to make such discrimination with exceptional efficiency, a practical aim of treatment would be to blur discriminative stimuli so that the child cannot discriminate between situations in which punishment may be contingent on misbehavior from situations in which punishment is absent. This blurring probably took place to some extent in this study since youngsters were punished on an intermittent schedule because cottage staff could not observe the pool table at all times.

Apparently little research has been done on the suppressive effects of intermittent or partial punishment. However, Kintz and Bruning (1966) found that partial punishment was less effective than continuous punishment in suppressing a well-learned response and in some instances may have strengthened the to-be-suppressed response. However, the conditions of their animal study were not comparable to those of the present study.

Two studies by Lovibond (1963) are more relevant. In the first, with animal subjects, he found that more trials with intermittent punishment were necessary to suppress a continuously reinforced (access to water) running response than with continuous punishment, but that the effects of intermittent reinforcement were also more "durable": the avoidance response was more resistant to extinction. However, in his second study, the suppression of enuresis in children required no more trials of intermittent punishment than continuous punishment. In addition, the durability of the suppression was considerably greater for the intermittent procedure: many more trials were required to extinguish the avoidance behavior conditioned by intermittent punishment. Future studies should permit comparison of partial and continuous punishment.

It may be assumed that the offenses consisted of behavior which occurred because of previous failure by social forces to shape acceptable pool-playing behavior. Presumably, in addition to punishment (in Phase I and III), concurrent peer group social reinforcement and reinforcement intrinsic to playing the game served to maintain acceptable behavior while misbehavior was suppressed. Presumably, also, the misbehavior which did occur continued to be followed by social reinforcement from the delinquent group, even though punishment led to a reduction in its rate of emission. The rapid recovery of misbehavior following the onset of no punishment (Phase II) indicates the punishment only suppressed behavior.

Since no effort was made to measure desirable pool-playing behavior, it is not possible to say how desirable behavior was modified in this situation. Essentially the situation appears to be an instance of passive avoidance-learning (Solomon, 1964). That is, the boys probably learned whatever behavior served to keep them from going to the time-out room. This may well have included a good deal of devious or underhanded misbehavior which produced social reinforcement from peers but avoided the punishment.

A more effective procedure probably would have included the reinforcement and shaping of socially approved behavior along with the punishment for misbehavior—a rewarded alternative (Solomon, 1964). The reward should be of a nature and magnitude sufficient to produce group social reinforcement for desirable behavior. Perhaps something like "good sportsmanship points" could be awarded. The strengthened desirable behavior should compete with misbehavior and prove more "durable" (resistant to extinction) than the suppression of misbehavior since behavior suppressed by mild punishment usually reappears eventually (Solomon, 1964).

Practical Considerations

From the point of view of institution management, the punishment imposed in this study would be considered extremely mild. This is of great importance in the training school situation. Frequently very harsh punishment is administered with little consideration of the contingent relationship between behavior and punishment (timing, duration of punishment, etc.). In the present institution there tends to be a rather benign, benevolent attitude of staff toward children. There is a frequent use of "counseling" and sometimes warnings to control children's behavior. The most severe punishment, which usually consists of placement in isolation, is seen as quite drastic and is delayed as long as possible. Frequently, children "test limits" or "see how far they can go" before severe punishment is finally invoked. Children quickly learn to discriminate staff whom they can test for long periods without repercussions from those with whom they must comply quickly. Sometimes even the imposition of punishment seems less important than the attitude, manner or "relationship" established with the staff member. As a consequence, it is frequently said that staff A runs a quiet shift and staff B runs an unruly shift. In any case it seems clear that in terms of day-to-day institutional supervision this approach of swift, brief, mild punishment does, in fact, work. It leads to the control of behavior in an institutional living-unit situation. It is relatively easy for staff to administer (although it is inconvenient for them to record data) ; it gives the child many more trials in which to shape up desirable behavior because of the brief length of isolation; and it appears to avoid bringing either strong group positive reinforcement or punishment into play which might produce numerous undesirable side effects. This approach contrasts with that used in other living units within the institution where the child may act out with increasing severity until he is finally placed in isolation. The staff may be extremely angry by this time and the youngster's stay in the isolation unit may last for several days. Prolonged isolation deprives him of opportunities to improve his behavior. In the training school, this is of great importance because of the fact that schools are crowded and it is necessary to have the youngsters learn as quickly as possible in a brief stay.

However, in spite of the fact that brief isolation is a useful tool for day-to-day control of institutional behavior, the "treatment" goal of socially desired behavior that can be maintained was not achieved. Considering the relatively rapid rate at which the rate of offending increased once the sanctions were removed, the effects of this training would not survive long enough to generalize to post-institutional situations. Punishment under varied conditions should increase generalization. At this point, then how one can use operant methods which will modify the behavior and make it "durable" so that it will generalize to situations outside of the institution is not clear. In other studies, experimenters are attempting to shape academic behavior using positive reinforcement which contrasts with efforts in the present study to eliminate undesirable behavior with punishment. It is believed that this behavior may prove more durable after institutionalization because of the fact that there should be positive social reinforcement available to maintain it.

REFERENCES

Ayllon, T.: Some Behavioral Problems Associated with Eating in Chronic Schizophrenic Patients, Paper read at American Psychological Association, Chicago, 1960.

Ayllon, T.: Intensive treatment of psychotic behavior by stimulus satiation and food reinforcement. *Behav Res & Therapy, 1:*53-61, 1963.

Ayllon, T. and Azrin N. H.: Reinforcement and instructions with mental patients. *J Exp Analysis Behav, 7:*327-332, 1964.

Ayllon, T. and Azrin N.H.: The measurement and reinforcement of behavior of psychotics. *J Exp Analysis Behav, 8:*357-383, 1965.

Ayllon, T. and Haughton, E.: Control of the behavior of schizophrenic patients by food. *J Exp Analysis Behav, 5:*343-352, 1962.

Ayllon, T., Haughton E. and Hughes, H. B.: Interpretation of symptoms: Fact or fiction? *Behav Res & Therapy, 3:*1-7, 1965.

Ayllon, T. and Michael, J.: The psychiatric nurse as a behavioral engineer. *J Exp Analysis Behav, 2:*323-334, 1959.

Bandura, A., Ross, D. and Ross, S. A.: Vicarious reinforcement and imitative learning. In Staats, A.W. (Ed.): *Human Learning,* pp. 45-50. New York, Holt, Rinehart and Winston, 1964.

Birnbrauer, J. S., Bijou, S. W., Wolf, M. M. and Kidder, J. D.: Programmed instruction in the classroom. In Ullman, L. P. and Krasner, L. (Eds.): *Case Studies in Behavior Modification.* New York, Holt, Rinehart and Winston, 1965.

Buehler, R. E., Patterson, G. R. and Furniss, J. M.: The reinforcement of behavior in institutional settings. *Behav Res. & Therapy, 4:*157-168, 1966.

Burchard, J. and Tyler, V. Jr.: The modification of delinquent behavior through operant conditioning. *Behav Res. & Therapy, 2:*245-250, 1965.

Cohen, A. K.: *Delinquent Boys: the Culture of the Gang.* Glencoe, Ill., Free Press, 1955.

Kintz, B. L. and Bruning, J. L.: Punishment and compulsive avoidance behavior. *J Comp Physiol Psychol* (in press), 1967.

Lovibond, S. H.: Intermittent reinforcement in behaviour therapy. *Behav Res & Therapy, 1:*127-132, 1963.

Patterson, G. R. and Anderson, D.: Peers as reinforcers. *Child Dev, 35:*951-960, 1964.

Redl, F. and Wineman, D.: *Children Who Hate.* Glencoe, Ill., Free Press, 1951.

Redl, F. and Wineman, D.: *Controls from Within.* Glencoe, Ill., Free Press, 1952.

Schrag, C.: *The Prison.* Cressey, D. R. (Ed.): New York, Holt, Rinehart and Winston, 1961.

Schwitzgebel, R.: A new approach to understanding delinquency. *Fed Probation, 24:*20-24, 1960a.

Schwitzgebel, R.: Delinquents with tape recorders. *New Society* 14-16, Jan. 31, 1963b.

Schwitzgebel, R.: *Street Corner Research: An Experimental Approach to the Juvenile Delinquent.* Cambridge, Mass., Harvard University Press, 1964.

Schwitzgebel, R. and Kolb, D. A.: Inducing behavior change in adolescent delinquents. *Behav Res & Therapy, 1:*297-304, 1964.

Shulman, H. M.: *Juvenile Delinquency in American Society.* New York, Harper, 1961.

Siegel, S.: *Nonparametric Statistics for the Behavioral Sciences.* New York, McGraw-Hill, 1960a.

Slack, C. W.: Experimenter-subject psychotherapy: a new method of introducing intensive office treatment for unreachable cases. *Mental Hygiene, 44:*238-256, 1960a.

Slack, C. W.: *Psychotherapy with Juvenile Delinquents.* Paper read at American Psychological Association, Chicago, 1960b.

Solomon, R. L.: Punishment. *Am Psychologist, 19:*239-253, 1964.

Tyler, V. O. Jr.: *Exploring the Use of Operant Techniques in the Rehabilitation of Delinquent Boys.* Paper read at American Psychological Association, Chicago, 1965.

Wolf, M., Risley, T., and Mees, H.: Application of operant conditioning procedures to the behavior problems of an autistic child. *Behav Res & Therapy, 1,* 305-312, 1964.

Chapter 11

"AVERSIVE GROUP THERAPY"
SOMETIMES GOOD MEDICINE TASTES BAD

ROBERT B. LEVINSON, GILBERT L. INGRAM *and* EDWARD AZCARATE

W E OFFER THEM GOLD but they see it as dirt" is a slightly de-terged expression of the frustration correctional workers express regarding their attempts to establish therapeutic relationships with inmates, What the correctional worker sees as a positive treatment approach, many inmates view as a waste of time and a big bother.

There are always a number of inmates in almost every institu-tion who are chronic visitors to the segregation unit. These habi-tués spend a few days in segregation almost every month for some infraction of rules; and it is clear that placing them in segregation has little effect. Inmates who regularly frequent segregation units circumvent the rehabilitative role of the institution. They have found a way to beat the system with the thought in mind that "You guys gotta let me go sooner or later."

Taking this into consideration, psychologists at the National Training School for Boys in Washington, D.C., proposed using group therapy for its "aversive" quality. It was "aversive" in that the value system of the offender was temporarily adopted by the correctional workers. Chronic referrals to segregation were requir-ed to attend what *they* viewed as useless group therapy sessions.

PROCEDURES

Specific entrance and exit requirements were established for the "aversive" group-therapy members.* In order to be eligible

---

Reprinted with permission from *Crime and Delinquency*, pp. 336-339, 1968.

*For a description of the regular institutional program at the National Train-ing School, see "Rational Innovation: The Cottage Life Intervention Program," U.S. Bureau of Prisons, Washington, D.C., 1964.

159

for the group, a boy had to have been in segregation at least once a month for three successive months. Attendance at the group therapy sessions—held once a week for an hour and a half—was mandatory until the boy met the exit requirement: three successive months without going to segregation. Once this exit criterion was met, the inmate was free to discontinue his group attendance or to continue attending group sessions for as long as he wished.

These conditions were explained to each eligible inmate in an individual interview prior to his placement in the "aversive" therapy group, and they were scrupulously followed throughout the period of this project. The initial group consisted of eight inmates. As these original members left the group, they were replaced by other eligibles; thus, a constant number of participants was maintained. The project was discontinued when the number of group members dwindled because of a lack of eligible boys.†

Results

Of the seventeen inmates who completed at least three months in "aversive" group therapy, eleven earned their way out and six exited for other reasons—expiration of sentence (three), transfer to another institution (two), and placement on a work-release assignment (one). Only one inmate elected to remain in the group beyond the date he became eligible to leave. (He was eligible to leave after three months but left after seven months, when he was placed on a work-release assignment.)

It took an average of 5.9 months for the inmates to *earn* their way out of the group; the range was from three to ten months. In regard to the amount of misbehavior before and after entering "aversive" group therapy, Table 11-I compares the number of misconduct reports on inmates for the six-month period before entering the group with the number in the six-month period after having entered it.*

---

†This was not solely the consequence of this project, since it was at about this time that the Bureau of Prisons changed its policies regarding the use of segregation units.

*One of the boys who earned his way out of the group and three who left without satisfying the exit criterion did not remain in the institution for this six-month period. They are not included in the table figures.

Of the inmates who met the exit criterion, three had no misconduct reports for the six-month period following entrance into "aversive" group therapy; none of the inmates who left the group without reaching the exit requirement maintained a misconduct-free record. In addition, six of those meeting the exit requirement were eventually placed on work-release, while only one of those who did not meet this criterion was given a work-release assignment.

Aside from these quantitatve results, the content of the sessions proved interesting. The initial reaction of those placed in "aversive" group therapy was either indifference or hostility. Amusement and bravado were displayed when the common-factor purpose of the group became clear to its members. This continued for several weeks and was succeeded by the development of a pecking order.

Almost all the members in the "aversive" group-therapy program were entrenched, antisocial leaders among the institution's population. However, in this group situation, exposure and confrontation soon produced attempts to establish a "suprapower" hierarchy. This development became a focal point for group discussion, leading into such areas as why certain individuals "run the stuff" on others and why the victims permit it.

In this setting it was difficult for group members to remain noncommittal or to straddle the fence on issues under discussion. Verbal attacks on the therapists followed as the group attempted to avoid what was becoming an unpleasant experience for all participants—unpleasant in that they failed to dominate one another, and facts about themselves which they preferred not to think about would be brought to their attention.

Both the rules established for this therapy group and the therapists were tested repeatedly, particularly by new members who continually sought ways to avoid attending the group sessions. For example, one boy volunteered for extra work so he would not be available for the group meetings. Surprisingly, these avoidance tactics of the neophytes were countered by the "timers," who made it very clear that the new members had to toe the line just as the older members had done. These pressures, generated by the group itself, made the prospect of members earning their way out all the more attractive.

The satisfactions that usually accrue to therapists conducting group sessions were absent in this project. Co-therapists may be required in "aversive" group therapy in order to cope with efforts by the group to manipulate a single therapist and to support each other in the postmortem discussions of the sessions.

When leaving the group, almost every member made a part-

TABLE 11-I

AVERAGE NUMBER OF MISCONDUCT REPORTS BEFORE AND AFTER "AVERSIVE" GROUP THERAPY

| | Average No. Misconducts | | |
| Exit Criterion | 6 Mos. Before | 6 Mos. After | Percent of |
	(N = 13)		Change
Attained	4.0	2.3	—42.5
Not attained	5.8	3.3	—43.1
Total group	4.4	2.5	—43.2

ing comment to the effect that the group had done nothing for him. However, in response to the question, "Then, why have you stayed out of segregation?" the frequent answer was: "To get out of this damn group!"

DISCUSSION

The idea of group therapy being labeled "aversive" rankles many therapists. The principle suggested by this project is akin to the palliative, "Sometimes good medicine tastes bitter." In other words, it was only from the perspective of the particular recipients that the group sessions were "aversive"; this was *not* the therapists' view. However, by adopting this approach, the therapists were able to capitalize on the "negative" motivation of the inmates.

For correctional workers, motivating inmates to participate in treatment programs has always been a problem. Therefore, application of learning theory methods to behavior modification offers the correctional worker a powerful tool. Insight into human behavior, obtained in the laboratory situation, can be applied profitably in real-life situations.

This project illustrates some of the principles involved in these new strategies of treatment. First, the nature of the problem is stated in terms of the specific goals to be achieved—decrease the number of inmates making frequent trips to segregation. Second, the target group is identified and a "handle" specified which has meaning for this group. Handles may be positive, such as rewards; or aversive, as in this project—the determinant (positive or negative) being fixed by the *target group,* which may or may not agree with the values of those conducting the project. Third, the use of this handle is made contingent on behavior which is both attainable and under the control of the target group. (It was explained that the inmate would continue in these group therapy sessions until *he* was able to stay out of segregation.) Fourth, the target group is kept informed concerning its progress. (The group often began its sessions with a discussion of who was getting close to the exit criterion and how long other members had to go.) Fifth, the rules of the game are adhered to without any deviation. (When each group member attained the exit requirement, his decision concerning continuation in the group was irrevocable.)

Admittedly, the number of boys involved in this project was small; therefore, results must not be over-generalized. Nevertheless, there appears to be clear evidence that the "aversive" group therapy approach is worth further investigation.

REFERENCE

Ullman, L. P. and Krasner, L.: *Case Studies in Behavior Modification.* New York, Holt, Rinehart and Winston, 1965.

Chapter 12

MODIFICATION OF CLASSROOM BEHAVIOR OF INSTITUTIONALIZED FEMALE ADOLESCENT OFFENDERS

DONALD H. MEICHENBAUM, KENNETH S. BOWERS *and* ROBERT R. ROSS

T HE EFFECTIVENESS of operant procedures in establishing and maintaining appropriate classroom behavior has been demonstrated with conduct problem children (O'Leary and Becker, 1966; Quay, Werry, McQueen and Sprague, 1966), and retarded children (Birnbrauer, Bijou, Wolf and Kidder, 1965; Birnbrauer, Wolf, Kidder and Tague, 1965; Birnbrauer and Lawler, 1965). The goal of establishnig appropriate classroom behavior is a major concern with institutionalized adolescent offenders who have a long history and high incidence of inappropriate classroom behavior. Generalized social reinforcers such as praise, teacher attention, and positive feedback, often minimal effects or negative effects upon their classroom behavior. The marked disruptive behavior of institutionalized adolescents in many cases precludes the possibility of the teacher administering an academic program.

Institutionalized adolescents differ markedly in many aspects from the school-age children who have been used in classroom reinforcement programs. The girls used in the present program were much more responsive to immediate peer reinforcement of

Reprinted with permission from *Behavior Research and Therapy*, 6:343-353, 1968. (Pergamon Press)

The authors gratefully acknowledge the cooperation of the administrators, teachers and staff of the Ontario Reception and Diagnostic Center, Galt, Ontario, and the Lincoln Heights School, Waterloo, Ontario. The authors are indebted to the following students whose careful observations made this research possible: A. Fedoravicius, J. Johnson, J. Knox, V. Koop, R. Morris, S. Notar, B. Palmer and B. Taub.

inappropriate behavior than immediate negative reinforcement by the teacher, or more severe delayed negative reinforcement administered by staff supervisors. The high frequency and potent value of peer reinforcement is consistent with the ward observations of institutionalized adolscent girls made by Buehler, Patterson and Furniss (1966).

Another characteristic of the institutionalized delinquent's undesirable classroom behavior is that the nature of her classroom misbehavior is quite varied topographically. Despite the manifest variety of undesirable classroom responses, however, apparently diverse misbehaviors do seem to have a certain functional equivalence. A student can try to gain the teacher's attention by walking out of the classroom, by throwing pencils or chalk, or by swearing. One consequence of the marked variety of misbehavior which results in the same reinforcement (e.g. teacher's attention) is that extinction or punishment of one particular response (e.g. swearing) results in an immediate decrease in the frequency of that response and a subsequent increase in other inappropriate responses (e.g. throwing objects) which lead to the same reinforcement. Adolescent delinquents thus pose a problem for operant procedures not encountered in work with populations which manifest highly stereotyped response units (e.g. schizophrenics, autistic children, retardates). The present study attempts to deal with this problem by dichotomously categorizing classroom behavior as either appropriate or inappropriate. The hope was that appropriateness of behavior could be defined and reliably identified in the context of a classroom situation. An advantage of the dichotomous, appropriate-inappropriate classification scheme, is that the delinquents have little opportunity to manipulate the observers by shifting from one kind of misbehavior to another when they discern the pertinent response-reinforcement contingencies. By making all inappropriate behavior functionally equivalent insofar as it leads to the postponement or elimination of desired consequences, we utilize to advantage the principle of the functional equivalence of behavior that otherwise threatens to undermine treatment efficacy. Moreover, in light of the inverse relationship between number of diagnostic categories and reliability, it was reasonable to expect fairly high interobserver reliability (Miller and Bieri, 1963).

Preliminary observations of the classroom behavior of these adolescents revealed that in most instances appropriate classroom behavior was available in their behavioral repertoires but was emitted sporadically. Thus, the goal of treatment was to maintain appropriate classroom behavior at a high level rather than to shape new responses. The relative effectiveness of different schedules of reinforcement on maintaining appropriate classroom behavior was examined. The behavioral consequence of operant treatment in one classroom on behavior in other nontreated classrooms was also examined.

Attempts to modify classroom behavior with operant procedures have been characterized by careful and intensive training of the teachers. The present study attempted to modify classroom behavior by means of a strong reinforcer (money) without staff training.

In order to assess the overall effectiveness of the operant treatment program, a group of noninstitutionalized peers in a nearby community school was assessed for comparative purposes.

In summary, the present investigation proposed (a) to establish the reliability and efficacy of a dichotomous behavior classification in the assessment of classroom behavior; (b) to establish the effectiveness of monetary reinforcement upon the appropriateness of classroom behavior for institutionalized female adolescent offenders; (c) to determine the differential effectiveness of various schedules of reinforcement on behavior change; (d) to compare the classroom behavior of adolescent female offenders with that of normal age peers before and after treatment.

METHOD

Subjects

Subjects were ten adolescent female offenders institutionalized in a special unit in a training school complex. Each girl had been selected from the total population of girls in training schools in Ontario on the basis of their apparent inability to profit from a training school program. The girls had been found to be completely unmanageable in their home settings, in foster home placements, in institutional settings and in training schools. They were described as manipulative, rebellious, uncontrollable, hostile, aggressive, and term "adolescent psychopath" was often used as the diagnostic label for them. Most had previously had a considerable amount of involvement with psychologists and psychiatrists prior to their committal to training school. They evidenced a heterogeneous variety of behavior problems such as assault, truancy, promiscuity, absconding from institutions, suicidal gestures, and vandalism. All presented major management problems in the classroom. They were inattentive, disobedient, insolent, and frequently disrupted the class by fighting, swearing, incessant talking, threatening the teachers, or simply walking out of class. All were academically retarded by at least one grade, although intellectually the majority fell within the normal range. Their mean age was 15 years, 4 months (S.D. = 1·18), and mean length of present institutionalization 240 days (S.D. = 76·32).

The girls were divided into two classes. Class I $(N = 4)$ worked at the remedial eighth grade level and devoted most of its time to academic course-work Class II $(N = 6)$ also worked at the eighth grade level, but devoted 20 percent of its time to commercial courses such as typing and clerical skills. Each class of girls had two teachers, one in the morning and the other in the afternoon. Two observations, of approximately 60 min each were made in morning classes and two in afternoon classes at varying times in order that all classroom behavior was sampled. The study began in the middle of May when five male psychology interns were available to begin classroom observation, and lasted until the end of June when school terminated. The fact that the modification program was implemented so late in the school year means that a considerable history of habitual misbehavior had to be overcome in a very short period of time.

The girls were in school 6 hr per day on each weekday except for one afternoon and one morning per week, when they were involved in group therapy sessions or sewing instruction groups. The group therapy meetings had been going on for several months before the onset of the present study.

A control group of twelve nominstitutionalized girls from a nearby community school were also assessed on the observational measure. Teachers at this school were instructed to submit names of 12 girls (four with average classroom behavior, four above average, and four below average). They were observed daily for 2 hr for a period of 2 weeks.

Observations

A major objective of this study was to develop a highly reliable observation technique which would be sensitive to the varied types of inappropriate behavior manifested. A time sampling observational technique was used. Observations were made on a 10-sec-observe, 10-sec-record basis. During the record period the observer indicated whether the behavior during the prior observe-period was appropriate or inappropriate, and briefly described any inappropriate behavior. This procedure was continued until all girls in the classroom were observed and was then repeated throughout the period of observations which averaged 60 min. Within a 1-hr observation period in a classroom of six girls, approximately 30 observations were made on any particular girl.

Inappropriate classroom behavior was defined as any behavior which was not consistent with the tasks set forth by the teacher, i.e. behavior which was not task-specific. If a girl during her 10-sec observational period manifested any single instance of behavior which was not conducive to academic performance she was marked "inappropriate." A single instance of inappropriate behavior resulted in the entire 10-sec period being marked inappropriate. This stringent criteria facilitated reliability and provided a rigorous test of the effectiveness of the present treatment program.

The time sampling observational measure did produce certain problems initially. The girls quickly determined the time sequence of observations, and the observers looking at a particular girl became a discriminative stimulus to behave appropriately only during her 10-sec period. In fact, one girl who sought to sabotage the program learned to anticipate the sequence of observations and attempted to get other girls in trouble during their respective 10-sec observational periods. Fortunately, during the treatment phase, the other girls extinguished this subject's attempt to get them in trouble. The use of multiple observers and randomizing sequence of observations constitute two means by which this problem was eventually overcome.

Procedure

The project involved four phases. Phase I was the baseline period during which the observers secured operant rates of the girls' classroom behavior. The observers were in the classrooms for two weeks during the operant period. The first week was spent becoming familiar with the classroom routine, and training raters on the observational measure. The second week's observations provided the baseline measures. At first, the girls repeatedly attempted to interact with the observers and the teachers reported that the girls' classroom behavior deteriorated when the observers were present. The observers persistently ignored the girls and the girls' interactions with them diminished.

The teachers were instructed to continue teaching in their typical fashion throughout the research program. No attempt was made to have them modify their teaching methods or their methods of controlling the girls.

The treatment procedure was iniated in Phase II. The girls were instructed that they could earn money (reinforcement) if they behaved appropriately in the afternoon classroom. They were told the definition of appropriate and inappropriate classroom behavior and given several examples of both. They were told that they would be observed in the morning classes as well, but that their behavior in the morning class would not affect how much money they would receive. The general importance of developing appropriate classroom behavior and good work habits was also mentioned. Every 10 min in the afternoon classes the girl received a slip of paper from one of the observers indicating the percentage of appropriate behavior (frequency of appropriate behavior over total number of observations made within a 10-min period, times 100). Throughout the treatment program each girl met daily with one of the psychology interns for banking hours. During this period each girl was told the amount of money she had earned and the frequency of her inappropriate classroom behavior. The girls received no feedback concerning morning classroom behavior. During Phase II of the study, a girl could earn $2 a day if she obtained 100 percent appropriate behavior for the observations during the afternoon class. A differentially weighted payment scale (logarithmically derived) was used such that a given high percentage of appropriate behavior (e.g. 100 percent) was reinforced by considerably more than twice the amount of money paid to only 50 percent appropriate behavior. During this phase of treatment a girl could lose money already earned, and zero percent appropriate behavior resulted in nothing earned. Money was placed in the girl's account at the end of each week. The girls had access to the money on weekends. For almost all girls the possibility of earning $8 a week was a very strong incentive.

The treatment approach in Phase III was modified slightly. The afternoon class was treated in Phase III in exactly the same manner as in Phase II. During Phase III, appropriate classroom behavior in the previously untreated morning class was also reinforced. However, because of the girls' requests for immediate feedback in terms of money earned, a change in the nature of feedback was made in Phase III. Secondary reinforcers such as tokens have been used in many operant programs. Nevertheless, care must be taken to avoid making the secondary reinforcement too distant from the primary reinforcement. Prior to Phase III, the feedback of percentage appropriate behavior had to be later translated into money values. Finally the money receipts could be traded in for cash each weekend. The feedback modification in Phase III shortcircuited this process. The girls were told that instead of receiving slips of paper indicating percentage of appropriate behavior, the slips would indicate the amount of money (denominations of 25, 20, 15, 10, 5 or 0 cents) they had earned. During the 2 hr of morning observation, six slips of paper would be dispensed to each girl, permitting a girl to earn $1.50 a morning if she manifested 100 percent appropriate behavior. If the girl manifested no inappropriate behavior during a specified period of observations she received a slip reading 25 cents: if one inappropriate behavior, 20 cents; two, 15 cents; three, 10 cents; four, 5 cents; five or more, zero cents. In the afternoon class during Phase II and III, the feedback slips indicating the percentage of appropriate behavior were dispensed on a fixed interval (FI) schedule (every 10 min). In the morning class during Phase III, they were dispensed on a variable interval (VI) schedule for each girl with the constraint that a minimum of five 10-sec observations was made for a particular girl before dispensing feedback. Thus, the time when reinforcement was dispensed varied on a random basis and was unpredictable.

The girls' classroom behavior during Phases I and II was marked by daily and hourly fluctuations from appropriate to inappropriate behavior. The inclusion of feedback on a VI schedule in the morning class was designed to foster maintenance of appropriate behavior at a high level.

Phase IV introduced a further modification designed to increase the maintenance of appropriate classroom behavior. Reinforcement in both morning and afternoon class during Phase IV was dispensed in the same manner as in the morning class of Phase III, viz. VI schedule of reinforcement with feedback consisting of money values. However, during Phase IV the girls were instructed for the first time in the treatment program that if their classroom behavior was inappropriate they could lose money they had earned the previous day. For every percentage point of inappropriate classroom behavior they obtained on a certain day, they would lose one and a half cents of what they had earned the previous day. For example, if a girl earned 80 cents one day and received an average of 70 percent appropriate on the following day, she would lose 45 cents from the previous day's earnings (30 percent inappropriate times one and a half cents). A girl could not lose more money than she had earned the previous day and go into debt, which might result in a loss of incentive. This modification was included in order to attempt to gain control of daily fluctuations in percentage appropriate behavior. Also during this phase (for reasons of diminished funds) the amount of money available for reinforcement was cut from a potential of $3.50 a day to $1.50 if the girl behaved at a 100 percent appropriate level during all classroom observations.

In summary, the treatment program included four phases: Phase I—operant period; Phase II—feedback on FI schedule only in the afternoon class; Phase III—FI feedback afternoon class and VI feedback morning class; and Phase IV—VI feedback both morning and afternoon classes tied with possible loss of previously earned reinforcement.

RESULTS

An exceptionally high reliability between raters was found which reflects the sensitivity of the observational measure in classifying the behaviors into appropriate or inappropriate categories. During the operant period, 3194 pairs of observations were made of the institutionalized adolescents' classroom behavior. The raters disagreed on the appropriateness or inappropriateness of behavior on only 190 of these pairs of observations, yielding agreement of 94 percent. Similarly, in the classroom with noninstitutionalized girls, 1569 pairs of observations were made on which two independent raters disagreed on only 18 observations, yielding agreement of 98 percent. Most of the disagreements occurred in discriminating between daydreaming behavior and paying attention. Often a girl would have her head on her desk, from the vantage point of the observer it was difficult to assess if the girl was daydreaming or listening to the teacher. Similarly, if a girl was staring at her book it was sometimes difficult to determine if she was in fact reading or merely passing time. Future research should include academic performance measures such as amount of material recalled as the criterion of appropriate behavior.

One additional reliablity check was made. Since the same observers were making observations during the operant phase and the treatment phase, it was deemed neecssary to check their reliability against raters who were naive to the study in order to insure against a subtle shift in criterion of inappropriate behavior or experimenter bias (Rosenthal, 1966). During the treatment phase, 685 observations were made by two naive observers and psychology interns who had participated in the study throughout. They disagreed on only 55 observations, yielding agreement of 92 percent. This result indicated that there was no shift in criteria of what constituted inappropriate behavior between the operant and the treatment phase of the study.

The time sampling measure was sensitive in discriminating beween appropriate and inappropriate classroom behavior of adolescent noninstitutionalized females. The mean percentage appropriate behavior for normal girls classified by their teachers as above average was 94 (S.D. = 6·86); average 84 (S.D. = 13·51); and below average 69 (S.D. = 12·87). The difference between the above and below average girls was significant at less than the 0·05 level. The teachers' average rank ordering of the 12 girls on the basis of their estimation of appropriate classroom behavior correlated 0·85 with mean percentage appropriate classroom behavior. These results indicate the discriminant validity of the observational measure in a normal classroom setting.

The inclusion of the noninstitutionalized girls provided a comparison group for the treated institutionalized girls. The mean percentage appropriate classroom behavior for the noninstitutionalized girls was 83 (S.D. = 17·38), with a range from 40 to 99 percent. The mean percentage appropriate classroom behavior for institutionalized girls during the operant period was 45 (S.D. = 30·15), with a range from 0 to 100 percent. The difference in percentage appropriate classroom behavior between noninstitutionalized girls and institutionalized girls during the operant period was significant at the 0·01 level. The inappropriate behavior of the institutionalized girls during the operant period was not only more frequent but more intense. For example, inappropriate verbalizations during operant period for institutionalized girls was characterized by swearing and insolence; whereas for noninstitutionalized girls it consisted of quietly talking to one's neighbor. Future research should attempt to assess the intensity of inappropriate behavior as well as its frequency.

The pretreatment behavior for the institutionalized girls also indicated that appropriate classroom behavior was in their repertoires since nine of the ten girls obtained at least 80 percent ap-

propriate classroom behavior for two observational periods, and
two girls secured above 90 percent appropriate classroom behavior. As noted previously, the task for the treatment program was
clearly to foster prolonged maintenance of appropriate classroom
behavior, and to reduce frequency of inappropriate behavior.

The effectiveness of the treatment program in modifying the
girls' inappropriate classroom behavior is reflected in (a) the
mean percentage of appropriate classroom behavior for baseline
vs. treatment phases for the ten institutionalized girls (Table
12-I) ; (b) the group performance curves for the two separate
classes (Figs. 12-1 and 12-2) ; and (c) the individual perfomance
curves (Table 12-II). A consistent pattern of results was obtained.
The operant period was marked by a generally high level of inappropriate classroom behavior. The introduction of reinforcement in the afternoon class had a sudden and dramatic effect. The
girls' behavior in the afternoon class quickly improved while
their initial behavior in the morning class remained the same as
in the operant period. It is important to note that the girls had
their first opportunity to spend the money they had earned between days nine and ten. Following the occasion of this initial,
direct reinforcement, classroom behavior in the afternoon class

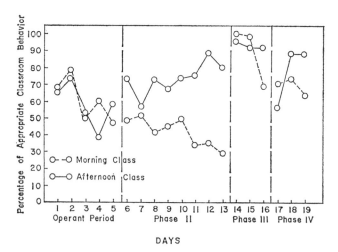

Figure 12-1. Mean percentage appropriate classroom behavior for Class I
(N = 4) for operant and treatment periods.

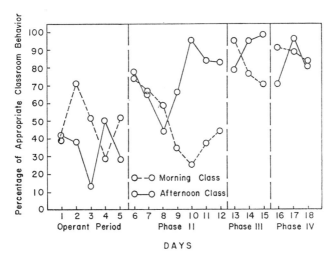

Figure 12-2. Mean percentage appropriate classroom behavior for Class II (N = 6) for operant and treatment periods.

improved quite substantially in Class II, while appropriate classroom behavior in the morning decreased below the operant level. A similar pattern was apparent in Class I. One girl reported: "If you don't pay us, we won't shape up." Clearly, the girls were manipulating the psychologists into initiating payment in the morning class and were offering appropriate behavior in the morning class as the possible reward. The girls proved to be effective modifiers of behavior. During the remainder of the treatment, the girls received reinforcement in both the morning and afternoon classes.

TABLE 12-I

MEAN PERCENTAGE APPROPRIATE CLASSROOM BEHAVIOR FOR 10 INSTITUTIONALIZED GIRLS DURING OPERANT AND TREATMENT PERIODS

	Phase I	*Phase II*		*Phase III*	*Phase IV*
	Operant Period	*First Week*	*Second Week*		
Morning class	54·20	52·13	36·29	84·50	78·17
Afternoon class	46·00	65·25	82·86	92·00	80·00

TABLE 12-II

INDIVIDUAL CLASSROOM BEHAVIOR FOR TEN INSTITUTIONALIZED GIRLS DURING OPERANT AND TREATMENT PHASES

Ss		Phase I*					Phase II Days								Phase III			Phase IV		
		1	2	3	4	5	6	7	8	9	10	11	12	13	14	15	16	17	18	19
Ss Class I																				
S-1	Morning	54	64	60	53	20	18	28	36	0	80	10	49	32	100	100	99	38	abs	64
	Afternoon	20	85	57	12	38	30	10	11	12	88	40	92	97	97	100	93	28	73	90
S-2	Morning	62	70	33	63	abs†	43	56	32	59	41	50	45	24	100	94	92	96	84	97
	Afternoon	76	80	40	29	88	81	63	90	85	92	90	78	70	100	88	73	92	100	88
S-3	Morning	84	94	54	72	46	62	48	32	66	31	abs	12	13	100	98	26	63	64	39
	Afternoon	75	50	58	56	10	93	83	100	87	37	abs	96	75	93	80	100	44	80	86
S-4	Morning	71	84	55	55	72	72	75	66	57	45	42	abs	48	100	98	51	85	71	53
	Afternoon	89	80	52	58	96	90	71	87	87	77	95	abs	78	90	100	100	61	100	abs
Ss Class II																				
S-5	Morning	56	45	27	15	abs	20	46	64	0	3	21	9	*‡	100	50	50	79	100	52
	Afternoon	0	0	0	0	abs	79	41	27	75	97	95	99	*	95	99	abs	45	100	100
S-6	Morning	15	74	35	0	abs	97	62	32	87	abs	66	97		96	98	99	abs	88	100
	Afternoon	58	50	0	84	27	74	38	0	94	abs	95	91		95	97	100	89	100	100
S-7	Morning	45	60	74	10	44	76	71	81	18	17	14	abs		100	88	66	abs	100	97
	Afternoon	0	10	48	15	27	90	96	89	65	100	100	100		73	100	100	100	100	abs
S-8	Morning	20	76	66	40	31	77	69	45	13	13	43	0		90	33	22	87	abs	53
	Afternoon	53	40	22	20	39	65	32	22	40	90	26	87		32	97	abs	40	100	70
S-9	Morning	75	92	73	70	75	91	91	86	87	70	68	84		96	93	97	100	100	99
	Afternoon	90	51	13	30	62	91	96	82	81	96	95	97		95	100	100	53	99	100
S-10	Morning	27	79	31	35	54	83	54	41	0	abs	13	31		85	92	88	98	50	100
	Afternoon	55	65	12	20	4	64	90	47	45	92	98	29		89	80	95	100	79	37

*Phase I = Operant period, days 1-5; Phase II = FI feedback afternoon class, days 6-13; Phase III = FI feedback afternoon class, VI feedback morning class, days 14-16; Phase IV = VI feedback both morning and afternoon class tied with possible loss of previously earned reinforcement.

†Abs. = absent, girl was absent from class due to illness, or medical examination.

‡Ss in Class II were absent from school on day 13.

During Phase III, the girls were given feedback on a VI schedule in the morning and continued on Fl schedule in the afternoon. The introduction of reinforcement in the morning class was dramatically effective in fostering appropriate classroom behavior. Percentage appropriate behavior jumped from 29 to 100 percent in Class I, and from 44 to 95 percent in Class II. In order to achieve a score of 100 percent appropriate behavior, each of the girls had to behave perfectly in all of her 10-sec time samples for two complete hours. This sudden rise in appropriate behavior was attributable to the introduction of reinforcement and also to the fact that the girls had developed a discriminated repertoire of appropriate classroom behavior during the previous phase of treatment. The previous training increased response availability, or response strength of appropriate classroom behavior which was quickly transfered to a situation in which it was rewarded. The mean percentage appropriate classroom behavior in the afternoon class was 92 (S.D. = 9·50) where feedback was dispensed on FI schedule and 84 (S.D. = 8·45) in the morning class where feedback was dispensed on a VI schedule (nonsignificant). However, Figures 12-1 and 12-2 indicate a decreasing trend in classroom performance under the VI schedule. Even though the VI schedule led to a precipitous rise in appropriate classroom behavior, the girls perceived the reinforcements as unpredictable. The unpredictableness of reinforcement on the VI schedule seems to have caused the drop in the appropriateness of classroom behavior.

Thus far, the treatment program had significantly increased the mean level of appropriate classroom behavior. However, there remained the problem of some girls who occasionally regressed in their classroom performance to their former pretreatment level. Although these behavioral reverses were becoming less frequent, a reinforcement schedule was selected which would make the girl pay for such drops in behavior. During the final phase of treatment, feedback was dispensed on VI schedule in all classes and in addition, the girls lost money from previous days' earnings if they behaved inappropriately. The introduction of this regime also resulted in a slight drop in appropriate classroom behavior from the high level obtained in Phase III. This appeared to be related to the girls' negative reactions to the possibility of the loss of money previously earned and a decrease in the amount of money they could earn. Furthermore, those girls most directly affected instigated and reinforced misbehavior on the part of their peers. With the end of the school year approaching, the effectiveness of the treatment program to attenuate peer reinforcement of inappropriate behavior diminished. Even with these factors, the institutionalized girls' mean level of appropriate behavior (79 percent) did not approach their mean pretreatment level (45 percent) and was not significantly different from the mean level of noninstitutionalized girls (83 percent). An analysis of the descriptions of inappropriate classroom behavior for institutionalized girls revealed that not only the frequency of inappropriate behavior decreased, but also its nature and form changed as a function of the treatment program. Both the teachers and observers reported that the topography of the girls' inappropriate classroom behavior more closely approximated that observed in noninstitutionalized classrooms.

DISCUSSION

The present investigation demonstrated that high frequency inappropriate classroom behavior of female institutionalized adolescent offenders is readily modifiable by means of an operant procedure. Prior to treatment, the institutionalized girls manifested almost twice as much intense inappropriate classroom behavior as noninstitutionalized peers. Even though the teachers were not trained in operant procedures, the treatment program showed that with monetary reinforcement, disruptive classroom behavior of such girls can be reduced to the level of noninstitutionalized adolescents, and peer reinforcement of inappropriate classroom behavior is attenuated.

It is difficult to assess the relative merits of the two schedules of feedback used in the present study (FI and VI) because of (a) the short period of time available; (b) the contamination of order and time effects; and (c) varying amount of money dispensed under the two schedules. Further research is needed to assess the relative effectiveness of such schedules in modifying behavior in such situations. However, the results suggest that factors of complexity, perceived unpredictability, and temporally remote secondary reinforcement undermine the effectiveness of an operant approach. The limited time available for the treatment program did not permit phasing out of monetary reinforcement or transferring to the teachers the control of reinforcement.

The present study indicated that institutionalized female adolescent offenders present particular problems for behavior modification programs based on operant techniques and suggested some solutions to these problems. Most of the problems were related to the girls' skill in manipulation, the potency of peer reinforcement, and the wide range and variability of their inappropriate behavior. The latter problem precluded preselection of behavioral categories and definition of specific response classes. The use of a reliable dichotomous recording technique which treated the variety of classroom misbehavior as functionally equivalent, dealt adequately with the problem of behavioral complexity and variety. The attenuation of peer reinforcement of misbehavior in the present study was accomplished by means of a potent reinforcer, viz. money. Further research along the lines of making reinforcement contingent upon group performance, or reinforcement of the group contingent upon an individual's behavior, may lead to even better control of peer reinforcement. The behavior to be reinforced was largely present in the girls repertoire during the operant period and the goal of treatment was to maintain it at a high level rather than to shape new responses. The use of intermittent schedules of reinforcement, and withholding reinforcement as a function of fluctuations in appropriate behavior are two techniques to handle this problem. The need to phase out reinforcement and to pair potent reinforcers with social reinforcement is also indicated.

The possibility of applying operant procedures to the modification of other inappropriate behavior of institutionalized adolescents is clearly indicated.

REFERENCES

Birnbrauer, J.S., Bijou, S.W., Wolf, M.M. and Kidder, J.D.: Programmed instruction in the classroom. In *Case Studies in Behavior Modification.*

Ullmann, L. and Krasner, L. (Eds.): New York, Holt, Rinehart & Winston, 1965.

Birnbrauer, J.S. and Lawler, Julia: Token reinforcement for learning. *Mentally Retarded, 2:*275-279, 1964.

Birnbrauer, J.S., Wolf, M.M., Kidder, J.D. and Tague, Cecilia, E.: Classroom behavior of retarded pupils with token reinforcement. *Journal of Experimental Child Psychology, 2:*219-235, 1965.

Buehler, R.E., Patterson, G.R. and Furness, J.M.: The reinforcement of behavior in institutional settings. *Behavioral Research and Therapy, 4:* 157-167, 1966.

Miller, H. and Bieri, J.: An informational analysis of clinical judgment. *Journal of Abnormal Social Psychology, 67:*317-325, 1963.

O'Leary, K.D. and Becker, W.C.: Behavior modification of an adjustment class: a token reinforcement program. Unpublished manuscript, University of Illinois, 1967.

Quay, H.C., Werry, J.S., McQueen, Marjorie and Sprague, R. L.: Remediation of the conduct problem child in the special class setting. *Exceptional Child, 32:*509-515, 1966.

Rosenthal, R.: Covert communication in the psychological experiment. *Psychological Bulletin, 67:*356-367, 1967.

Chapter 13

A TOKEN ECONOMY IN A CORRECTIONAL INSTITUTION FOR YOUTHFUL OFFENDERS

LOREN KARACKI *and* ROBERT B. LEVINSON

O<small>N</small> J<small>ANUARY</small> 14, 1969, the Robert F. Kennedy Youth Center (KYC) began operation with the arrival of 85 youthful offenders. Designed to replace the century-old National Training School in Washington, D. C., KYC is an open, cottage-type institution nestled within a scenic valley near Morgantown, West Virginia. With capacity set at 325, the Center receives Federal law violators, ages 15 to 19, whose homes generally are in the eastern half of the nation.* The largest offender category, by far, consists of Dyer Act violators (persons who have crossed a state line in a stolen automobile). Other major offense categories include drug law violators, postal law violators, and individuals who have committed crimes on Federal property.

The treatment program at the Center incorporates a number of innovations. Prominent among these are: (a) a differential treatment program based upon a behavior typology developed by Quay, *et al.* (see References) ; (b) an educational/vocational program built around various vocational clusters;† and (c) a token economy system which enables the performance of students—inmates—to be evaluated and rewarded.

In this article, the token economy system will be discussed—

Reprinted with permission from *The Howard Journal of Penology and Crime Prevention, 13:*20-30, 1970. (Howard League for Penal Reform)

*Youthful offenders from the western part of the nation are sent to the Federal Youth Center, Englewood, Colorado.

†Developed under contract by Learning Systems, Inc., Washington, D.C.

first, by describing how the system operates; second, by indicating some of the advantages seen in this approach over more traditional institutional reward systems; and, finally, by providing a preliminary assessment as to how the token economy system has functioned thus far. Before proceeding, however, a brief description of other aspects of the program at KYC is in order.‡

STANDARD STRUCTURE AT KYC

Differential Classification

When a new student—as offenders are referred to at KYC—is received at the institution, he is sent to the Reception Center where he remains for approximately two weeks. While there, he undergoes extensive testing, including the administration of test instruments especially developed by Quay and his colleagues for rating students along various behavioral dimensions. Based upon this test profile, the newly admitted student is classified into one of five behavioral categories or BC-types: BC-1 (inadequate-immature); BC-2 (neurotic-disturbed); BC-3 (psychopathic-aggressive); BC-4 (subcultural-gang oriented); and a more recently established and as yet untitled BC-5 category, which is a subgroup of BC-1 and BC-4. He is then assigned to the particular cottage where his BC-type is housed.

Once assigned to his regular cottage, the student becomes the responsibility of that cottage's classification committee. The cottage committee consists of the cottage supervisor (a caseworker), the student's counselor (a correctional officer/counselor), and a member of the teaching staff. Cottage committee members familiarize themselves with the student's case, and in consultation with other members of the staff, develop and monitor a treatment and training program relevant to the particular needs of the student. Since the program at KYC consists primarily of academic and vocational training during the day and an evening cottage program, the main task of the cottage committee is that of involving the student meaningfully in these areas. In addition, however, at-

---

‡A more detailed description of program is found in Gerard, Roy, *et al.: Differential Treatment . . . A Way to Begin.* Robert F. Kennedy Youth Center, Morgantown, West Virginia, May, 1969.

tention must be given to such matters as release planning, the student's medical and religious needs, and assignment to chores for two hours per day.

Housing Units

Cottages are designed to handle up to 55 students. They are staffed by a cottage supervisor (a social worker), an assistant cottage supervisor (a correctional supervisor), two or more correctional officer/counselors, and enough correctional officers to provide 24-hour coverage. Each cottage operates more or less as an autonomous unit and has responsibility for developing and implementing a program especially suited for the BC-type individual it houses.

In the case of the BC-1 or immature group, for example, since these students characteristically are weak and dependent individuals who behave in childish and irresponsible ways, the major program objective is to establish a secure and nonthreatening environment in which "growing-up" can be stressed. The approach taken is a combination of individual counseling—"fatherly" talks—and group activities such as town meetings and group discussions.

In contrast, since the BC-3, or psychopathic group, consists of rather aggressive, manipulative individuals who frequently become institutional "trouble-makers," the primary objective in that cottage has been to provide an environment in which their energy can be absorbed while control is still maintained. Consequently, emphasis has been placed upon athletics and other forms of physical activity, with only limited effort made to establish verbal interaction through individual or group counseling.*

The Program Day

During weekdays, students usually are scheduled for six hours of training. This program represents a major effort in integrating

---

*The treatment approach for this group is based upon an experimental program developed at the National Training School in Washington, D.C. See: U. S. Bureau of Prisons: *Project R.E.A.D.Y.* (Reaching Effectively Acting-out Delinquent Youths). Washington, D.C., U. S. Bureau of Prisons, 1968. See also: Quay, Herbert C. and Levinson, Robert B.: The Prediction of the Institutional Adjustment of Four Sub-groups of Delinquent Boys Mimeo, 1969.

vocational training with academic instruction. The program is structured around several vocational clusters such as aerospace, graphic arts, and electronics. These, in turn, are subdivided into various segments such as power technology, wood and plastics technology, and metals technology, to name three under the aerospace label. The academic and vocational training a student receives in each vocational cluster is specifically geared to the knowledge and skills necessary for employment in that vocational field. In this manner, the practical value of classroom instruction is made apparent.

Nearly two hours of a student's day are spent on a chore detail. The work performed contributes to institutional maintenance and is not regarded as having any specific treatment value for students. Religious instruction and medical treatment are also provided. An effort is made to maintain community contact through such modalities as town visits, furloughs, and work/study release.

Class Levels

Another aspect of the program at KYC is a class level or privilege system. All students begin at the *trainee* or lowest class level. They must demonstrate their ability to progress in their program before they can be promoted to the next level of *apprentice* and eventually to the highest class level—*honor student*. The higher the level, the greater the advantages. For example, while trainees can only wear institutional issue khaki clothing, apprentice students are permitted to wear civilian clothing during evening hours and weekends while honor students wear regular clothes whenever they wish. Similarly, whereas trainees are not permitted to leave the institution, apprentices are eligible for town trips and study-release while honor students are also eligible for home furloughs, work release, and parole.

OVERVIEW OF THE TOKEN ECONOMY SYSTEM

A major element of the program at KYC is the token economy system or the method by which students are, in effect, rewarded for appropriate behavior. Based upon operant conditioning principles of behavior modification through application of external rewards, this approach to retraining has been successful in such diverse fields as mental health and work with the mentally retarded and emotionally disturbed (e.g. Ayllon, Teodore and Azrin, 1969). Its application in the field of corrections, however, has been limited, mainly being restricted to small experimental studies.* Consequently, the token economy at KYC represents one of the more ambitious undertakings of this nature to date in the field of corrections.†

Student Earnings

The token economy at KYC provides a method by which student earn "points" for good behavior. The points have a monetary value (one point = one cent) and can be used for the purchase of various goods and services. Points are earned in two ways: (a) through a regular token economy system by which students earn points on a weekly basis while functioning in the areas of cottage, school, and chores; and (b) by a bonus point system in which points can be immediately awarded youths for certain positive kinds of behavior.

In the regular system, the amount of points a student can earn in any week is dependent upon his class level at KYC. trainees can earn up to 750 points with 250 coming from the cottage area, 375 from school, and 125 from chore detail; apprentices earn at a rate of 10 percent greater than trainees; and honor students earn at a rate 20 percent greater than trainees.

Rating forms are used by staff to evaluate student performance. Regarding school, for example, the form contains such items as arrives on time, uses class time productively, plans work, and so forth. The basis for evaluation is deliberately flexible so that

---

*A recent list of 50 institutions in the United States and Canada involved in token economy systems contained only three institutions for confined offenders. Krasner, Leonard and Atthowe, John, Jr.: Token Economy Bibliography, Mimeo, 1968. For examples of programs in correctional institutions involving token economics or other operant learning techniques, see Reference no. 2 at end of this chapter.

†The token economy at the George Junior Republic in Freeville, New York (which considerably predates the one at KYC), also represents a comprehensive approach along similar lines.

one student may be scored on a variety of behavioral items while another may only be evaluated in the one area where he has evidenced problems in the past. Rating forms are completed by Sunday of each week, and on Thursday students receive an earnings statement indicating points received and their current financial status.

The bonus-point system (the second method by which students can earn points) differs from the regular economy in that rewards are immediate and no limit exists on the number of bonus points a student can earn over a given period of time—although there is a limit on the number of bonus points any individual act can be awarded. It is expected that bonus points will be used primarily to reward especially meritorious behavior. For example, the successful completion of a unit of study by a recalcitrant student or assisting staff in an emergency situation are acts which may warrant issuance of bonus points. Such bonuses consist of slips of paper on which a student's name is written; these are given directly to the student by the staff member.

The bonus-point system, with its emphasis upon immediate and unlimited rewards, is more consistent with the tenets of operant conditioning theory which hold that new behavioral learning is more likely to occur if desired behavior is rewarded immediately every time it takes place. It is, therefore, an effective device for "shaping" new behavior. The problem, of course, with this approach is that it tends not to be the manner by which society rewards its members. Consequently, the weekly token economy system, with its reliance upon delayed gratification and definite limits to rewards, represents a system more nearly approximating conditions outside the institution. It is hoped that this combination of approaches to rewarding positive behavior will prove to be a more effective treatment tool.

Student Spending

Points earned are nontransferable from student to student. They are used in a variety of ways, some of which reflect voluntary spending and others involuntary charges against student accounts, as follows.

1. *Savings.* All trainees are required to deposit 40 percent of their net earnings in a savings account, apprentices 20 percent, and honor students whatever they may voluntarily choose to set aside. Three percent simple interest is paid on deposits which are "frozen" until the student's release. Students who run away or who are transferred to another institution for disciplinary reasons automatically forfeit their savings.

2. *Room rental.* Trainees pay a room rental of 70 points per week, apprentices 140 points, and honor students 280 points. Differences in rental rates reflect variations in accommodations and privileges associated with place of residence. The living area for trainees consists of small cubicles separated by shoulder high partitions; apprentices have private rooms without sink and toilet facilities; and honor students have private rooms with sink and toilet.

3. *Earnings tax.* Each student is charged a weekly earnings tax of 3 percent of his gross earnings which is placed in a general fund for his cottage. These funds are used to sponsor social events such as dances and splash parties, and to pay for property damage in the cottage.

4. *Fines.* Students can be fined for misconduct. In one case, for example, a youth was fined 500 points for having taken a bottle of India ink for use as a tattooing agent.

5. *Commissary and snack bar purchases.* Points can be used to purchase such items as cigarettes, soap, and toothpaste from the commissary and candy bars, soft drinks and ice cream from the cottage snack bar. Purchases are made with "spending cards" which students obtain by writing checks against their spending accounts. Each spending card is worth 200 points. Printed on it are values of five and ten points which are punched out by staff as purchases are made.

6. *Recreation and special services charges.* Many leisure time activities available at KYC must be paid for by the students. It costs to see a movie, to shoot a game of table pool, or to use the gymnasium or swimming pool beyond the prescribed program. Other privileges also carry a charge. Trips to town for special events, for example, cost points and a charge is made for renting civilian clothing for the occasion. While no set formula exists for determing how much an item or service should cost, generally the charges are in line with actual prices in the free community.

7. *Miscellaneous charges.* Other ways in which points can be used include the purchase of civilian clothing, rental of cameras, a charge for overdrawn checking accounts, and a tariff on items sent to students from outside the institution by friends and relatives.

ADVANTAGES OF THE TOKEN ECONOMY SYSTEM

It can hardly be said that there is something new or revolutionary in a correctional method which provides external rewards for positive behavior. On the contrary, such reward systems tend to be the very cornerstone upon which most institutional programs are built. This principle is reflected in such well-established practices as parole, "good time," custody grading, and institutional work-pay systems. Further, the token economy system does not eliminate other institutional reward systems. Rather, its contribution is one of strengthening and enhancing these other aspects of the total institutional program. Nevertheless, the token economy at KYC is sufficiently different from other monetary reward systems to give it a rather unique and experimental character; and found in these differences is its potential for greater correctional effectiveness. The advantages of this system follow.

1. *Inclusiveness.* Most institutional monetary reward systems are based solely upon work-assignment performance. As a result, it is quite possible for an offender not to participate in a significant segment of the institutional program and yet receive full monetary reward, provided his noncompliance is manifested outside the work situation. In contrast, the token economy system extends into virtually all aspects of a student's life at the Youth Center. Students are not only evaluated on how they perform in their chore details but also in school and in their cottages. Consequently, it is extremely difficult for a youth to "beat the system"—remain detached from his program—without adversely affecting the amount of points he earns.

2. *Flexibility of application.* Not only do most monetary reward systems apply only to the work situation but they also tend to be administered along rather narrowly prescribed and inflexible lines. Inmates are paid simply for being in the work area or their pay is based upon the extent to which they maintain production schedules. In either case, the basis for evaluaiton is quite restricted and usually has little real bearing on individual situations. In contrast, the basis for evaluation at the Youth Center is extremely flexible and broad-based. It is possible, for example, for one student to be rewarded mainly in terms of how he conforms to institutional rules and regulations and for another to be evaluated primarily on the basis of progress toward obtaining a high school degree or on his behavior in cottage group

sessions. In this manner, staff are able to direct the token economy system towards what appears to be a particular treatment and training need of a youth and to shift focus as circumstances warrant.

3. *Universality.* Another weakness or shortcoming of usual institutional monetary reward systems is that they frequently exclude certain members of the offender population, thus contributing to gross inequities among inmates. This is usually the case with a work-pay system where there are not enough jobs to go around or when new admissions are not assigned to work details until after completing the orientation period. At KYC, all students participate in the token economy system from day of arrival to day of departure. As a result, variations in student earnings should reflect actual differences in behavior rather than merely fortuitous circumstance or worse.

4. *Self-contained nature.* A problem with some institutional monetary reward systems is that they are easily undermined by funds received from friends and relatives outside the institution. Consequently, differences which existed among offenders on the outside tend to be repeated inside the institution, and for those receiving such funds, the motivation to comply with institutional standards is often reduced. In the extreme, excessive pressure is placed on marginal family resources to provide funds for some incarcerated offenders while affluent "racketeers" buy their way through their confinement period.

At the Youth Center, money sent to students is held for them until they are ready to leave and cannot be used in their spending account. Furthermore, restrictions are placed on the kind of items a student can receive from outside the institution, while those which are permitted, as noted earlier, are subject to a tariff. In this way, the attempt is made to make the student soley dependent upon his own efforts and the token economy system for his source of goods.

5. *Variety of choice.* In many institutions, what an inmate can do with his funds is limited to what is available in the commissary and snack bar. At the Youth Center, students not only enjoy these privileges, but have many other goods and services available to them. They can buy telephone calls home or pay for items ordered from a mail order catalog; they can pay to attend selected events in the community such as athletic games, concerts, plays; they can pay to attend dances and parties; they can pay to use recreation equipment and facilities during their leisure hours, and so forth. This variety of choice makes the token economy system significant and meaningful for the KYC students.

INITIAL EXPERIENCES

The KYC token economy has not been an easy system to operate. The seemingly countless forms and unrelenting deadlines necessary to operate the system on a current basis have required an enormous effort from institutional personnel, and at times have taxed the patient of even the most sanguine staff member. Nevertheless, the expectation is that it will prove to be both an effective population control device and a powerful treatment tool.

Since the program at KYC has only been in operation for a brief period, any effort at assessing the token economy system at this time would be premature, particularly since the evaluation, in part, is dependent upon obtaining follow-up information on students after release. It is possible, however, to comment on how the token economy system has operated thus far.

Within the framework of operant conditioning theory, consideration must be given to the following actions: (a) determining the desired behavior; (b) observing and recording occurrences of the desired behavior; and (c) providing appropriate rewards. It is within this context that the following discussion proceeds since problems have been encountered in each area.

Determination of Behavior to be Rewarded

It is important to note that the principles of operant conditioning theory provide a method of changing behavior but *not* a method for selecting the behavior to be changed. Ultimately, therefore, the success or failure of any program of this sort depends on the ability of staff to select appropriate behavior.

In this regard, problems have arisen since staff have shown a tendency to become "form bound"; that is, they frequently rely upon the various rating forms mainly devised to suggest general ways students could be rewarded, rather than developing individualized behavior goals. This in itself would not be a problem if the purpose of the token economy system were merely to assure that students got up on time in the morning or remained seated in class; in other words, if the purpose was simply to run a "smooth" institution. As it is, since the token economy is also seen as contributing directly to offender rehabilitation, an effort must be made to relate it to the specific treatment and training needs of students.

Admittedly, this is no easy task. Frequently what needs to be changed is not so much specific, observable behavior as such intangibles as attitudes and values. Moreover, one rarely finds at KYC such behavior as phobic reactions, serious withdrawal, tics, enuresis, or persistent assaultive behavior, actions which readily lend themselves to treatment by operant conditioning techniques.* It is necessary, therefore, that cottage staff and school personnel receive assistance in this endeavor. This is being provided by psychologists on the Center's staff and by consultant psychologists.

Along these lines, a recent innovation has been the use of a reinforcement "menu" as part of the admission unit testing program.† This will enable cottage personnel to individualize rewards since each student indicates those things he finds most pleasurable.

Observing and Recording Behavior

Numerous minor problems have arisen over such matters as communicating to staff behavior to be observed and devising forms for recording this behavior when it occurs. There has been, however, a persistent problem in the perception of how points are credited to students. It was originally intended that each student would begin each week with a clean slate and would *accumulate* points throughout the period as he demonstrated positive behavior. As it was, the forms for recording behavior were structured in such a manner that many students thought they began each week with the full quota of points and would *lose* points for mis-

---

*The difficulty in relating the token economy to individual treatment and training programs is stated somewhat differently by Tyler and Brown. "In a school for delinquents, the size of living units, the limited number of staff, the large number of youngsters, and the numerous responsibilities of the staff members make it difficult to set up individualized programs without extra staff to record data and administer contingencies with precision." (Tyler and Brown, 1967, p. 1.)

†This is an adaptation of a reinforcement survey schedule developed by J. R. Cautela and R. Kastenbaum, *Psychology Reports, 20:*1115-1130, 1967.

conduct. Consequently, rather than functioning as a positive reward system to promote new behavioral learning, the token economy system appeared to be another way to punish student misconduct. Efforts are now being made to redirect the system along intended lines.

Rewards for Behavior

A third problem area concerns the use of points earned. Somewhat unexpectedly, however, this involves those who *provide* the points rather than those who *spend* them, since it is essentially a budgetary problem which has arisen. Indeed, from the standpoint of the students, the reward system would seem to be working exceedingly well, since by objective standards, it has fostered what can be called an "economy of abundance." That is, in addition to paying all involuntary charges against their accounts, students appear to be earning enough points to satisfy their wants for such "basic teenage staples" as candy bars, soft drinks and cigarettes and still afford such extras as dances, games on the pool table, movies, etc. During the last week in July, for example, the average student began the week with over thirteen dollars in his spending account while earning over six dollars during the week. It is no wonder, therefore, that he could spend, on the average, more than three dollars for commissary goods and another dollar for snack bar items during that week without causing a serious drain on his spending account.

It is noteworthy that this "economy of abundance" appears to have contributed to a positive institutional climate among students. At least there seem to be fewer instances of theft and related forms of misconduct at KYC than is usually the case in institutions for young offenders.

In order to appreciate the budgetary problem which has arisen, a distinction needs to be made between "hard" and "soft" items in the token economy. "Hard" items are those which must be paid for with real money from the token economy budget. Primarily this consists of money spent by students for consumable goods and money set aside for savings. "Soft" items, in contrast, are those which are not charged to the token economy budget either because they are paid for from other budgets or because no actual costs are involved. Transportation to town, for example, is a "soft" item, because although students must pay to go to town, the actual cost of their transportation is paid from another budget.

Based upon original estimates, approximately $2.50 was set aside for each student per week to cover the cost of hard items. As it turned out, over five dollars a week is being used for hard items, or twice the budgeted amount. This suggests that staff may be too generous in the rewarding of points to students. It also indicates that additional planning needs to be done to develop more noncost or "soft" items on which students can spend their funds. These areas are currently under review and some modification of the token economy system is expected.

Another issue concerns the rewards themselves. A few students have occasionally refused to perform desired behaviors because they feel too few points are being awarded. The value that students place on points is inverse to their need for them. As points accumulate in their spending accounts over the weeks, some feel they can afford to "loaf." While this is disconcerting for staff and may present some management problems, such a turn of events may not be totally undesirable. It does get across to the student the idea that "the good life" can be earned by staying within the law. The problem, of course, is to insure that good things are being *earned* and not given away in an unrealistically generous environment.

CONCLUSION

This discussion of the experience to date with the token economy system at KYC has concentrated on problems encountered. This should not overshadow the general impression that the token economy has had a good start and appears to have received acceptance by both staff and students. Thus, while problems remain, the token economy at KYC has proven to be a workable system and one which deserves further testing and refinement.

REFERENCES

1. Peterson, D.R.: Behavior problems of middle childhood. *Journal of Consulting Psychology, 25*:205-209, 1961.

Peterson, D.R., Quay, H.C. and Cameron, G.R.: Personality and background factors in juvenile delinquency as inferred from questionnaire responses. *Journal of Consulting Psychology, 23*:395-399, 1959.

Peterson, D.R., Quay, H.C., and Tiffany, T.L.: Personality factors related to juvenile delinquency. *Child Development, 32*:355-372, 1961.

Peterson, D.R., and Quay, H.C.: The Questionnaire Measurement of Personality Dimensions Associated with Juvenile Delinquency. Mimeo, 1964.

Quay, H.C.: Personality dimensions in delinquent males as inferred from the factor analysis of behavior ratings. *Journal of Research in Crime and Delinquency, 1*:33-37, 1964.

Quay, H.C.: Dimensions of personality in delinquent boys as inferred from the factor analysis of case history data. *Child Development, 35*: 479-484, 1964.

Quay, H.C., and Quay, Lorene C.: Behavior problems in early adolescence. *Child Development, 36*:215-220, 1965.

Quay, H.C.: Personality patterns in preadolescent delinquent boys. *Educational and Psychological Measurement, 26*:99-110, 1966.

Quay, H.C., Morse, W.C., and Cutter, R.L.: Personality patterns of pupils in special classes for the emotionally disturbed. *Exceptional Children, 32*:297-301, 1966.

2. Ayllon, Teodore, and Azrin, Nathan H.: Token Economy: *A Motivational System for Therapy and Rehabilitation.* New York, Appleton-Century-Crofts, 1969.

3. Burchard, John D.: Systematic socialization: a programmed environment for the habilitation of antisocial retardates. *The Psychological Record, 17*:461-476, 1967.

Buchard, John D. and Tyler, Vernon, O., Jr.: The modification of behavior through operant conditioning. *Behavior Research and Therapy, 2*:245-250, 1965.

Callihan, W.W.: A Training Program for Teenage Male Residents with Histories of Delinquent Behavior, Mimeo, 1967.

Cohen, H.L., Filipczak, J.A. and Bis, J.S.: Case project: Contingencies applicable for special education, to be published in Weber, R.E. (Ed.): *A Book on Education and Delinquency.* Office of Juvenile Delinquency and Youth Development, Department of Health, Education, and Welfare.

Ross, R.R.: Application of Operant Conditioning Procedures to the Behavioral Modification of Institutionalized Adolescent Offenders. Mimeo, 1967.

Tyler, V.O., Jr.: Exploring the Use of Operant Techniques in the Rehabilitation of Delinquent Girls. Paper read at American Psychological Association meeting, Chicago, 1965.

Tyler, V.O., Jr.: Application of operant token reinforcement to academic performance of an institutionalized delinquent. *Psychological Reports, 21*:249-260, 1967.

Tyler, V.O., Jr., and Brown, G. Duane: The use of swift, brief isolation as a group control device for institutionalized delinquents. *Behavioral Research and Therapy, 5*:1-9, 1967.

Tyler, V.O., Jr., and Brown, G. Duane: Token Reinforcement of Academic Performance with Institutionalized Delinquent Boys. Mimeo, undated.

Chapter 14

SOME VARIATIONS IN TECHNIQUES OF CONTINGENCY MANAGEMENT IN A SCHOOL FOR DELINQUENTS

CARL F. JESNESS *and* WILLIAM J. DeRISI

T HIS CHAPTER describes several classrooms functioning in a behavior modification program at the Karl Holton School, a California Youth Authority institution for boys. The programs were developed as part of the Youth Center Research Project, a four-year research-demonstration project begun in 1968 to compare the effectiveness of two different approaches to the treatment of delinquents. The approach at Holton was based on behavior modification principles, while the adjacent institution used group-therapy procedures (transactional analysis) as its basic treatment technique.

The Karl Holton School for Boys is one of three institutions at the Northern California Youth Center near Stockton, California. The institution is designed to house approximately 390 wards in eight 50-bed living halls. During the time of the study the age-range was 15 to 21, and the average age was 18. The

The Youth Center Research Project was supported by PHS Grant No. MH 14411 NIMH (Center for Studies of Crime and Delinquency). The grant was made to the American Justice Institute which worked closely with the California Youth Authority in the development and implementation of the project. We are particularly grateful for the contributions to this paper made by several teachers at the Karl Holton School whose individual creative talent was responsible for the development of unique classroom operations: Mrs. Carol Galvez (the use of immediate reinforcers in the classroom), Mr. Pete T'Souvas, (the arts and crafts class), Mr. Jerry Brent (the auto shop), Mr. Kyle Wiesenberger (the large team-teaching classroom), and Mr. Larry McVicar (the classroom for lower maturity adolescents).

school's program combines an intensive educational program with a behavior modification program.

All eight living-units and all classrooms in the Karl Holton school operate under a microeconomy and a parallel parole-contingent point system. To be recommended to the Youth Authority Board for release, each boy needs to accumulate a predetermined number of behavior change units (BCUs). To obtain more immediately desired comforts, materials, services, and recreational opportunities, the youth must earn Karl Holton dollars. For each BCU earned toward release, the boy gets one dollar for his more immediate needs.

Three different kinds of behaviors are identified and managed in the Karl Holton program. The first is "convenience behavior," not always crucial to the subject's becoming a nondelinquent, but important to the efficient, orderly function of the institution. "Academic behavior" refers to educational achievements and skills. "Critical behavior deficiencies" (CBDs) identified by use of the Behavior Checklist (Jesness, 1971) are those seen as most likely to increase the probability of the subject's failing or succeeding on parole. Forty-five percent of the ward's points must be earned by convenience behaviors, 28 percent by academic behaviors, and 27 percent by the correction of critical behavior deficiencies. Each of these program elements is described in detail in the Holton program manual, which serves as a guideline for the youth counselors in the Karl Holton school.

EDUCATIONAL PROGRAM

The faculty at Karl Holton is organized into terms, each having three teachers. Each team is responsible for the education program of one residence hall of 50 wards. These teachers are also part of the hall treatment-team. In one case, where a broader curriculum best meets the needs of a particular group of wards, two teaching teams have been combined to serve a 100-ward unit, and the teachers have departmentalized their course offerings. One teacher on each teaching team is designated as the "lead" teacher and is responsible for coordinating the efforts of that team.

Most of the teaching staff at Holton have shown considerable

ingenuity in establishing contingency-managed classroom procedures suited to their subject matter and the needs of their students. What follows is a description of several of these programs
selected as illustrative of the many creative innovations in classroom operations that have evolved, as well as some of the problems
encountered. Included are sections describing (a) the evolution
of a program to meet needs of lower-maturity adolescents, (b)
procedures for introducing immediate, tangible reinforcers, (c)
the use of multiple behavior contracts in an auto shop program,
and (d) a student-managed arts and crafts class.

A Program Which Meets Needs of Lower-Maturity Adolescents

In March, 1968, the first behavior modification program at
the Karl Holton School for Boys began in Yuba Hall, the living
unit to which boys of the lowest maturity level were assigned.*
This program initially differed markedly from the one that later
evolved. The purpose of this paper is to describe the changes that
took place over the several years of the project.

Yuba Hall's population averaged 48 wards in March, 1968.†
About one-third of the population was classified at the lowest
maturity level (I_2), and the other two-thirds at the I_3 level, as
Cfm's (Immature Conformists). Many wards, especially those
called "I_2, Unsocialized Passive," had poor study habits and high
rates of disruptive behavior. The Yuba students generally scored
lower on achievement tests than all others in the institution.
Grade-level scores in reading comprehension averaged 4.4, and
of the average of 48 subjects in the hall, there were at least 15 who
scored below the third-grade level.

The reinforcement program, based on operant conditioning
principles, was implemented both in the classroom and on the
living unit. Each ward was initially given a blank, 150-item card.
Wards were reinforced with checkpoints entered on the cards for
acceptable behaviors, which were defined in very simple terms.

*This special program was funded by an ESEA Title I appropriation. Initiated
shortly before the start of the Youth Center Research Project, it provided extra
personnel and consultants to Yuba Hall for several months.

†When the enriched staffing provided by the funds was reduced, it became
necessary to assign only 35 boys to the living hall.

The behaviors included promptness in arriving at and departing from class, and task management, i.e. getting work completed immediately, seeking help when needed, and so on. Check marks were also given for academic performance. Academic assignments were subdivided into small tasks. When a student successfully completed a task, he received checkpoints on the card he carried.

No contracts were written during this initial behavioral program in Yuba hall. Under this system, students were intermittently reinforced by the teacher or teaching assistant, who had a prescribed number of points that could be given out each hour. The teaching staff continually circulated through the room helping students with their tasks and awarding checkpoints contingent upon the students' performance.

The students could use these checkpoints to buy items both in the classroom and the hall. The first menu consisted of items that were considered by staff to be reinforcing. Later, the students suggested adding other items. Staff opened a store in the hall where students could buy cigarettes, candy, soda, pens, stationery, and other items.* They could also buy rugs and keys for their rooms, and pool-playing privileges.

In the classroom the teacher operated a reinforcement center which contained music, puzzles, upholstered chairs, and many types of games. Ten-minute outside breaks also proved highly reinforcing. In class, the variety of reinforcers available meant that desired behavior could be reinforced either by awarding checkpoints on the cards, or by granting extra break-time or reinforcement privileges.

In the beginning the program had the following limited objectives: (a) using positive reinforcement rather than negative reinforcement or punishment as a means of behavior control; and (b) improving study habits (beginning tasks without being told, organizing the work, and finishing it).

The classroom teacher attempted to provide the student with an activity for every minute of the day. The room was divided into

---

*Because funds for material reinforcers were no longer made available after the first year of the program's operation, it was necessary to run the program thereafter using reinforcers already available in the institution.

five major areas: the achievement area, the reinforcement center, the exploratory area, the order area, and the time-out center. The student did most of his academic work in the achievement area. It was the goal of the system to keep the student working successfully in this section.

If the student became frustrated or was having other problems in the achievement area, the teacher could intervene in several ways. He first determined if the task was within the capability of the student. If not, the student was assigned a more appropriate task. Other means of intervention included using the order center and the exploratory areas where tasks were designed to hold the student's attention and prepare him for return to the achievement area. The order center was so named because the tasks offered here were designed to be of help in teaching the boys to organize materials. Some of these tasks were following simple lists of directions, working crossword and other puzzles, and playing a game called *Instant Insanity*.

The exploratory center was designed by the teacher to develop the student's independent learning skills and improve his ability to solve problems. The teacher or teaching assistant provided tasks that were left to the student to complete. To do so he had to explore alternative solutions. For example, simple science experiments required searching in more than one reference source.

If a student behaved unacceptably, and extinction failed to solve the problem, he was placed in the time-out area where he received no points or attention. The area was at the rear of the classroom, and was separated from the rest of the class by a wooden partition. The student was usually placed in time-out for about ten minutes. In most cases he was the one to decide when he was ready to come out. If the problem behavior persisted, he had to return to the hall for a short time.

Several characteristics of this classroom program set it apart from others. The students were not told specifically which behaviors would be reinforced, and they were not placed on contracts. Goals or objectives were common to the total group, and individual goals were not set. Points given on the hall were, as in the classroom, for general behaviors such as keeping bed areas clean and making positive comments in community meetings. Points had no connection with parole, day passes, or length of stay in the institution.

When this program was first initiated, no explanation was given to the students. On the first day of class the students were assigned new desks and given blank checkpoints cards. Those who sat down quietly were given points and a candy bar. As they began working, those attending to their tasks were given other reinforcers. When the wards returned to the hall, all those arriving on time received points. A new pool table had been set up for them, and the new hall-store was shown to them.

Within a very few days almost all of the students adapted to the system. From the start it was obvious that the program made control much easier. Students who had been behavior problems began to attend to their work, and most of the disturbances in the class disappeared. The teacher more readily established routine procedures, such as hand raising. At the time the program began, students had been prone to yell out to get the teacher's attention, but they changed rather quickly after receiving points for raising their hands. Soon the whole class conformed, and even as the amount of reinforcement was gradually decreased, the established hand-raising behavior was maintained.

This program continued for about nine months with few alterations. The first major changes occurred in January, 1969, when the checkpoint card was replaced by the Karl Holton bankbook. This was used in much the same way as the card. Dollars earned were recorded in the bankbook, just as points had been written on the card. The bankbook was easier to use because the card system required excessive paper work. The students could keep better track of their bankbook than they could of the cards, and they could more easily see their account balances.

The next major change was the introduction of contracts for academic work. Specific amounts of reinforcement were set up for specific assignments. Contingency contracts were written for behavior problems that arose in the class. New items such as trips, day passes, and personal clothing wear were added to the hall's *RE* (reinforcement) menu.

Another major change required the specification of individual objectives, both academic and behavioral. General goals were still set for all the students, but contracts were utilized to solve individual problems. At this time, dollars in the bankbook still had no connection with referral to parole.

During this period the classroom operated in much the same manner as it had during the period when checkpoint cards were used, with the only real difference being the use of contracts. The areas of the classroom (*RE,* order, exploratory and time-out) helped to facilitate teacher intervention. The instructor believed the key to the effectiveness of the system was the use of intermittent reinforcement on a variable-ratio schedule. Students received dollars (scrip) for completion of contracts, but from time to time they received other reinforcers, too, for desired behavior or academic performance.

During the first months of the program several constructive changes occurred in the classroom. Disruptive outbursts decreased, students were highly motivated to complete tasks, and most management problems disappeared. The need to use the order, exploratory, or time-out areas decreased.

With the introduction of the bankbook system and contracting, the teacher decided to change the design of the classroom. The need for the order and exploratory areas had greatly diminished, and the amount of staff time needed to operate them outweighed any positive use they might have had; hence, they were removed. This change had no apparent ill effects on the performance of the students in the class.

The class continued with the system of bankbooks, dollars, contracts, and intermittent reinforcement for about ten months. During this period the teacher's ability to write contracts improved, the *RE* area was made more attractive, as was the total appearance of the room. The students appeared to take personal pride in the classroom. When visitors came, student behavior seemed to improve even more, whereas previously it had not.

The final major change in the system was the introduction of the Behavior Change Unit (BCU) system, whose main feature was the direct connection of points to referral to parole. More specific goals were set for each student, and the general behaviors expected of all students were listed as "convenience" behaviors. The amount of intermittent reinforcement had to be limited to avoid inflation of the economy, because although use of bonus money was encouraged, hall and teaching staff had difficulty in coordinating all components of the economy.

All material in the curriculum had to be assigned point values. Individual student contracts were suited to individual needs. Intermittent reinforcement was still used, but to a much lesser degree than in the past.

The major disadvantage of the program, as compared with the operant conditioning procedures, was the restricted use of immediate reinforcement, because of limits imposed by the institution-wide economy. Immediate reinforcement appeared to have been important in maintaining behavior control with the immature students on Yuba Hall, and behavior problems gradually increased as a result of decreasing its emphasis.

The teacher, therefore, began to look for new ways to provide immediate reinforcement, ways that would not disrupt the hall economy, and that did not demand expenditure of funds for material reinforcers (the funds simply were not available). The classroom *RE* area became a primary means of doing so. The area was first increased in size. Art materials, a wide variety of music (jazz, rock and soul), magazines, books, and many more games were placed in the area. Items discarded by others as of having no value proved to have value to the students. Old maps of California, calendars, manila folders with metal clips, colored pencils, paper, and almost any type of classroom supplies were prized. The teacher learned that effective reinforcers were readily available in the normal classroom environment. He began to make more frequent use of the *RE* area as an immediate reinforcer. A student who came into class and began work immediately was told, "For the very good job you are doing today, you may have ten free minutes in the *RE* area." In addition, as an institution-wide policy, students who achieved a 90 percent level of performance in all their assigned classes were served waffles and punch once a month.

To help increase the value of the hall's generalized reinforcer (Karl Holton money), staff would about every four months bring from home such items as old coffee pots, shirts, or magazines to auction off to the students. These sales were an exciting feature of the behavior modification program for both students and staff.

One final comment should be made. As each new element of the program was introduced, most wards reacted negatively. When staff and boys met as a community to talk over problems and program changes, several wards would threaten not to go along with the changes; but in most cases they quickly saw fit to comply, usually within a few days.

Procedures for Introducing Immediate, Tangible Reinforcers

"Mrs. Galvez, I need a pencil to do some work. I can't buy one because I don't have any money."

"You don't have any money? What's the reason for that?"

"Well, I'm in the hole."

"Why?"

"Back at the hall they just let us spend money we don't have, so I just keep spending it. Nobody knows how much you have anyway because the banker is the only one that knows how much money each dude has. Besides that, I'm always getting fines for doing things wrong."

"I see. How many others are in the hole?"

"I guess right now there's about thirteen guys."

"That doesn't seem quite right. How far in the hole are you?"

"I'm not sure, but I think about one thousand dollars."

"*A thousand dollars!* How on earth do you ever expect to get out?"

"I don't know and I really don't care."

"Do you know that in order to go to the parole board your debts have to be cleared?"

"It's not real money and I don't care about the board anyway. I just wish I could get transferred out of this joint. I wish they would send me some place where I could just do my time and get out."

"You certainly do appear to have a problem. Here, take this pencil for now and we'll see if anything can be done."

This was the dilemma a teacher faced on her first day in a classroom to which boys were assigned from a living hall with a poorly regulated microeconomy. The unit housed youngsters who seldom presented serious antisocial behavior problems in the classroom;

rather they were somewhat withdrawn boys who were prone to do very little work. The achievement level in reading and arithmetic for these boys aged 16 to 19 extended from grade two through grade twelve.

The students were operating within an institution-wide token economy system in which referral to the Youth Authority Board was contingent on performance. When a student earned the prescribed number of Behavior Change Units (BCU's), he was recommended for parole. Thus, a student could earn his way out of the institution faster by earning at a higher-than-average rate. Along with each BCU earned he also earned spendable "money," the amount of which was recorded in the bankbooks but not issued in tangible form.

Several flaws were apparent in the system as it operated on the hall housing the students of this classroom, flaws that gave rise to the several problems described above. The first was inflation, resulting from some staff's failure to charge for reinforcers, while wages and prices remained the same. The second was the lack of tangible reinforcers. BCU's and "money" were abstract quantities, mere numbers in a ledger. No tangible money was used. Students could buy items on hall and school menus, but wards who kept no record of their earnings or purchases frequently found themselves "in the hole" (bankrupt). Official "posting" of everyone's balances came but once weekly. Some wards found themselves having to earn their way out of bankruptcy before referral to the board. Students too deeply in debt because of over-spending or fines for misbehavior quickly lost interest and were not motivated to perform within the program. Although relatively few boys on the hall were bankrupt, the teacher decided that a more effective motivation system was necessary to improve performance of all students in her classroom.

She and the project behavior specialist designed a six-month experiment to test the effectiveness of a unique reinforcement system for her classroom. They designated a period of time for collecting baseline data, time for applying the new system, and time for a "reversal period" in which the old procedures would be reinstated to see if the behavioral deficiencies would return.

They did return, and so the special system was again established.

The new system called for the issuing of a tangible currency to be used in the classroom for purchasing a variety of high-interest back-up reinforcers immediately available in the classroom. (The institution point system remained intact and students still earned BCU's for all school work completed.)

The classroom was rearranged. Students went to the teacher's desk, which was called the Contracts and Clearance section, for their assignments from her. As in all other classrooms in the institution, academic assignments were all written in the form of contingency contracts. Tests corrected by two student proctors who ran the Corrections and Testing section were also taken to the teacher for clearance, in order that their performance could be supervised. The proctors' task was critical; they had control over all test materials in the classroom, and passing the tests was the last step in completing contract tasks. A high degree of honesty was therefore required of these proctors, and the teacher frequently but inconspicuously checked their work.

A third job of responsibility was given to the student who ran the Banking and Purchasing section. The banker did the bookkeeping on the checking and savings accounts and collected money for all menu items purchased. The banker also paid out money for work completed. To avoid the stealing or transferring of money, all money was imprinted with the recipient's name, the date, and the banker's initials. The banker's work was audited frequently, but at irregular intervals.

Near the door was the desk of the "timekeeper," also a student. He noted the time of entry and exit of each student, kept track of the time each student was on a break, and collected the money for these breaks (tearing it up to prevent re-use).

Near the teacher's desk was placed a plain wooden bench, and the area labeled the Welfare section. Here students worked when they did not earn even the small amount required to rent their desks, chairs, and school materials. The welfare section was intended to facilitate immediate and frequent reinforcement of any approximation to the desired academic behavior. In fact, it was used less than six times in six months. On those occasions, the teacher interpreted the student's behavior, or lack of it, as a consequence of her failing to apply reinforcers properly and she was careful to identify and reinforce approximations of more adaptive behaviors needed to get a student off welfare.

She introduced the new student to the classroom by giving him a detailed, programmed orientation package that was also recorded on tape to enable the student with reading difficulties to listen to the words as he read them. Each student was required to take a progress check at the end of the orientation and to pass at least 80 percent of the items.

Students earned their basic pay by adhering to posted convenience behavior descriptions. Mere conformity to the convenience behaviors paid the student five dollars per period—which was just enough for his chair, desk and book (as shown in Figure 14-1). Earning beyond this subsistence level required completing aca-

MENU			
Pad of Paper	$150	Outside classes (tuition)	$200
(Paper (10 sheets)	$10	Book rental (per period)	$1
Large brown envelopes	$50	Desk (per period)	$1
Small white envelopes	$20	Floor space only (per period)	$1
Eraser rental	$1	Rest room	$5
Eraser purchase	$50	*WORK HALF-HOUR*	
Pencil rental (per period)	$1	*WITH NO CHECKS*	
Pencil purchase	$25	Sleeping	$150
Paper notebook	$50	Non-task activity	$25
Magazines	$25	Library (25 minutes)	$25
Pencil cap eraser	$10	Coffee	$35
Ink pen	$100	Deposit on coffee cup	$10
Pen refill	$50	Smoke breaks (10 minutes)	$10
Pencil clip	$25	Smoke break deposit	$5
Transcript review	$350	Tea	$35
Raffle tickets	Price varies	Sugar	$5
Chair (per period)	$1	Coffeemate®	$5
Desk & chair (monthly)	$35	Coffee refill	$15
Book Rental (monthly)	$15		

Figure 14-1. Menu for the experimental classroom program.

demic contracts. Students could earn up to $200 per week in class-room money.*

Inappropriate behavior was placed on a response-cost basis, just as it was in the overall institution program. One incidence of misbehavior reduced payment one dollar for that 45-minute class period. Any additional incidents resulted in forfeiture of the entire five dollar convenience-behavior payment.

Serious incidents of misbehavior were handled by temporary isolation of the student from the rest of the class. During this time-out period he was not able to earn points or money, or obtain any of the usual reinforcers. If ten minutes of this restriction was not sufficient to control the behavior, he was sent or removed from the classroom and returned to his living unit under time-out conditions. Wards were returned to the program as soon as inappropriate behavior was suppressed. All but a very few students responded to brief isolation in the classroom, so that referral to the living unit was seldom necessary.

All students enrolled in the class at the time this revised class-room program was instituted were required to go through the orientation program. Every student began the first day with zero dollars.

Initially, several students wished to sit on the floor to do their work, rather than pay for a desk. They were instructed, however, that as long as they were earning money they were required to pay rent for floor space, just the same as anyone in the community would pay rent even for land. It did not take long before they preferred to work at their desks. The students soon found that it was not difficult to earn money if the class rules were followed. Most became quite cautious with their money and in deciding upon the best way to spend it. Many bought desks and chairs on the monthly plan so they would be assured of having sufficient funds for the necessities. Coffee, a recent addition to the menu (see Figure 14-1), added a new attraction to the classroom atmosphere and provided another immediate, tangible reinforcer.

---

*The institution-wide system providing BCU points and "hall money" for appropriate behavior in the classroom (convenience behaviors) and for academic performance was continued in this new program, even though only classroom "money" was allowed to be spent in the classroom.

Many students were upset with the new program and for a few days lost convenience behavior points. The change in behavior can be noted in the data charted in Figure 14-2. Baseline

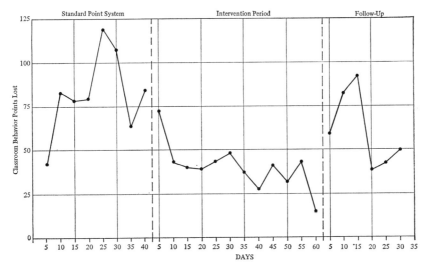

Figure 14-2. Effects of immediate-tangible reinforcers on classroom behavior.

data were recorded for the 39 school days preceding implementation of the new program. During that period convenience behavior points lost averaged 84.6 per five-period day. Average population in the classroom was 15 per period. During the intervention period of 62 school days, the average number of convenience behavior points lost dropped to 40.7 per day, or a 52% improvement in classroom behaviors.

During the reversal period the students were told that they would no longer receive special classroom money and would be going back to the old system in which menu items would be purchased with hall money. Everything in the classroom associated with the new system was removed and all menu items that were not available before the new system was introduced were removed. The data collected during the 30-day reversal period indicated that the average loss of convenience points was 48.9 per day, representing a 17% increase above the intervention period.

There was a sharp increase in inappropriate behavior during the first 15 days of the reversal period. These data may be interpreted as reflecting an emotional response to returning to a system of operation that was not favored. (The threat of aversive consequences and the removal of reinforcers typically produce such behavior in a variety of organisms.) After the first 15 days the students' rate of inappropriate behaviors went down somewhat, but the rate continued to be higher than that for the experimental period.

As a further illustration of the effects of the new program, the convenience behavior points lost by six students chosen at random is shown before the new program was implemented, during the time the program was in effect, and during the reversal period. These data presented in Table 14-I were quite typical for all class members. It will be seen that for some students the special feature of the revised classroom management plan had a rather dramatic impact on their behavior. Four of the six returned to their previous poor performance rate in the reversal period.

As a result of this experiment, the experimental classroom management system was reinstalled. An indirect result was the modifying and improving of the basic economy and the contingency management system in the wards' living unit.

TABLE 14-I
AVERAGE DAILY CONVENIENCE BEHAVIOR POINTS LOST FOR SIX
RANDOMLY SELECTED STUDENTS

Student	CB's Lost Before	CB's Lost During	CB's Lost After
A	10	2	2
B	2	2	2
C	7	5	8
D	15	5	12
E	11	7	15
F	10	2	12

This section dealt with a set of problems that can arise in contingency-managed classrooms, resulting from a breakdown in the reinforcing values of generalized intangible reinforcers (points). The solution to the problem described here involved the use of tangible reinforcers applied immediately, student participation in the operation of the classroom, and an experimental approach to evaluating the effects of intervention. A second solution, of course, would have been to repair the faltering living hall economy and reestablish the potency of the general institution-wide reinforcers. This was done as a result of efforts not directly related to the experiment described in this paper, but this experiment did help to point up the need.

The Use of Multiple Behavior Contracts in an Auto Shop Program

Vocational classes have usually concentrated on teaching mechanical skills that help prepare students to enter the job market. Traditionally, only limited emphasis has been placed on the social skills and interpersonal behaviors needed for effective work performance.

The vocational auto mechanics program at the Karl Holton school was originally organized in the traditional manner, with primary emphasis on the teaching of vocational skills. However, with the introduction of the behavior modification program, the shop class appeared to present a unique opportunity for helping these inmates develop other important job-related social skills. The auto shop program was elective. All students enrolled had asked for assignment in the class, so just being in the auto shop program was itself reinforcing. The student's motivation to remain in the class to learn the skills of auto mechanics provided leverage to increase the students' repertoire of useful and adaptable social behaviors. With most of the students, the need was apparent.

The typical ward in the Karl Holton auto mechanics class was $17\frac{1}{2}$ years of age and was approximately three years behind his expected level of academic achievement. Over 85 percent of the students were high-school dropouts and almost all were at best apathetic towards academic achievement. Their attitude was typically exemplified by such comments as: "This math is too hard;" "How come I've got to go to school anyhow;" "What good is this English going to do me?" However, because of their already established interest in auto mechanics, these same students found auto shop strongly reinforcing and they were consistently eager to begin work. Although students from all residence halls were assigned to the class, the majority came from Tioga Hall, most of whose residents were classified as *Mp* (manipulator) or *Na* (acting-out neurotic). Their behavioral deficiencies generally included resentment of authority, a reluctance or inability to cooperate effectively with peers, poor communications skills, quickness to anger and physical aggression, and low stress-tolerance. Their programs were not based on these general characteristics, however, but on an objective evaluation of each student's strengths and deficiencies. Areas of behavioral deficiencies were determined from the behavioral profile (BCL printout), which was a composite of ratings made by the caseworker, teacher and one other staff member from the living unit. When a ward was assigned to the auto mechanics class, his behavior profile served as the basic source for an initial statement of objectives. In addition, interviews with each student helped to further assess his needs.

In the interviews, most of the students expressed much interest in learning auto mechanics, but showed marked deficiencies in many of the social skills needed to get a job. Many of the youths were uncertain about their future job plans, and typically responded inappropriately in a classroom setting. Many of them misperceived the auto class as a place where they could simply "fool around" with engines, and somehow absorb the skills needed to become expert auto mechanics. The instructor faced the problem of dealing with these unrealistic preconceptions without dampening the students' enthusiasm for the class.

Orientation

When a new student entered the class, efforts were made to insure that his initial introduction to the class was a pleasurable experience. An orientation (some pages of which are shown in Fig. 14-3) explained the convenience behavior system and the shop safety program. Each new student was required to pass a progress check on this material with a minimum score of 80 percent. The reinforcement for passing was ten dollars in token money. If a student failed orientation progress checks, he received personal instruction from an advanced student or from the shop instructor.

Figure 14-3. *Below.* Auto shop orientation sheet. Examples from the shop orientation handout.

O R I E N T A T I O N

Vocational Auto Shop
Room 26

A.   WELCOME TO AUTO SHOP.

B.   THIS ORIENTATION BOOKLET WILL ANSWER A NUMBER OF QUESTIONS ABOUT OUR PROGRAM.

C.   READ THIS BOOKLET OVER, AND THEN CONTACT THE INSTRUCTOR. HE WILL ANSWER ANY QUESTIONS YOU MIGHT HAVE.

D.   YOU WILL BE GIVEN A VERY EASY PROGRESS TEST TO BE SURE YOU UNDERSTAND OUR PROGRAM. GOOD LUCK!

G. M. BRENT, *INSTRUCTOR*

A. IT'S VERY SIMPLE, CONVENIENCE BEHAVIORS ARE THOSE BEHAVIORS EXPECTED FROM ALL OF US. TO BE PROMPT, POLITE, FOLLOW RULES, AND DO YOUR ASSIGNED WORK.

B. BESIDES BEIN GEASY TO DO, YOU WILL EARN POINTS (CB's) WHICH WILL HELP YOU COMPLETE YOUR PROGRAM AT KARL HOLTON SCHOOL.

3B.2 Progress Check_____

WHAT ARE BCU's

A. SHORTLY AFTER YOU ARRIVED AT KARL HOLTON SCHOOL, YOU WERE GIVEN A SLIP TELLING YOU HOW MANY BCU's THAT WERE TO BE EARNED BY YOU. OBOUT 30% OF THE BCU's WERE IN THE SCHOOL CLASSES.

B. YOU MAY EARN BCU's IN SCHOOL BY COMPLETING ASSIGNMENT CONTRACT.

C. EVERY 10 POINTS THAT YOU EARN IS WORTH 1 BCU.

D. EXAMPLE: IF YOU COMPLETE A CONTRACT IN SCHOOL WORTH 250 PATS., YOU HOVE EARNED 25 BCU's.

E. REMEMBER: YOU CAN WORK AT YOUR OWN SPEED.

5E. Progress Check_____

HOW TO EARN RE's

A. RE's = REWARDS FOR POSITIVE BEHAVIOR.

B. BY DISPLAYING POSITIVE BEHAVIOR IN THE CLASS-ROOM, YOU CAN EARN "FUNNY" MONEY TO BUY.

WHAT'S A CONTRACT

A. A CONTRACT IS AN AGREEMENT BETWEEN TWO PEOPLE.

B. EACH ASSIGNMENT IN AUTO SHOP WILL BE A WRIT-TEN CONTRACT BETWEEN YOU AND THE INSTRUC-TOR.

C. THE CONTRACT WILL TELL YOU WHAT TO DO, HOW TO DO IT, AND THE TEST. THE CONTRACT WILL ALSO TELL YOU HOW MANY POINTS THE ASSIGNMENT IS WORTH.

D. ALSO, THE CONTRACT MUST BE COMPLETED TO RE-CEIVE POINTS.

A series of manipulative tasks, arranged hierarchically from the most simple to the more complex, tested the entering student's mechanical skills. This entry level test, shown in Figure 14-4, served as the basis for negotiating the initial job contract. There were individual contracts for each task listed in the entry level test, and for all other skills taught in the course. Depending upon their ability and speed, the students completed from 80 to a maximum of 160 contracts during their average eight months study at the institution.

Multiple Behavior Contracts

Multiple behavior contracts have been a unique feature of the auto shop program. In order to shape appropriate social behavior, such simple courtesies as the use of "hello" or "good morning," the habit of knocking on the office door prior to entering, the use of "please" and "thank you" are included in a multiple behavior contract (see Figure 14-5). These contracts have proved to be effective.

The percentage of multiple behavior contracts successfully completed by 35 boys enrolled in the auto shop program during the last six months of 1970 was recorded. The criterion for successful completion was the performance of both an auto mechanics skill and a social behavior on a single trial. Successful first trial performance rose from 64 percent to 83 percent in four months, and stabilized near 90 percent. These data indicate that social skills may be improved by pairing their performance with a reinforcing curriculum and with the other reinforcers normally found in a shop class.

When negotiating for a new contract, the student was required to use the social behavior he had already learned. If he did not, he was not given a progress check, and did not receive a new contract. Inappropriate social behaviors were otherwise systematically ignored. As the jobs in his contracts became more complex, and the correct social behaviors more permanently a part of his behavioral repertoire, greater reliance was placed on the instructor's approval as the basic reinforcer. Beginning at this stage, only skill-oriented contracts were written, unless a social deficiency was again noted.

KARL HOLTON SCHOOL FOR BOYS
VOCATIONAL AUTO MECHANICS
ENTRY LEVEL CONTRACT

NAME_____ DATE_____

Instructions

The purpose of this contract is to determine how much you know about basic jobs in auto mechanics. Also, to determine your knowledge of tools and how to use the right tool for the job.

Be sure and call for a progress check when indicated. Take your time.

JOB ONE: Select the tools necessary to disassemble a hydraulic brake, proceed to disassemble the brake, (prog. chk.) Assemble brake, and perform minor adjustment. (prog. chk.)

_____ _____ Points_____
    Completed   Incomplete

JOB TWO: Select the tools necessary to disassemble a steering gear unit, disassemble the steering gear (prog. chk.) assemble steering gear and adjust (prog. chk).

_____ _____ Points_____
    Completed   Incomplete

JOB THREE: Select the tools necessary to remove spark plugs, remove spark plugs. (prog. chk.) Perform adjusting operation (gap____). (prog. chk.) Reinstall the spark plug, use the correct tool for tightening spark plug.

_____ _____ Points_____
    Completed   Incomplete

JOB FOUR: Select the tools necessary to remove distributor points, and condensor. Remove points and condensor from the distributor assigned to you. (prog. chk.) Assemble the distributor parts, and adjust the contact points to (_____). (prog. chk.)

_____ _____ Points_____
    Completed   Incomplete

You will be scored on accuracy of tool application, use of *Motors Manual,* and job skill. Your final score will be used to determine the area where you have encountered difficulty.

Final Score_____

_____ _____ _____
    Instructor   Date   Student

Figure 14-4. Entry level contract.

VOCATIONAL AUTO MECHANICS
JOB CONTRACT

Student's Name _____ JOHN DOE _____ Contract No. ___5___

JOB TITLE
How to Overhaul A Rochester Two Throat Carburetor

What To Do

Step One: Check out proper tools and manual, remove airhorn and throttle (progress chk) remove float and main jets (progress chk) remove power pump and check valves (progress chekd)

Step Two: Be able to properly identify all carburetor parts for instructor (progress chk) use manual to obtain float level and float drop measurements (progress check)

Step Three: Reassemble float parts in carburetor body, make proper adjustments (progress check) complete reassembly of carburetor, contact instructor for final progress check.

School Points _____85_____

Behavior Objectives

The student agrees to perform the following behavior(s):
The student will use at least one of the following words during his conversation with the instructor at progress check time: "please", "excuse me", "may I", "thank you"
The student will receive ___$.50___ for each positive response during progress check.

School Points_____

Bonus Points_____

Read Contract Rules

1. Contract must be completed before money or points are given.
2. Charge for lost contracts will be $50.
3. Each progress check must be initialed by the instructor.

_____   _____   _____
Instructor   Date   Student

Figure 14-5. Multiple behavior contract.

A variety of reinforcers were used in this program. The academic points earned through the fulfillment of each contract were augmented by short-term reinforcers applied through using scrip money printed exclusively for use in the auto shop. The money was used as the payoff for contracts, and as an immediate source of reinforcement whenever the instructor saw a behavior occurring that he felt was especially in need of being strengthened. This money proved to be an effective reinforcer because it enabled the student to buy immediately available items including the use of hotrod magazines, extra time in the library, break-time, cups of coffee, and other items on the reinforcement menu. The menu was updated frequently so that high interest items could be added and low interest items removed, and thus retain its attractiveness to the boys.

Other kinds of reinforcers were also used. Some boys especially appreciated the opportunity to progress into specialties such as work on transmissions, small engines, or multiple carburetors. Outside trips to auto parts and equipment supply stores were sometimes made available. For some wards, working as a shop manager or as a proctor was sufficient reinforcement to maintain appropriate behaviors over a long period of time. In addition, the instructor was careful to verbally reinforce all desired behaviors as well. This wide variety of reinforcers made it almost a certainty that high strength reinforcers could be found for each person in the class.

Self-Management Stress Contracts

The ultimate goal of the Karl Holton program was to develop young men capable of efficient self-management. Therefore, as the boys progressed in the program and the minimal social behaviors seemed well-established, a series of self-management demands were introduced that served both as a situational performance test and as an opportunity to teach new behaviors. These goals were accomplished by having each boy write his own job contract, specifying the goal to be achieved and the reinforcement he was to receive for its attainment. He was required to set appropriate objectives for himself, clearly specify the tasks to be accomplished, state the criteria for success, and the time in which the contract was to be accomplished. For example, "To properly operate the wheel balancer," the student needed to develop a contract that described the mechanical skills involved, and estimate the time needed to do the task.

Specifying the time needed for contract completion introduced an element of stress that enabled additional behaviors to be learned. The instructor was convinced most of these boys needed to develop greater tolerance for stress before they would be able to hold a job. Initially the stress imposed was relatively slight, for the time limits were liberal and the reinforcement schedule was rich. Even so it was apparent that some anxiety was engendered in most of the boys by the mere presence of the time limit. If the stress appeared to be too high, the time limits were liberalized in the next contract and only gradually increased. When stress became too great, certain behaviors predictably appeared, the most common being verbal abuse and the rejection of further contracts. If these reactions occurred, the student was required to confer with the instructor and told to allow himself slightly more time to subsequent contracts.

Obviously, all students could not be expected to achieve equally. However, the self-management procedure appears to have been at least partially effective with all students who participated in the program. Of the first 26 students involved after the contracting technique was initiated, seven completed 80 percent of their stress contracts, 16 completed 77 percent, and two completed 45 percent. Only one, who completed just 12 percent of his contracts, could be considered a failure.

Case Studies

The rate of achievement varied substantially from one student to another. Data from three students with similar severe behavioral deficiencies are illustrative. Interviews and conferences tended to confirm the initial ratings on the behavioral checklists, indicating that the three wards were all verbally hostile toward authority figures, quarrelsome and argumentative with peers, and reluctant to follow orders. Each of these behaviors, therefore, was included as a specific target for a series of multiple behavior contracts.

Data were collected for four weeks. Each student's contract performance and social behaviors were evaluated and recorded daily. The instructor used a mechanical counter or tallied behaviors on a piece of masking tape attached to his sleeve. A plus mark was recorded for each positive social response and a minus sign for each negative response.

Figure 14-6 shows the rate of contract completion over the four-week period. Student A completed 19 of the contracts, student B completed more than 30, and student C, whose BCL profile was initially the most deviant of any of the 51 boys assigned to the living hall, completed 15 contracts, an astonishing accomplishment for him.

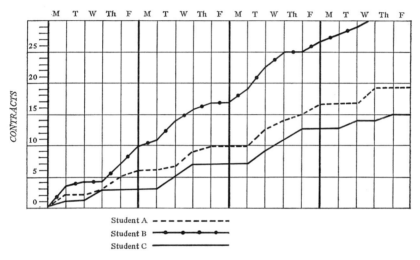

Figure 14-6.

Continued observation indicated that the behavioral improvement of the three wards tended to stabilize. Students A and B required only intermittent reinforcement to maintain their level of achievement. Student C, however, required a richer reinforcement schedule to maintain his. All three students continued to perform satisfactorily, so that by the end of their stay at the institution they achieved the following results:

Student A—final class grade B; 140 out of a possible 160
contracts completed,
Student B—final class grade B; 130 out of a possible 160
contracts completed,

Student C—final class grade C; 116 out of a possible 160 contracts completed.

Six months after their release on parole all students appeared to be doing well. Two of them returned to public school and the third was employed as an apprentice auto mechanic.

Summary

Although at the termination of the project, contingency management techniques had become an established part of the auto mechanics course, the instructor of the program believed that only a small part of the method's potential had been realized. There was, for example, every indication that the strong interest in auto mechanics could be used effectively as an inducement to increase the student's progress in academic courses such as math and reading, as well as a reinforcer for developing increased social effectiveness. One important requirement of such a program is to determine the most desirable and useful reinforcer for each student individually. This can be the starting point for promoting varied and sometimes dramatic behavioral growth.

A Student-Managed Arts and Crafts Class

The arts and crafts class at the Karl Holton School is an elective course that accepts students from all eight of the living halls at Karl Holton. Students work with a wide variety of ceramics, leather, wood, metal and other art materials. This section describes changes made in the contingency-management program in order to solve two problems that were present from its inception.

The first problem arose because the halls operated on slightly different monetary bases. This meant that five dollars in Karl Holton money was worth more to one boy than to another living in a different hall. Thus, rather than being able to rely on the generalized Karl Holton reinforcers, the instructor had to supplement them by installing a self-contained reinforcement system.

The second problem was that the instructor was ordinarily so busy serving as janitor, supply clerk, and disciplinarian that he had little time left to teach. Primarily through his own creative efforts, the organization of the class was changed in a manner that freed the instructor from these chores. As the structure finally evolved, the instructor was able to devote almost all of his time to teaching.

The primary goals of the arts and crafts program are to strengthen prosocial behaviors and to strengthen behaviors approximating creative arts activities. The procedures used to accomplish these goals include:

1. The use of transitional contingency contracting in which the students assume more and more control for setting the task and their own reinforcement schedule.

2. The use of student managers who actually run the arts and crafts classroom.

3. The establishment of proper stimulus conditions in the classroom which help to maintain its reinforcing value.

4. An internal token economy based upon sources of reinforcement that are available in the classroom itself.

Orientation

On their first day of class, the students are warmly greeted by the instructor, taken on a tour of the shop, and introduced to the contract manager who hands the student an envelope containing nine dollars in scrip, a welcome letter (Figure 14-7), and the student orientation checklist (Figure 14-8). As the new student completes the tasks on the orientation checklist, he has the contract signed by the appropriate person, and immediately receives five dollars in scrip. He then takes a progress check to determine if he understands the contracting system (see New Student Orientation *Progress Check*).

TO THE "ARTS & CRAFTS" FUN CENTER . . . .

where you "EARN" while you "LEARN" . .

Enclosed you will find a gift of nine dollars of our Arts & Crafts money from us to you with no strings attached . . .

Actually, there is sort of a hidden string attached -- that is, once you start spending this money you'll want to earn some more so that you can spend some more . . . . . . Well, that's what it's all about . . .

Technically speaking, this class is a "CONTINGENCY MANAGED CLASS" -- which simply means that if you produce "X" behavior you will receive cash - $ $ $ Arts & Crafts cash -- like the money you received in this envelope. This money is redeemable in products or services provided uniquely by us. To help you learn how to earn this money we have a "Contract Manager" who will assist you in making your initial contracts, as most money earned is earned through written contracts.

In the shop near the office hanging down from the ceiling you will see signs briefly explaining the "FIVE LEVELS OF CONTRACTING" * * * read these and learn them -- and if you have any questions the Contract Manager will be glad to answer them for you. When you feel that you understand all of these levels then ask the Contract Manager for a progress check. He will then ask you a series of questions. Below is the reward for the number of questions consecutively answered correctly . . .

" GOOD LUCK "

1 - a smile from the
    contract manager
2 - $1.00
3 - $3.00
4 - $6.00
5 - $10.00
6 - $15.00

Mr. Pete T'Souvas
Art "Fun Center" Director

Figure 14-7.

ARTS AND CRAFTS
Room 21

STUDENT'S NAME_____ Mr. T'Souvas
DATE_____ Art Director

NEW STUDENT ORIENTATION CHECKLIST

Have person in charge initial here when completed: _____

1. Receive introductory letter from Contract Manager _____
2. Receive safety instructions from Safety Supervisor _____
3. Pass safety test—Receive test from the
   Contract Manager _____
4. Receive explanation of tool and supply checkout
   from toolroom man _____
5. Receive explanation from contract manager on
   contracting and spending _____
6. Receive explanation on how to earn convenience
   behavior and academic points from the Shop Manager _____
7. Receive a pay job from the clean-up contractor _____
8. Receive an explanation from the Shop Manager
   the art activities available and other requirements
   of the Arts and Crafts Program _____
9. Receives an explanation of the clay processes from
   the Ceramic Superintendent _____
10. Be assigned to a critique group by the shop
    manager who will explain its purpose to you _____
11. Take progress check from the shop manager _____
                                                    Passed

Be sure that all eleven items are initialed. When they are you can
turn this sheet in to the contract manager and he will give you
five dollars of our money.

Figure 14-8. New Student Orientation Checklist

NEW STUDENT ORIENTATION PROGRESS CHECK

STUDENT'S NAME_____
DATE_____

PART I
Arts and Crafts Contingency-managed Shop

*Note: Place a check mark by the choice you think is correct. When
no choices are given, fill in the blanks provided.*

1. Developing the student's interest toward learning is a fundamental task of education. In this program developing the student's i n t __ __ __ __ __ toward art activities is also a fundamental task.

2. *Interest* comes about through *motivation*. For a person to be *motivated* means that there is a *reason* why the person *moves, performs, responds,* or *takes action*. If a person makes a move, we can say that something m __ __ __ __ __ __ __ d him to make that move.

   For a student to be m __ __ __ v __ __ __ d in this program we use Arts and Crafts money and points. Money and points give the student *reason* to m __ v __ toward art activities, p e __ __ __ __ __ with art materials, r __ __ __ __ __ d to art materials, and to t __ k __ a c __ __ __ __ with art materials.

3. Money m o __ i __ a __ __ s many people.

4. Money can give many people reason to t __ k __ a c t __ __ __ __.

5. Arts and crafts money can buy items which the students would like to have. Students can earn arts and crafts money by producing art projects. Therefore, arts and crafts m __ n __ y can give many students reason to t __ __ __ a c __ __ __ __ arts materials.

6. If producing ten pencil sketches can earn a student enough money to buy a gold chain which he would like to have, then giving the student r e a __ __ __ to t a __ __ a c __ __ __ __ with pencil and paper is called __ __ __ v __ __ __ __ __.

7. In order for a student to *perform* a certain art task he must be m __ __ __ __ __ __ __ __.

8. For a person to be motivated means that there is a reason the person
   _____a. took action, moved, performed or responded.
   _____b. wants to learn art.
   _____c. likes education.
   _____d. none of the above.

9. In this program earning arts and crafts money is *contingent* upon p e r f __ __ __ __ __ g certain art tasks.

10. *Depends upon* means the same as c o n t __ __ g __ __ __ upon.

11. The title of this program "Arts and Crafts Contingency Managed Shop" means that the money earned here is c o __ __ __ __ __ __ __ t, upon the *performance* of an art task here.

12. Agreeing with a student to pay him ten dollars for ten pencil sketches is a form of c o n t __ __ g __ __ __ __ m a n-__ g e __ __ __ t.

13. To make the above agreement official or legal it should be put in writing and signed by the manager and the student. The official agreement in writing is called a c __ n __ r __ c __.

14. The person who writes the *contract* with you and who pays you for successfully completing the *contract* is called the c o n t __ __ __ __ m a n __ __ __ __.

15. *Contingency contracts* written here pay off in arts and crafts money for the desirable *performance* of some art activity. Which is an example of a *contingency contract?*

_____a. "Take this five dollars and buy yourself something."

_____b. "Make a ceramic bowl and you will earn ten dollars of our arts and crafts money."

PART II

Understanding Student Management and Shop Procedures

Note: True or false — circle the correct answer.

T F 16. Arts and crafts money can only be spent in arts and crafts.

T F 17. Arts and crafts money can be spent *only* by the person whose name is written on the money.

T F 18. All contracts are written with the shop manager.

T F 19. The purpose of small group critiques is to evaluate art projects.

T F 20. You may purchase items from the menu from either the contract manager or the art director.

T F 21. Greenware should never be glazed.

T F 22. Goggles or face shields *must* be worn when using any machine tool.

T F 23. There are seven levels of contracting in this program.

T F 24. You must be working on a contract to purchase items from the menu.

T F 25. Being late to class may cost you convenience behavior points.

T F 26. 36 academic points for one class period is considered outstanding.

T F 27. You may go into the toolroom and help yourself to tools.

T F 28. Students may work on art projects of their interest.

T F 29. The projects you make in arts and crafts are yours to keep.

T F 30. The shop manager's job is to assist students who want help.

T F 31. You obtain a pay clean up job from the clean-up contractor.

T F 32. The ceramic superintendent is in charge of the whole shop.

T F 33. You may not smoke in the shop.

T F 34. You may earn points as well as money on contracts.

T F 35. You may use your arts and crafts money to buy something from another student.

Matching: Draw a line connecting every two that match in number 36.

36. art director   issues and collects tools
     clean-up contractor   makes clay mold projects
     contract manager   arranges small group critiques
     ceramic superintendent   explains the use of machine tools
     shop manager   pays for completed contracts
     safety supervisor   rates the student managers
     toolroom attendant   assigns clean-up jobs

37. You will lose some convenience behavior points if you

_____a. drink coffee in the shop.

_____b. leave class without permission.

_____c. talk with a friend during class.

_____d. all of the above.

_____e. none of the above.

38. If you weren't sure on how to adjust the drill press, you would ask the

_____a. shop manager.

_____b. safety supervisor.

_____c. a friend.

_____d. contract manager.

39. The small critique group is for

_____a. Working on art work together.

_____b. Evaluating each other's art work.

_____c. Friendly conversation.

If he passes this assignment he earns an additional $15. If he does not pass the progress test he is given individual instructions by the contract manager, and is retested.

After fulfilling his orientation contract, the student is free to choose any arts and crafts activity. Almost any techniques or modes of expression and any approximations to creative art are reinforced. If a student wishes to learn the technical aspects of being a commercial artist, he is not discouraged; neither is he discouraged from pursuing any specialized or limited aspect of the work. He is not forced to do anything he does not want to do, but all students are encouraged to experiment with and explore the various media.

The importance of creating a pleasant environment is stressed by the instructor. He believes that the physical surroundings influence the students and affect the quality of their performance. The students have voluntarily enrolled in the class and the instructor does whatever he can to insure that they continue to want to be there and continue to perceive the arts and crafts room as a place of satisfaction and enjoyment. The room is attractively decorated, and pleasant music is played while the students work on their arts and crafts projects. The instructor believes that the total learning environment should be made as positively reinforcing as possible.

Menu

To make a purchase from the reinforcement menu the student must be working on a contract or have already completed a final series of advanced contracts. The menu contains a list of items and services, shown in Figure 14-9, that are attainable only in the arts and crafts class and only by means of the special arts and crafts scrip (see Figure 14-10). All scrip is stamped by the contract manager with a special stamp, and as added protection against stealing or gambling, the student's name is written on the money. Prices and items are adjusted at least once a month as some items tend to lose their reinforcing strength with repeated exposure.

The money earned in the shop can only be spent in the shop. Thus, the arts and crafts program provides backup reinforcers for its own arts and crafts scrip. Most scrip is earned by students through successful completion of written contracts. The contracts provide that $3 in scrip can be earned for approximately one hour of performance. Bonus scrip can also be earned on most contracts for quality and effort beyond expected standards. A typical contract is shown in Figure 14-11. The student contract manager negotiates all contracts and supervises all purchases from the menu. Every morning he makes up a new accounting sheet onto which is transferred the previous day's balance. At the end of the

```
                        M E N U
                   ARTS and CRAFTS
Unfinished Projects from
Ceramic Molds                        Other Items

Girl with fruit hat         $15    Gold or silver chains (each) $ 3
Stein                       $15    Earring findings (set)       $ 2
Buddha                      $ 8    Cuff links (set)             $ 2
Mustache cup                $ 7    Velour paper (15"x20")       $ 1
Indian head                 $ 5    Leather (6"x6")              $ 1
Cuban dancer—man            $ 5    Lacing for leather—per foot  $ 1
Cuban dancer—woman          $ 5    Canvas boards (12"x12")      $ 3
Cat                         $ 3    Matt boards (22"x28")        $ 6
All medium size mugs (each) $ 5    Framing stock (per foot)     $ 1
All small mugs (each)       $ 7    Plastic sheets (per sq. ft.) $ 6
All large mugs (each)       $ 7    Wallet kits (each)           $ 9
Fish vase                   $ 4         This Month's Special
Tie rack                    $ 2               $30
Small madonna and child     $ 1         Acrylic paint set
Large madonna               $ 4            includes:
Bust of Jesus               $ 4     12 colors—1"x3" tubes
All jewelry cases (each)    $ 2           2 brushes
All ash trays (each)        $ 3    One 12"x16" canvas board
Zodiac platter              $ 9       One small palette
Birds (each)                $ 1    Take this set to the hall and
                                   paint in your leisure time.
                                       — Save your money —
                                     Only three sets available
Paintings or drawings matted (each) $2.
Buy an extra hour in arts and crafts only $5 an hour.
Lunch outside KHS $200.
Chess game with instructor $10.
Outside trip to art gallery $100.
```

Figure 14-9. Arts and crafts menu.

day the sheet is turned into the classroom instructor and checked for accuracy.

Student Management

The key to enabling the instructor to be freed from the many housekeeping tasks in the arts and crafts class is the use of student

Figure 14-10.

managers. Even more important, student managers and the other students gain important experience. Boys who are responsible for the management of their own educational affairs have an opportunity to develop needed social skills. They find their learning activities taking on more meaning, and they have the opportunity to observe and emulate the prosocial behavior of student managers acting in positions of responsibility.

Six student managers are used in the arts and crafts class: contract manager, cleanup contractor, ceramic superintendent, safety supervisor, tool room attendant, and shop manager. For each of these managers, a very detailed job description is provided along with a self-progress checksheet that enables him to know if he is satisfactorily performing the tasks required. They are paid in arts and crafts scrip contingent upon the quality of their job performance as determined by the progress rating sheet. There are several avenues for beoming a manager and most students have that opportunity during their involvement in the course.

The student manager system underwent continuous revision during the project. The essential problem was to give real author-

CONTRACT

"ARTS & CRAFTS"

CONTRACT LEVEL 3 PART 2 DATE 1/14/71

I JOE JONES do solemnly & sincerely agree to perform the following task or tasks:

PAINT A NIGHT SCENE

ON A 18" X 24" CANVAS

PANEL USING ACRYLIC

PAINTS.

.... and I, BILL SMITH, contractor, agree to pay the above named contractee $6.00 AND 70 POINTS for successfully completing the above task or tasks. Furthermore, *bonus* money may be awarded if the above tasks demonstrate quality and/or effort beyond the expected standards.

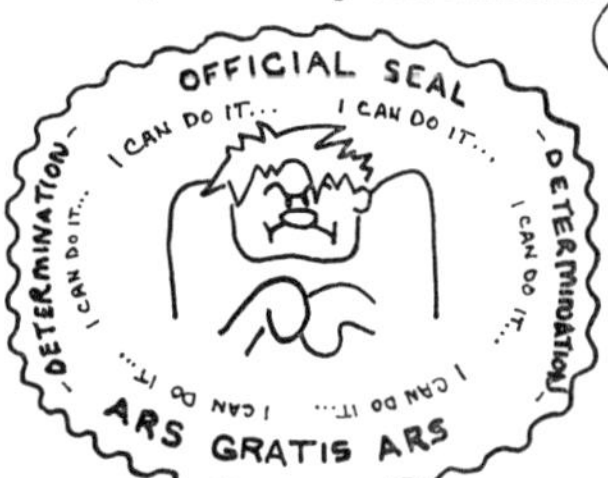

Bill Smith
CONTRACTOR'S SIGNATURE

Joe Jones
CONTRACTEE'S SIGNATURE

1/15/71
date of ~~completion~~

SAMPLE

Figure 14-11.

ity to the managers, and yet be sure the authority was not abused. The instructor found that the best way to do so was to make sure that the manager's tasks were clearly specified, and that periodic checks of manager performance were made by the instructor.

Transitional Contracts

Every conscientious teacher wants to do more than teach arithmetic, composition or geography. He also wants to teach such traits as self-control and self-discipline. Often these types of goals are included as a part of the stated objectives of a school program. Usually, however, no specific techniques or means for achieving these goals are offered.

Contingency contracting provides an explicit way to teach desired social behaviors. The aim of contingency contracting is to lead the student from manager (other)-controlled to student (self)-controlled activities. The method by which a student may be led to managing his own contracts has been called transitional contracting (Homme and Tosti, 1971). This system is an integral part of the arts and crafts program.

After the new student passes the orientation check, which insures that he understands the contracting system, he is given his first contract by the student manager. From that point on, he takes more and more responsibility for determining what the task will be and what the reinforcer will be. Five levels of self-management are provided. Eight different transitional contracts have to be completed before the highest level, the fifth level, is reached. At this level the contracts are student-controlled "macro" contracts, which require the completion of several smaller "micro" contracts (see Figure 14-12). A level-five contract reads something like this: "Each day for five days I will complete one self-managed contract, for which I will recieve $15." If a student successfully completes the contract he moves to Phase II of level-five contracting, the most advanced phase, which requires completing twenty self-managed contracts instead of five. This series is the last of the written contracts the student is obliged to complete in the program. From then on the contracts are verbal. The manager (M)

I _____ PROMISE TO COMPLETE _____ SELF
    CONTRACTEE

MANAGED CONTRACT(S) EACH DAY FOR _____ DAYS

...... AND I _____ AGREE TO PAY THE
                 CONTRACTOR

ABOVE NAMED CONTRACTEE _____

_____

_____

. FOR SUCCESSFULLY COMPLETING THE ABOVE TASK.

_____
CONTRACTEE'S SIGNATURE

_____
CONTRACTOR'S SIGNATURE

DATE BEGAN _____

DATE COMPLETED_____
    & PAID

(Remember to save all your self managed contracts to verify this contract)

Figure 14-12.

and the student (S) establish the task (T) and reinforcer (R) in various combinations.

Conclusion

In a student-managed classroom or shop, the teacher's housekeeping, record keeping, and disciplinary tasks are almost totally eliminated. The instructor's role becomes increasingly that of assigning new managers to various positions, individualizing instruction, and developing ways the students can become more effective in operating and directing their own educational affairs. Freed from many nonteaching tasks, the instructor has more time to spend on art instruction with individuals—a highly satisfying activity. In this program, no one has failed, because the system makes failure almost impossible.

REFERENCES

Homme, L. and Tosti, D.: *Behavior Technology: Motivation and Contingency Management.* San Rafael, Individual Learning System, 1971.

Jesness, C. F.: *The Jesness Behavior Checklist.* Palo Alto, Consulting Psychologists Press, Inc., 1971.

Jesness, C. F.: The Preston typology study, an experiment with differential treatment in an institution. *Journal of Research in Crime and Delinquency, 8:*38-52, 1971.

PART
FOUR

Modification of Delinquent Behavior
in the Community

INTRODUCTION

JEROME S. STUMPHAUZER

INSTITUTIONS FOR DELINQUENTS, or rather the people that support and run such institutions, have failed miserably. They have not failed if their goal has been to punish youth; they are certainly punitive. They have not failed if their goal has been to protect society; these youth are temporarily put away. But if their goals have indeed been to *rehabilitate, correct,* or *educate,* then they have grossly failed. There is evidence that the *opposite* is closer to the fact—that delinquents become more sophisticated criminals during their stay in *correctional* institutions (see Ch. 6). The professional community has been aware of this for some time, and the public is just beginning to be awakened to the crime of punishment. A recent cover story in *Time* magazine (January 18, 1971) dealt with United States prisons as schools for crime, and *Look* magazine has opened many eyes with its recent article, "How to Make a Criminal Out of a Child" (Mangel, 1971). The chapters in Part Three represent positive attempts at more effective institutional programs for delinquents, but we must focus predominantly on community programs, if we wish to not only stop, but prevent adolescent crime. After the fact, too little-too late programs have not stemmed the tide of growing juvenile law breaking and related problems. The papers provided here are attempts by behavior therapists to respond to this need.

A recent book, *Behavior Modification in the Natural Environment* (Tharp and Wetzel, 1969) is well written and highly recommended reading for anyone seriously interested in modifying or preventing delinquent behavior in the community. I find their premise completely acceptable, that ". . the environment, in which the individual is embedded, is principally responsible for the organization or disorganization, the maintenance or change, the appearance or disappearance of any behavior (p. 7)." What's more, this leads to the inescapable conclusion that intervention, or more importantly *prevention,* should take place in the natural environment (family, school, peer relationships, social structure) of the youth and not in an artificial institution, from which he will be discharged to his same environment armed with newly learned antisocial behaviors. Tharp and Wetzel see three important future directions for the helping enterprises: the use of the natural environment, behavior therapy, and reliance on nontraditional or nonprofessional workers. This last development needs further discussion. Our attempts at one-to-one intervention, of professional and client, of doctor and patient, and of probation officer and probationer, have clearly not met the needs of society in either mental health or corrections. On the one hand, there are not nearly enough professionals to intervene on a one-to-one basis, and on the other hand, the applicability of the model most often followed, the illness model, has been seriously questioned and in some cases rejected entirely (Ullman and Krasner, 1965; Tharp and Wetzel, 1969; Stuart, 1970). Instead, Tharp and Wetzel, for example, have suggested the use of the lay public as the *natural* controllers of behavior: the parent, teacher, spouse, sibling, friend, or employer. These authors suggest a consultative triad, in which a behavioral consultant, trained in the principles of behavior therapy, helps a mediator (e.g. a parent) modify the problem behavior of a child. Tharp and Wetzel discuss their own such work in Tucson, Arizona (see Ch. 17) and clearly explain the implementation of such intervention in the natural environment for those interested in following their exemplary work.

In Chapter 15, Buehler clearly presents a strong case for behavior therapy in *open* social systems (*closed* social systems being those in which the individual's membership is controlled by behavioral, physical, legal, or quasi-legal restrictions). Strictly speaking, institutions are closed systems, but so are many of the systems in the community or natural environment. For the younger child, membership in both the family and school is compulsory. For open systems, where client participation *is* elective, Buehler lists senior high school, college, professional and trade schools, and the training programs under current welfare organizations. Buehler points to the need for behavior therapy in such social systems and presents his own attempts at behavior therapy in a Job Corps center. The purpose of the Job Corps was to provide vocational training for untrained youth; the youth were free to leave at any time they desired. Buehler, too, used nontraditional mediators and focused on social living behavior within the shops and class-rooms, and specific job-related behavior. Social reinforcement and tokens were used and only limited success was achieved. Buehler cogently explores some of the natural agents of behavioral control (e.g. informal peer system) working against the success of the pro-ject, and he suggests an experimental model for further behavior therapy experimentation in open social systems.

The next two chapters explore behavior therapy applied to probation of delinquents. While probation takes place in the community, Buehler would consider it a closed system in that membership is required. Jamieson, a circuit court judge, finds in Chapter 16, that the most important function of probation to be that of changing the habits of probationers sufficiently to avoid further criminal behavior and to make this change long-lasting. Following the writings of H. J. Eysenck on crime, Jamieson sum-marily concluded that persistent criminal conduct is a learned response and can be unlearned or extinguished by application of learning theory and conditioning principles. One way in which judges can use these techniques in the court system is to make use of psychologists trained in behavior modification. Jamieson went so far as to suggest that judges can "order it to be done by experts, order the government to pay for it and make probationer's con-sent and cooperation a condition of probation." Ethical question (e.g. those of Holden, Ch. 2,) and questions of the necessary moti-vation of the probationers, may be raised against so strong a posi-tion. Jamieson's second suggestion would probably be more pala-table. In drafting the conditions of probation, judges should keep principles of learning theory in mind. This means they would need to know them. Goals would be to break up habits which lead to crime, help create new constructive and noncriminal activity, and to use small but immediate punishment for violations. No example of the use of these principles was given, but the following chapter meets this criterion.

A group from the Behavioral Research Project of the Southern Arizona Mental Health Center (Thorne, Tharp, and Wetzel, Ch. 17) outline some of the major principles of behavior modification, their use with juvenile probationers, and provide four case-histories. Following chiefly the operant conditioning principle of B. F. Skinner and associates, that behavior is governed by its consequences, Thorne *et al.* explain the possible applications of shaping and reinforcement contingencies. Aversive controls (punishment) may be used to reduce misbehavior, while positive controls (reward) may be used to teach new socially acceptable behavior. This chapter makes these contributions: it clearly explains the approach to probation workers, it provides good case examples, and it underscores the use of contingent positive reward and not just punishment. Larger scale application of this approach, with true experimental designs, is necessary to fully evaluate its potentials. Since there is such wide use of probation with delinquents, this particular approach warrants full-scale appraisal.

Chapters 18 and 19 present two behavior therapy techniques carried out in the community, in clinics, or in offices. If the client sought help himself and were free to attend or not attend sessions, then we could call it an open social system. Such therapy, which one might term "clinic" or "outpatient behavior therapy," could be extended directly into the community in what is called *in vivo* treatment. Psychiatric outpatient clinics per se, in which patient comes in to meet with professional, may become as outmoded or inadequate a model for providing effective help, as the hospital and institutions. Stuart (1970) convincingly argues for the demise of psychiatric hospitalization, offering behavior therapy in the community, family care, foster care, day care and other extramural services as better alternatives. If on the other hand, a youth were forced by parents or probation (see Jamieson, Ch. 16) to attend behavior therapy sessions, then Buehler would probably term it a closed social system. Both of these studies represent behavior therapy in the clinic. It is being suggested here that the trend will be more and more toward *in vivo* intervention (Tharp and Wetzel, 1969).

Cautela has developed a treatment approach, which he terms covert sensitization. Unlike desensitization (Wolpe, 1958), which attempts to decrease anxiety connected with certain stimulus situations, this procedure has a goal of *increasing* emotional reactions in specific situations. Maladaptive approach responses (e.g. homosexual behaviors), are repeatedly paired with noxious experiences. The procedure is much like aversive conditioning, except that aversive stimulation is carried out only in the patient's imagination, or *covertly*. Cautela, in Chapter 18, has extended this approach to the treatment of alcoholism, obesity, and certain delinquent problem behaviors. This represents the first attempt to use conditioning procedures with such behaviors as breaking-and-entering, glue-sniffing and automobile theft. Juvenile offenders are trained to imagine, for example, a car theft scene. As they approach the car, they are to imagine becoming increasingly nauseous and find relief only when they cease their theft behaviors. Through repeated pairings, an aversion to car-stealing develops. Although Cautela reports good results, his data are based on only a few case studies, with no measured changes in rates of these maladaptive behaviors reported, or any control or untreated cases. Cautela notes that there was no difficulty in gaining the cooperation of these juveniles in his behavior therapy program. While the above results are promising, more rigorous research is needed to determine possible large-scale applicability in treating delinquents.

In Chapter 19, MacCulloch, Williams and Birtles, present the only aversion therapy with a delinquent or predelinquent use, known to the editor, although aversion therapy has been widely used with adult alcoholics and sexual disorders (Jones, 1969; Rachman and Teasdale, 1969). Using anticipatory avoidance aversion therapy, MacCulloch *et al.* demonstrate, in a baseline design, the successful treatment of a twelve-year-old exhibitionist in eighteen sessions. The authors suggest the main usefulness of aversion therapy to be in cases where maladaptive approach behavior (e.g. exhibitionism and homosexual behavior), cannot be relieved. At this point, the potential application of aversion therapy to delinquency needs much more research to determine precisely when its use is both indicated and effective.

Aversion therapy and Cautela's covert sensitization do represent, in many ways, first attempts at conditioning conscience in delinquents, and fit what Eysenck (1957, 1964, 1965) calls the "Mowrer/Eysenck conditioning theory of conscience." If conscience is viewed as the result of repeated pairings of a given behavior or situation with aversive stimulation over many years, then certain character disorders, i.e. psychopathy, may be viewed as a failure at this kind of learning. Aversive conditioning procedures and Cautela's covert sensitization may represent treatment approaches for some delinquent behaviors, such as stealing, drug abuse, glue-sniffing and exhibitionism that have been particularly difficult to modify in other ways. Further exploration of this topic is certainly needed.

An entirely different kind of intervention technique with delinquents in the community or natural environment was developed first by Slack at Harvard, and then by his students Ralph K. and Robert L. Schwitzgebel and their colleagues. In their research-treatment program, termed "subject-experimenter psychotherapy" and "streetcorner research," at first they paid delinquents to take tests and talk into tape recorders (Slack, 1960). They extended this to treatment sessions in a church (R. K. Schitzgebel and Covey, 1963), and finally to a storefront (R. K. Schwitzgebel, 1964). They recruited delinquents on street corners, paid them to attend sessions, and found that attendance became regular, their attitudes became less hostile, and (even more surprising) the delinquents developed an attachment to the experimenters and to the various research settings. R. L. Schwitzgebel and Kolb, in Chapter 20, explain their street-corner research in more detail and present their findings in a matched control group design, with a three year follow-up. This perhaps represents the first attempt at behavior therapy with delinquents in an *open* social system and may, together with Buehler's work in Chapter 14, serve as a beginning model, a starting point.

Many have called for the breaking-up of large institutions in favor of smaller, home-like treatment centers within the community. An outstanding example of applying behavior therapy in such a setting is provided here by Achievement Place. In a baseline or individual experimental analysis design, Phillips (Ch. 21) used a token economy approach to modify the behavior of three "predelinquent" boys, all of whom had histories of minor legal offenses and difficulty in school. The three were declared "dependent-neglected" by the court and placed in the private home of the experimenter and his wife for a home-style, residential treatment program. A programmed environment was developed whereby points, earned in various ways, could be exchanged for certain privileges each week. After an initial observation period, target behaviors were selected in social, self-care and academic areas and subsequently modified through application of reinforcement contingencies. In a series of experiments, the frequency of aggressive statements and poor grammar were decreased, while tidiness, punctuality and amount of homework were all increased. It should be noted, as is typical of experimental analyses of behavior, that contingencies were repeatedly varied within each experiment, and control over the behavior was demonstrated. The Achievement Place concept was extended to home-based reinforcement for classroom behavior by Bailey, Wolf, and Phillips (1970). The boys were required to take a "report card" to school, where the teachers marked "yes" or "no" for various behaviors, such as "studied the whole period." *Yes's* gained privileges at home with encouraging results. Together, these studies represent a tenable model for small group-home behavior therapy with delinquents. Bailey *et al.* demonstrated that behavioral control can be effectively extended outside the home as well. This kind of setting seems far superior to traditional institutionalization and more congruent with a true philosophy of rehabilitation, relearning, and corrective experience.

One of the major trends in behavior therapy with children and adolescents has been in working with parents or the whole family in the community (see Liberman, 1970). Two excellent books are available both to aid the practitioner in helping families and for the parents to read and apply themselves. The first is

Patterson and Gullion's widely accepted *Living with Children: New Methods for Parents and Teachers* (1968); the second is Becker's *Parents Are Teachers* (1970). Both are clear, well written, and easily used in working with one family at a time or for training groups of parents. Both follow a programmed teaching format and both have definite application in helping parents modify the behavior of their delinquent children. Stuart (Ch. 22) has made a unique and far-reaching contribution to behavior therapy with delinquents in his development of behavioral contracting within the families of delinquents. In this chapter, he provides background, rationale, technique and a complete case study of behavioral contracting. One noteworthy aspect of his work is that he does not confine himself to a clinic, but rather moves directly into the community, into the home, to help the family. More data and research is obviously needed, but this technique shows great promise for work with the families of delinquents *in* the community—it certainly makes use of the *natural* controls on behavior, suggested by Tharp and Wetzel (1969.)

R. L. Schwitzgebel, one of the most forward-looking of behavior therapists, has brought our attention to use of technology in behavior therapy with delinquents and to the future potentials of a blending of behavior therapy into the technological revolution which we are just beginning. Holden (Ch. 2) warned the world of the coming of *1984*, with the advent of behavior therapy, and R. L. Schwitzgebel brought it to us, quite literally, in his 1969 paper, "A Belt from Big Brother"—and fifteen years early at that! Schwitzgebel, too, foresaw the trend toward direct *in vivo* intervention, of *behavior technology* in the natural environment, where instruments of technology are blended with human control and self-control. In this first attempt, he fitted delinquents with a belt, which they could wear during their usual activities in the community. Through a communication system, their behavior was monitored back at the laboratory and they, in turn, were reinforced via a vibra-tactile unit on the belt (not unlike a pat on the back). Obviously critics, hoping to preserve the so-called freedom of man, were quick to make known their horror at the thought of behavior being monitored by Big Brother back at the laboratory (presumably like that of Dr. Frankenstein). But Schwitzgebel sees psychotechnolgy as *pro*social, humane, and as a technology for the improvement of man "by making our physical environment and our physical selves increasingly responsive to human intention . . . (1970, p. 498)." There may be a threat to mankind from technology, but not from excessive behavioral control. Rather, the technological threat seems to be coming from the building of bigger and better weapons and from environmental poisoning.

> An instrument is essentially a passive tool. Although instruments and gadgets significantly influence our private and professional lives, we are not—or need not be—as Thoreau claimed, "tools of our tools." An instrument is not a substitute for creative thinking. (It is, in fact, more likely to be a result of it.) Nor are instruments a substitute for competent knowledge of the problem area or for adequate experimental design. Nonetheless, an investigator who is unaware of the possibilities afforded by present instrumentation in clinical practice, unnecessarily handicaps his own efforts.
>
> It is a worn-out truism that technology is changing our lives. However, it has not, as yet, for better or worse, changed much of clinical or social psychology. Maintaining and upgrading the quality of professional intervention is of utmost importance, and certainly what we can do and what we should do are not identical categories of action. Standardized tests and verbal interviews have served the profession well, but now technological innovations gave us new options. Let us take care to avoid the awkward situation of the aborigine who, having made a new boomerang, discovered that he could not throw the old one away." (1968, p. 455)

At present, and in summary, we still seem to be in the Dark Ages of penal corrections for young lawbreakers, where indeed a lot of kids do come out learning a "trade," i.e. come out knowing more criminal behaviors than when they went in. This is in spite of the fact that both more humane and effective means of changing the behavior of adolescents have been around for some time. Stuart (1970, p. 200) attempts to locate the possible sources of resistance, at least with regard to the mental health establishment.

> They may be prisoners of their training to some extent; that is, all have painstakingly acquired a competency through long years of

preparation and it takes great character for a man to summarily forsake one skill in order to develop another. In addition, therapists occupy positions of prestige and influence which are richly rewarding. . . Finally, psychotherapists tend to be highly articulate, and a radical shift in position would require public repudiation of formal positions developed over years of teaching, lecturing, and writing.

Much the same seems to be the case within the corrections establishment. Even worse, correctional institutions often seem to attract staff with authoritarian and punitive ways of interacting with inmates. They too, along with the inmates, scoff at terms like *rehabilitation* and *correctional* institution. Nothing short of wide-scale penal reform is called for, with an emphasis on community intervention, and more importantly, self-evaluating attempts at prevention, following and extending the model provided by the contributors to this text. It is only a beginning, but finally there has been a step forward.

REFERENCES

Bailey, J. S., Wolf, M. M., and Phillips, E. L.: Home based reinforcement and the modification of pre-delinquents' classroom behavior. *Journal of Applied Behavior Analysis, 3*:223-233, 1970.

Becker, W. C.: *Parents Are Teachers*. Champaign, Illinois, Research Press, 1971.

Eysenck, H. J.: *The Dynamics of Anxiety and Hysteria*. London, Routledge and Kegan Paul, 1957.

Eysenck, H. J.: *Crime and Personality*. Boston, Houghton Mifflin, 1964.

Eysenck, H. J.: A note on some criticisms of the Mowrer/Eysenck conditioning theory of conscience. *British Journal of Psychology, 56*:305-307, 1965.

Jones, M. R. (Ed.): *Aversive Stimulation*. Coral Gables, Florida, University of Miami Press, 1969.

Liberman, R.: Behavior approaches to family and couple therapy. *American Journal of Orthopsychiatry, 40*:106-118, 1970.

Mangel, C.: How to make a criminal out of a child. *Look*, June 29, 1971.

Patterson, G. R.: *Living With Children: New Methods for Parents and Teachers*. Champaign, Illinois, Research Press, 1968.

Rachman, S., and Teasdale, J.: *Aversion Therapy and Behavior Disorders: An Analysis*. Coral Gables, Florida, University of Miami Press, 1969.

Schwitzgebel, R. L.: Survey of electromechanical devices for behavior modification. *Psychological Bulletin, 70*:444-459, 1968.

Schwitzgebel, R. L.: A belt from big brother. *Psychology Today*, 2:45-47, 65, 1969.

Schwitzgebel, R. L.: Behavior instrumentation and social technology. *American Psychologist*, 25:491-499, 1970.

Schwitzgebel, R. K.: *Streetcorner Research: An Experimental Approach to the Juvenile Delinquent.* Cambridge, Harvard University Press, 1964.

Schwitzgebel, R. K. and Covey, T. H.: Experimental interviewing of youthful offenders in a church setting. *Journal of Clinical Psychology, 19:*487-488, 1963.

Slack, C. W.: Experimenter-subject psychotherapy: A new method of introducing intensive office treatment for unreachable cases. *Mental Hygiene, 44:*238-256, 1960.

Stuart, R. B.: *Trick or Treatment: How and When Psychotherapy Fails.* Champaign, Illinois, Research Press, 1970.

Tharp, R. G., and Wetzel, R. J.: *Behavior Modification in the Natural Environment.* New York, Academic Press, 1969.

Ullman, L. P., and Krasner, L. (Ed.): *Case Studies in Behavior Modification.* New York, Holt, 1965.

U. S. prisons: schools for crime. *Time*, January 18, 1971.

Chapter 15

SOCIAL REINFORCEMENT EXPERIMENTATION IN OPEN SOCIAL SYSTEMS

ROY E. BUEHLER

T HE PURPOSE OF THIS ARTICLE is not to debate the merits of social reinforcement learning. Rather, it is to raise some issues regarding under what conditions research and therapy which follow this paradigm can be done. In reading *Walden Two,* one inevitably keeps looking for some information as to how and under what conditions this unique social system was built. One can only conclude that it was built within what Meehl (1960) calls the "cognitive activity of a clinician" and not in a world made up of social institutional power structure, bureaucracies and, more importantly, people. To use a paradox, "Where in the world can social reinforcement research take place?"

It is one thing to go into a community or social system within a community, collect self-report or observational data, and then leave—quickly and without changing anything. This type of research is not disparaged. It yields much important information on human behavior. The behavior modifier, however, carries science a step further and adopts an experimental model. He sets out not only to measure behavior, he seeks to change behavior. Since he does not see behavior as mainly, if not solely, self-actional, but

This was originally presented at the Western Psychological Association Annual Meeting on May 4, 1967, San Francisco, California. Reprinted with permission.

The writer gratefully acknowledges the financial assistance provided by the OEO Research Contract 1393, and the research sponsorship provided by the Educational Systems Division, Litton Industries, Inc. in connection with the experiment for which this article constitutes a partial report.

instead as transactional, his experimental operations take him into the social systems of society—the family, the school, or whatever people are trained or treated by and among other people, and he has to change those systems in order to change his client or group of client behavior.

If behavior modification research requires a social system base, the question is open as to what kind of social system is required. The literature indicates that with rare exceptions such research has taken place in what may be labeled "closed social systems."* The term "closed" is used because client membership in the system is maintained by either behavioral, physical, legal, or quasi-legal restrictions. In correctional systems, whether residential or probationary, membership is by legal compulsion. In mental hospitals patients are either "committed" or "voluntary," but voluntarism is generally associated with very positive sanctions from significant reference groups in the patient's social environment. Likewise, for the deviant child being treated within the family social system, the family is a closed system because the child is not free to mount his tricycle and ride off when the behavior modifier arrives. Mama or papa keeps him home. The public school system, at least through junior high school, likewise may be called a closed system by virtue of compulsory attendance laws. The senior high school student is much more free to drop out, and also to "turn on and tune in" if he wishes. In short, in this context the term "closed" refers to a social system wherein membership decisions are not the prerogative of the client or his peer group but of staff persons who represent external authority.

There are many other social systems in society having training, treatment, rehabilitative, or similar behavior-changing objectives wherein client participation is elective. There often is, of course, some pressure from significant persons or reference groups for the client to enter or to stay, but the client makes the decision. This is largely true of the senior high school, both academic and vocational. It is true of colleges, professional and trade schools. It

*Goffman (Asylums, 1961) calls these "total institutions," primarily characterized by barriers to social intercourse, without and within. However, the fact that staff hold the keys which open doors for admission and exit suggests the more specific term "closed system."

is true of most of the training and/or rehabilitative programs under welfare and the current "war on poverty." It is also true that the literature on behavior modification is lacking in reports of experimental studies in such social systems.

As matters now stand, the population which does not meet the criteria for membership in closed social systems and which is dissociated from the behavior controls operant in family, school, or occupational systems of society is left untouched by reinforcement learning experimentation. These persons constitute a significant percentage of the population. Not all of them are officially labeled "offender" or "mentally ill." However, it cannot be assumed that behavioral deficiencies are not involved in their temporary or permanent dissociation from occupational and other legitimate social systems of society. Certainly, too, all members of this population do not volunteer to participate in the open social system programs designed for them; even when they do volunteer, it cannot be assumed that the programs shape their behavior up to snuff. So, must it be concluded that the only human behavior which is amenable to behavior modification research is that which appears in closed social systems? Will social learning principles apply only to "captive" and not to "free" populations? Until research and model-building which follow reinforcement learning principles is done on open social systems it must be concluded that a captive clientele is required.

And why must we so conclude? Let me restate in very brief and necessarily general terms some principles that are stated as essential in social reinforcement research. A primary principle is that behavior can be modified when environmental contingencies can be controlled appropriately. When the behavior modification program fails to obtain control over environmental contingencies, behavioral change is not likely to occur. Ayllon (1966) has put the matter very succinctly: "You arrange the situation in such a way that it is practically impossible for the child or patient to respond in any way but that which will lead to the specific reward . . . . You engineer the situation to make it virtually impossible for them to believe in any other way except the one which leads in the direction of the ultimate behavior you have specified."

This involves, of course, some drastic shifts from some of our most cherished traditions in behavioral science. Instead of seeking, in the training or treatment situation, to enlarge the range of freedom, permissiveness, voluntarism and other similar variables, the experimenter makes every effort to control the contingency system in the client's immediate environment. Instead of noncontingently dispensing tender, loving care to fill a big affectional vacuum, he ties these gifts to specific behavioral approximations of the treatment goal. Surely, Dr. Schaefer's (1966) patients are free to eat, but not before they earn their meal. They are free to live in a comfortable room in the hospital if they have earned it through the performance of certain required behaviors. Likewise, Cohen's delinquents in the National Training School (1966) are free to refuse the demands in the behavior modification program, but by refusing they reduce themselves to what Cohen calls "welfare" existence in the institution. Patterson, with his child clients (1966), establishes and maintains control over M&M® dispensing and expressions of mother-love, while Bijou at Ranier (1966), Lovas at UCLA (1966), and other researchers have depended upon parents, aides, teachers, or nurses to keep the doors locked so that the client cannot move away from the situation and receive conflicting contingencies from outside the experimental social system. In short, contrary to the "free and open universe" in which evocative therapy presumably has operated, behavior modification research takes place in highly restrictive social systems.

Space-imposed brevity at this point leads to some misunderstanding, unless the few instances of voluntarism are mentioned. Some delinquents volunteered to come into Schwitzgebel's laboratory, some clients volunteer for out-patient behavior therapy, some public school students voluntarily seek the school counselor for behavior counseling. In terms of theory construction and technique development, these certainly are essential endeavors. However, any assessment of coverage suggests that their numbers roughly approximate, in size, the congregation of already converted people who come to hear the sermon on sin.

This is, without doubt, an area in which even angels fear to tread, because it involves the rights and privileges of relatively free citizens. But by dropping the disease model, adopting a learning model, and defining learning in terms of operant conditioning through social contingencies, there have been opened some critical issues which are not yet closed. The label "offender" or "sick" made it unnecessary for the psychologist to identify the person whose behavior presumably must be modified. All that had to be done was inquire about the behavior which earned the subject either one of these labels. Then instead of trying to extinguish that behavior, the therapist set about to treat the "dynamics" which presumably were the cause of that behavior. After the treatment program reduced the "sickness" cues, a judge or psychiatrist would say that the person was no longer an "offender" or "sick." The social learning model, however, requires the identification of the behavior which is inappropriate, the person who thus behaves, and the social contingencies which maintain the inappropriate behavior. Among the problems which emerge once the disease model is no longer used is who decides what behavior is deviant? And what behavior is appropriate? We can say, of course, that the appropriateness of any behavior is determined by the culture, but cultures may be characterized by behavior which is exceedingly deviant and costly with reference to significant sectors of the population. Furthermore, a culture may be and often is made up of many subcultural systems which do not train their members for adaptation to the general culture.

Instead of the sickness model for identifying the deviant and his deviance, the researcher can substitute personality tests. Peterson (1965) reviewed such instruments and came up with an intra-trait correlation among tests of .30, which, he said, "is no cause for rejoicing." Even if the correlation were high, the relevance of these traits to behavior remains to be established. So again the behavioral scientist is thrown back upon what Bales (1950) stated is the "ultimate stuff or empirical phenomena which the social scientist can observe, record, interpret, and arrange in many ways." He lists "action or interaction" and "situation" as this ultimate stuff.

Now back to the question. When controls over the contingencies are not available anywhere in the lifespace of the potential client, what can be done? The position can be adopted that there is no behavior that needs modification unless it has been officially labeled as deviant, underachieving, delinquent, psychotic, neurotic, or criminal. Thus, the researcher depends upon the law enforcement and various administrative agencies to identify the research problem. This means, in effect, that behavior modification efforts wait until the behavior has become sufficiently costly to the community to necessitate putting the person in one or another of the various closed systems of society where his behavior can be reshaped. Another alternative has been suggested by Secretary McNamara and Sargent Shriver who propose a universal draft system beginning at age 16 for both sexes. However well-intentioned the authors of this proposal may be, the fact of the matter is that it would greatly increase the present formal controls over a much wider range of social behavior than that which presently obtains. If this did not have so many punitive possibilities, it might be viewed with more equanimity, but control without the reinforcement of the positive tends only to stop behavior temporarily and not to reshape it for the day the controls are lifted.

The alternative is to conduct experimental open social system research in terms of social reinforcement principles. Following is a brief description of a recent attempt to conduct an experimental subsystem within the larger social system of a Job Corps center. The details of the project are reported elsewhere (Buehler, Asrican and Sauer, 1967), and in this context the implications for open social system experimentation will be extracted.

Parks Job Corps Center, like all Job Corps centers, was an open social system. Its resident clients were free—legally, physically, financially, and administratively—to leave at any time they so desired, and many of them did. Furthermore, they had no officially defined behavioral deviances which the centers were expected to modify. The purpose of the Job Corps was to provide vocational training for untrained youth. A Job Corps center was a residential social system responsible for the behavioral activities of the residents 24 hours a day, seven days a week. However, there were few locked gates around a center or locked doors within a center. Members were free to move for social purposes from one residential unit to another. It was impossible to segregate a portion of the population from social contact with other members or with the community, as a means for controlling contingencies. In staffing, Parks Job Corps Center management did not, and could not had it tried, staff with behavior-modification-oriented people, because such people are still in very short supply. Persons were drawn from industry (open social systems), public schools (quasi-closed systems), juvenile courts (closed systems), mental hospitals (closed systems), the clergy (open systems), etc. This produces an extremely eclectic staff with reference to how to deal with residents' behavior. Consequently, as a corpsman moved about within the total social system of the center, he encountered a variety of staff-dispensed contingencies for any given behavior on his part. Furthermore, as sociologists who have researched residential institutions report, a resident culture arises which provides its own positive and negative sanctions within the peer group. The social system build-up process at Parks, as well as throughout the Job Corps program, was extremely rapid with large groups of newly arrived corpsmen being managed and trained by large numbers of newly hired staff members. In such a situation, again as institutional research has long indicated, much of the control of resident members' behavior passes from either the staff or the larger peer group into the hands of informal peer groups. In correctional literature these informal controls often get into the hands of the "Dukes" who establish and maintain a peer-group reinforcement system which is relatively immune to staff influence.

This is reported in no criticism of Parks Job Corps Center or any other Job Corps center. The Job Corps was launched quickly to meet an acute social need which other social institutions and agencies were not and still are not meeting. It is highly improbable, too, that there are any empirically validated models to which all behavior scientists would have given consent as alternatives to the general system adopted by the Job Corps.

The first question that had to be asked was, What are the target behaviors or common dependent variables in this enterprise? The clients were not officially classified as delinquent, mentally ill, or public nuisances. Obviously, too, they all were not Eagle Scouts. One general assumption was made regarding their expected initial behavior. In addition to being members of the so-called "poverty subculture," it was expected that the clients had not been conditioned to the more or less routine social behavior required for successful school progress and for retention of jobs. It was assumed that in addition to the achievement of technical skills, the corpsmen needed to acquire social-vocational skills required for membership in the vocational systems of society as well as the social systems of the community.

Two areas were investigated for criteria. The most immediate was social living behavior within the dormitory and daily attendance in the shops and classrooms. Since the outcomes of institutional programs where these behaviors are enforced through sanctions dispensed by staff alone without peer-group participation have not been impressive, the peer-group social system was seen as a potential dispenser of reinforcements to its individual members for socially accountable behavior in and outside the dormitory.

An additional area was sampled for target behavior. This is the specific job-relevant behavior required on the semiskilled level for job retention. The literature on vocational training is silent on this matter; its focus is on technical skill. So we interviewed 50 employers of entree level semiskilled employees in the San Francisco Bay Area. They were asked, "What behavior must a man show on a job in your business in order to keep his job?" From their total list of statements they rated 43 behavioral items as being essential for job retention (Buehler, Sauer and Gaustad, 1967). Insofar as any of these 43 items pertained to corpsman behavior in the Job Corps center, they were adopted as target behavior to be strengthened.

If the objective is to reinforce those peer-group behaviors which are necessary for establishing and maintaining a peer-group system which functions as behavior training agent, what behaviors do we look for? A search through the literature failed to locate a behavior rating scale specific to this task. The only alternative was to devise a tentative list of specific peer group behaviors necessary for cooperative decision-making and for carrying out group decisions.

The project used two kinds of reinforcers: (a) social—dispensed through interpersonal communication behavior, and (b) tokens which were exchangeable for certain limited commodities. The formal teaching situation was a daily group meeting, through which an adult mediator (or counselor) was expected to model and reinforce appropriate group problem-solving behavior with reference to the day-by-day management and operation of the experimental dormitory. Behavior in the group meetings was video-taped and coded in terms of appropriate or inappropriate acts and their reinforcing contingencies within the group. Also, individual behavior in work details necessary for dormitory maintenance was observed and coded. The nature, time, and membership of the details were determined by the peer group under strong pressure from the counselor.

After observing each subject in group meetings and work details, a list of negative behaviors was obtained; that is, behaviors which interfered with group-task performance. These operations thus produced a list of appropriate and inappropriate behaviors which were to be given positive or negative reinforcement by the counselor and peer group each time they occurred.

Since the Job Corps aimed at shaping racially integrated behavior, the random selection of incoming enrollees assigned to the experimental and control groups was controlled for racial distribution. Approximately one-half of new enrollees were Caucasian and the other half was made up predominantly of Negro, with some American Indians. These ratios were adopted for the experimental and control groups.

In this context only a brief summary of results can be given. The data indicate very definitely that only minimal success was achieved in building a peer-group social system capable of functioning as change agent. A small group of the subjects quickly formed informal peer-group relations with corpsmen on other dormitories scattered throughout the center, and as is apparently inevitable in large social systems, some of these informal peer groups were continuously dispensing reinforcements for behavior which had been identified in the project as inappropriate. There was no way to prevent the experimental group from receiving these conflicting contingencies from peers in and outside the dormitory. Other staff members who interfaced with the subjects outside the dormitory dispensed a variety of conflicting contingencies. The contingencies within the dormitory were uncontrollable for the simple reason that the doors were unlocked at all times, outside corpsman could come in with relative freedom, and innumerable inappropriate behaviors occurred behind closed doors without the counselor becoming aware of them. More importantly, it became apparent that corpsmen who were targets of aggression, etc., and who then fed this information back to the peer group in the daily meetings, received quick and effective punishment from some of their peers shortly after the meeting was over. In other words, the informal peer system could dispense rewards and punishments immediately and effectively. The counselor made every effort to reward open feedback, identification of behavioral problems of individuals and groups, and problem-solving behavior. Nevertheless, a minority of corpsmen in the experimental group, with the assistance of allies whom they brought in occasionally at night from the outside, soon were able to establish and consistently reinforce a "code of silence" which blocked peer-group problem-solving behavior.

Some issues could not be resolved. We could not control the behavior of the minority of subjects who were extremely threatened by the social-reinforcing peer-group system which we were trying to develop. We could not alter the contingencies which maintained inappropriate behavior in and outside the Job Corps Center. We could not, without denying the project's objectives, turn over control of the social system to informal groups which were dispensing reinforcements for inappropriate social-vocational behavior. So it became a power struggle between the counselor and a small minority of subjects who dispensed massive punishment for appropriate peer-group behavior. Furthermore, when a subject's behavior became so threatening to others as to require extreme action such as dismissal, the processing of the action through administrative channels delayed the dispensing of effective negative sanctions. Meanwhile the offender continued to stimulate fear and distrust among other corpsmen, some of whom resigned from the corps. Moreover, many rewarding commodities were not amenable to rescheduling in terms of behavioral contingencies. These included food, clothing, pay, and many fringe benefits. Other issues were involved but these appeared to have been most critical.

SOME INFERENCES FOR SOCIAL REINFORCEMENT PROGRAM-BUILDING IN OPEN SOCIAL SYSTEMS

There is a strong bias in favor of small institutions among those behavioral scientists who have researched the outcomes of both large and small institutions. Supporting evidence has been short on linkages between process and outcome variables, however. The data from the present study suggest that a reinforcement learning analysis of large versus small institutions will add support to the bias. The study suggests at least three reasons for this. The first is that the larger the institution, the more eclectic the staff tends to be, and consequently the more diverse and conflicting are the contingencies dispensed by the staff to the clients. The second factor is the tendency in large systems for rewards and punishments to become highly codified and controlled by staff members who do not interface directly with the client. Thus, rewards and punishments cannot be dispensed immediately upon the manifestation of behavior but are delayed through administrative processes. The codified reward and punishment system tends to be applied to all in spite of the obvious fact that what is reinforcing for one person may be punishment for another. The third factor is the inevitable and necessary client subculture which arises. In the larger institution, with its codified reward and punishment system, its eclective staff, and its large number of clients, it appears to be more likely that an underground, informal, and effective reinforcement system will develop and be controlled among the very clients who most need behavior reshaping.

These observations indicate that the typical problem of "escape from the contingencies" (Liberman, 1967) is greatly exacerbated in open social systems. Rather than abandoning behavior modification experimentation in such systems, the following experimental model is proposed:

1. The experimental social system should be relatively small, probably in the range of 20 to 100 clients, and not located as a subsystem within a larger institutional structure.
2. The situational, process, and outcome variables must be defined in behavioral terms.
3. All staff, including upper and middle management, should be carefully selected, trained, and supervised in the use of operant conditioning principles and techniques in management and program operations.
4. Increases in numbers of clients should follow the acquisition of appropriate behavior in the nucleus group of clients, lest the behavior which large numbers of new clients bring into the system destroy the emerging change agent, i.e. the social system's reinforcement system.
5. The locus of decision-making and action with reference to rewards and punishments should be among those staff members who interface directly with the clients.

If an open system model following these procedures could be empirically validated, further experimentation on administrative and other matters involved in increasing institutional size would be in order.

REFERENCES

Ayllon, Teodoro: Quoted in *Reinforcement Therapy*. Philadelphia, Smith, Kline, and French Laboratories, 1966, pp. 2, 3.

Bales, R. E.: *Interaction Process Analysis*. Cambridge, Mass., Addison-Wesley Press, Inc., 1950, p. 31.

Bijou, Sidney: Experimental studies of child behavior, normal and deviant. In Krasner and Ullmann (Eds.): *Research in Behavior Modification*. New York, Holt, Rinehart, and Winston, Inc., 1966, pp. 56-81.

Buehler, R. E., Sauer, John, and Gaustad, Gregory: Job-related Behavior Rating Scale, Final Report, Project B, OEO Research, Educational Systems Division, Litton Industries, College Park, Maryland, 1967.

Buehler, R. E., Asrican, Steve, and Sauer, John: A Social Reinforcement Experiment in an Open Social System. Final Report, Project C. OEO Research Contract 1393, 1967.

Cohen, H. L., Filipczak, J. A., Bis, J. S., and Cohen, J. E.: Contingencies applicable to special education of delinquents. Interim Report, National Training School, 1966.

Goffman, E.: *Asylums.* New York, Doubleday-Anchor, 1961.

Liberman, Robert: A View of Behavior Modification Projects in California, Unpublished (mimeographed) report. Laboratory of Social Psychiatry, Harvard Medical School, 1967.

Lovaas, O. I.: In *Reinforcement Therapy.* Philadelphia, Smith, Kline and French Laboratories, 1966.

Meehl, P. E.: The cognitive activity of a clinician. *The American Psychologist, 15*:19-27, 1960.

Patterson, G. R. and Brodsky, G.: A behavior modification programme for a child with multiple problem behaviors. *Journal of Child Psychology and Psychiatry, 7*:277-295, 1966.

Peterson, Donald R.: Scope and generality of verbally defined personality factors. *Psychology Review, 72*(1)48-59, 1965.

Schaefer, H. H.: Investigations in operant conditioning procedures in a mental hospital. In *Reinforcement Theory in Psychological Treatment.* California Mental Health Research Monograph No. 8, Buerau of Research, State of California, Sacramento, 1966.

Skinner, B. F.: *Walden Two.* New York, MacMillan Company, 1948.

Chapter 16

CAN CONDITIONING PRINCIPLES BE APPLIED TO PROBATION?

RONALD B. JAMIESON

Conditions of probation have three purposes: (a) to facilitate supervision of probationers by probation officers; (b) to protect the public against criminal acts by probationers; and (c) to change the habits of probationers sufficiently to make avoidance of crime by them habitual. Of the three, the last is the most important. Supervision of probationers is only a means to an end. Protection of the public can result only if good behavior of probationers becomes habitual. Conditions of probation should be so written and used as to create good habits in probationers.

David Dressler's *Practice and Theory of Probation and Parole* (Columbia University Press, 1959) contains an excellent discussion of probation supervision and conditions. It appears now, however, that modern learning theory and conditioning principles are sufficiently advanced to carry us beyond Dressler's discussion. Professor H.J. Eysenck, a distinguished psychologist, said the following in *Encounter,* October, 1964:

> Everyone is agreed that neurotic behaviour, as well as behaviour leading to crime or to preventable accidents, is learned. Although I have always stressed that there is a genetic basis for differential rates of learning and conditioning, it is clear that behaviour as such cannot be inherited but must depend on learning and conditioning. If this is true, then it would seem that psychologists who have spent almost a hundred years of carefully controlled scientific study on the way in which learning and conditioning proceed, the ways and means

*Reprinted with permission from *Trial Judges Journal, 4:*7-8, 1965. (American Bar Association).

of enhancing or retarding the acquisition of knowledge and skills, and the way acquired habits are extinguished, should have some practical suggestions to make in relation to what are undoubtedly very serious social problems.

Professor Eysenck is editor-in-chief of the journal *Behavior Research and Therapy* (Pergamon Press, Oxford, England), which began publishing in May, 1963. This journal is devoted to the use of learning theory and conditioning principles to control maladaptive behavior. In the first issue Professor Eysenck states that the main conception unifying the approaches to maladaptive behavior through learning theory and conditioning principles is "the belief that behavioral disorders of the most divergent types are essentially *learned responses,* and that modern learning theory (using that term in its widest sense) has much to teach us regarding the acquisition and extinction of such responses."

Criminal conduct, especially persistent criminal conduct, is a learned response. Being a learned response, it can be unlearned, extinguished as a response, by application of learning theory and conditioning principles. A good summary of learning theory and principles of conditioning is in Chapter 5 of Bernard Berelson and Gary A. Steiner's *Human Behavior: An Inventory of Scientific Findings* (Harcourt, Brace and World, 1964). The learned character of criminal behavior appears to be borne out by Berelson and Steiner's discussion (Ch. 15, pages 625-630) of what types of people are more likely to commit crime.

How can judges use learning theory and principles of conditioning to help people on probation avoid criminal conduct? The best thing judges could do would be to have trained psychologists devise and use suitable behavior therapy to extinguish the learned responses which led probationers into crime. This would not involve psychoanalysis or any attempt to probe into the probationer's unconscious. It would not be based on Freudian principles. It would be based on principles which go back to Pavlov and have been further developed by J.B. Watson, C.L. Hull, B.F. Skinner and others. Behavior therapy of this type is less speculative, expensive and tedious and more exact and scientific than psychoanalytic therapy. Apparently it gets good results in the vast majority of cases, which psychoanalysis does not.

Judges do not have the time or knowledge to carry on behavior therapy with probationers. But they can order it to be done by experts, order the government to pay for it and make the probationer's consent and cooperation a condition of probation.

Judges can keep learning theory and conditioning principles in mind in drafting conditions of probation. They can require the probationer to do things (a) which will tend to break habits and associations which led him into crime and (b) which will tend to create new habits and associations which will tend to lead him into constructive, noncriminal activity.

Most probationers are young, full of energy, and more or less gregarious. But their outlook and experience are often narrow and of the wrong type. They have too many bad friends, too few good ones. They misdirect their energy, spend too much of it on riding around in automobiles or drinking, and not enough of it on regular work, education, athletics, reading, hobbies, music, art, saving money, planning for themselves and their families for the future, etc. They do not spend enough time in constructive social groups, the YMCA, evening classes, etc.

In addition to the necessary general conditions relating to conduct, probation orders should include detailed, specific, specially tailored conditions, both negative and positive, designed to broaden the probationer's experience and outlook in constructive ways, to weaken his unwholesome associations, and to prevent the type of conduct and way of life that got him involved in crime. Probation supervision should be close and violations of probation conditions should be both detected and punished immediately. Small prompt punishment is the best.

It appears clear that modern learning theory and conditioning principles should enter into the drafting of probation conditions and into the supervision and treatment of probationers under them.

Chapter 17

BEHAVIOR MODIFICATION TECHNIQUES: NEW TOOLS FOR PROBATION OFFICERS

GAYLORD L. THORNE, ROLAND G. THARP, *and* RALPH J. WETZEL

P ROBATION work with juvenile delinquents, as the authors have viewed it, has not been very rewarding to the probation officers and not very helpful to the youngsters. Far too many youngsters fail probation by committing further offenses and, unfortunately, a significant percentage move on to adult crime. Probation officers frequently point to their large caseloads and lack of professional training as causes for low success rates. The former certainly warrants concern, whereas the latter is probably overemphasized. The position of this article* is that juvenile probation officers could be considerably more effective than they are presently even with large caseloads and no graduate training.

Such a position is based on the burgeoning evidence that has become available recently in the field of mental health. Great changes are underway. The importance of the following is diminishing in modern treatment approaches: Talking therapies as a major curative method; the medical disease model; primary reliance on highly trained therapists; institutions operating as quasi-psychiatric centers; and the emphasis on "psychiatric" causation (particularly psychoanalytic) for antisocial behavior. The abandonment or severe curtailment of these traditional approaches has led to some badly needed changes.

Reprinted with permission from *Federal Probation,* June, 1967, pp. 21-27. (United States Department of Justice).

*This article is based on data gathered from the Behavioral Research Project which is supported by the Office of Juvenile Delinquency and Youth Development, Welfare Administration, Department of Health, Education, and Welfare.

The application of *behavior modification* techniques is certainly one of the most exciting and refreshing of the new treatment innovations. The techniques follow from operant learning theory—a theory that is elegantly simple, easily taught, dramatically effective, and useful in an almost unlimited number of settings (Grossberg, 1964; Schwitzgebel, 1964; Ullmann and Krasner, 1965; Wolpe, *et al.,* 1964). The juvenile probation officer is in a key position to take advantage of these new techniques. This was recently pointed out by Judge Ronald B. Jamieson (1965) in his recommendation of the use of conditioning principles in probation work.

> Judges can keep learning theory and conditioning principles in mind in drafting conditions of probation. They can require the probationer to do things (a) which will tend to break habits and associations which led him into crime and (b) which will tend to create new habits and associations which will tend to lead him into constructive, noncriminal activity (p. 7).

BEHAVIOR MODIFICATION TECHNIQUES

What are behavior modification techniques? Briefly, they represent the systematic application of a reinforcement learning theory largely developed by B. F. Skinner and his associates. The basic premise is: *Behavior is governed by its consequences.* Only observable behavior is dealt with; fantasies, dreams, the unconscious, ego, etc., are not considered legitimate data. The goal of modifying behavior is accomplished by altering consequences. One technique of such an approach involves the determination of these consequences (or more technically *reinforcers*) and applying them when a desired behavior is approximated.

A child's reinforcers can be determined by carefully observing his behavior. Each child has an idiosyncratic list of reinforcers which one can rank from most to least important. Aside from candy for young children, and money for all others, it is seldom that reinforcers can be accurately specified without observation and inquiry. In working with predelinquent children, the authors determine a "reinforcement hierarchy" by inquiring directly from the child and from his parents as to what motivates him—the people, things, or events which he seeks.

There are two general types of reinforcement schedules used to modify behavior. The first is a "positive schedule of reinforcement," and is characterized by such reinforcers as praise, attention, privileges, money, food, TV, use of the car, etc. Changes in behavior promoted by such a schedule tend to be relatively rapid and durable. The second is an "aversive schedule of reinforcement," and is characterized by such reinforcers as threats, physical punishment, confinement, withdrawal of rewards and privileges, ridicule, ostracism, etc. Psychologists have shown that behavior changes promoted on the latter kind of schedule tend to be relatively limited and temporary.

In actual practice the type of schedule used to modify behavior is usually mixed, i.e. both positive and aversive. The key to modifying behavior lies with that which is given the major emphasis. Many delinquent and predelinquent children are being raised primarily on an aversive schedule, and unfortunately the steps usually taken by public agencies to correct such behavior are also very likely to be aversive—e.g. being expelled from school, incarcerated. The challenge, from a behavior modification viewpoint, is how to get the youngster onto a more balanced schedule of reinforcement.

The Concepts of Shaping and Contingency

Two more concepts are needed to round out the general description of operant principles before dealing with specific procedures to change behavior. The first is *shaping,* a term used to describe steps or approximations to a desired goal. When a behavior is selected as a goal, then all responses that approximate this goal are reinforced and all other responses are not reinforced. For example, when an otherwise very capable youngster is getting all failing grades in school, one should not immediately ask for A's on his work. Instead, he should be shaped toward A's by rewarding D's and all behaviors approximating those needed for academic success (attending, opening book, completing some of the assignments) . Once D's are attained, the reward criterion can be gradually increased to C's, then B's, and finally A's. The same process would be used for antisocial behaviors. To illustrate, a boy who habitually fights could be rewarded for going a full day without a fight, then two days, then five days, until it was felt that he had learned new nonaggressive ways of relating to peers.

The second is the concept of *contingency* and it is absolutely essential in understanding operant principles. Contingency means that the consequences of an event are made dependent upon whether the event occurs. For example, telling a child he may have an ice cream cone only if he behaves means that ice cream is contingent upon good behavior; or, if parole depends upon acceptable prison behavior, then acting-out prevents parole. It is a very simple and straightforward concept that we deal with in a variety of ways during our daily lives. However, failure to understand the importance of rewarding or punishing *on contingency* is commonplace and can utterly destroy learning.

Alternatives to Traditional Therapy

The possible use of probation officers as agents to implement behavior modification would be highly consistent with some current outlooks on treating problem children. The traditional use of highly trained psychotherapists has not been particularly successful with children. The creation of an artificial relationship between a youngster and a caseworker, psychologist or other individual, takes considerable time and skill, yet its effectiveness can be questioned. However, the use of natural relationships (e.g. parents, friends, relatives, teachers) for bringing about changes in a youngster can be efficient and powerful. Parents have the primary responsibility for their children, and if they even display a modicum of cooperation, there is a potential for bringing about behavior changes of a meaningful and durable nature.

The agents used on the Behavioral Research Project of the Southern Arizona Mental Health Center to teach new child management techniques to parents and teachers are all subprofessionals—bachelor's degrees or less. They were trained and are supervised by the authors. The training techniques could easily be taught to probation officers to improve their effectiveness.

The typical probation officer's effectiveness with youngsters could be improved with operant techniques because of the ways in which they usually fulfill their present roles. When a probation officer enters a child's life, his "treatment" plan is traditionally built around points of law, the prestige of the judge, threats of incarceration, the punishments and restrictions he can create in the home and community, lectures on bad behavior and society's right of revenge, lists of "Do Not" rules to follow, and the use of his presence in the home or school to prevent certain misbehaviors. Psychologists would describe this as an aversive schedule of reinforcement—only unpleasant or punishing consequences are used. They would also predict that such a reinforcement schedule will only produce circumscribed learning (Bandura, 1962; Skinner, 1953). The latter is further complicated by the fact that additional contacts with the child's parents rarely occur (while he behaves), so the changes in their behavior are not reinforced by the probation officer and thus not maintained. This represents a considerable waste of effort in a large percentage of cases, i.e. one instance of threat from the juvenile court motivates only a small number of parents to change their ways.

The error of focusing one's attention on misbehavior is certainly not unique to probation officers. It is a commonplace occurrence in schools and homes. Schoolteachers particularly tend toward this, seldom realizing that the use of attention in this manner actually *stimulates* and *maintains* misbehavior in a large number of youngsters. It is, of course, only logical that probation officers must focus their initial attention on misbehavior since they have almost no other occasion for being in contact with a child. However, this does not justify the continuation of such a focus.

Probation officers should make use of their aversive controls, which can temporarily reduce misbehavior, and then build a treatment or rehabilitation plan around positive controls that would teach new socially acceptable behaviors. The whole purpose of behavior modification techniques is to introduce reinforcement contingencies that will encourage the emergence of nondeviant behaviors. The latter can rarely be done without teaching parents new child-management techniques; juvenile probation officers are usually very remiss about doing this.

Some Case Examples

Perhaps several cases from the Behavioral Research Project will illustrate some of the alternatives available in working with the teachers and families of misbehaving children. All of this work was carried out by subprofessional staff, so in every case a juvenile probation officer (trained in operant techniques, of course) could have done the same.

Case 1

Claire is a bright, moderately attractive 16-year-old who was referred to the project for truancy, poor grades, and incorrigibility at home. The parents were divorced six years ago and the mother now supports the two of them as a maid. The father is out of state, as is Claire's older married sister.

When the referral came from a local high school, it stated that Claire was going to be expelled for truancy. The staff persuaded them to hold up expulsion for several days, which they were willing to do.

The mother was eager for help, although she lacked the physical or emotional resources to assist very much. Claire had been staying home from school for days and was now threatening to run away. Her mother had withdrawn all money, the use of the telephone, and dating privileges. These were all very powerful reinforcers to Claire but unfortunately, her mother had not provided any clear way for Claire to earn them back.

Obviously, the most pressing problem was Claire's truancy and it was imperative that an intervention plan be prepared immediately to prevent suspension from school. Also, Claire's attending school would be very reinforcing to mother who was at this time somewhat dubious that a "noncounseling" approach would be successful. By winning her confidence it would be possible to begin shaping her to regard Claire in a more positive perspective, which would be necessary before a more amicable relationship could be worked out between them.

An intervention plan was agreed upon by mother, Claire, and a staff member. Telephone privileges and weekend dates were contingent on attending school all day. The school attendance officer would dispense a note to Claire at the end of each day if she had attended all of her classes. On presenting the note to mother, Claire earned telephone usage (receiving and calling out) for that day. If she received four out of five notes during the week, she earned one weekend date night, and five out of five notes earned two weekend date nights. Phone usage on the weekend was not included in this plan.

Much to mother's astonishment Claire accepted the plan. Mother herself felt the plan "childish" and was apprehensive about Claire complying with it. Staff emphasized the necessity and benefit of praising Claire whenever she brought a note home. This would be difficult for mother, who was inconsistent, ineffectual, and emotional in all her relations with Claire. However, she was given support through several brief phone calls every week.

Despite frequent family upsets, Claire attended school regularly from the first day of intervention. The plan was altered (in technical terms the schedule was "thinned") after a month so that Claire would receive only two notes a week. A note on Wednesdays would mean she attended all her classes on Monday, Tuesday, and Wednesday. This was backed up by the privilege of one weekend night out. A second note on Friday meant full attendance on Thursday and Friday, which was backed up by a second weekend night out. The telephone privileges were taken off contingency. About seven weeks later the notes were stopped entirely.

The results were quite impressive. During the first 46 days of school (baseline period), Claire missed 30 days of school (65.2 percent absent). While working with the project for less than three months, she was illegally absent twice (6.6 percent). She was *never* illegally absent again following termination, which covers the entire second semester of school. Grades were beyond redemption during the first semester mainly because of absences, thus causing her to fail two subjects. This dropped to one failure during the second semester.

According to her counselor at school, Claire continued to experience a poor relationship with her mother but did begin expressing positive attitudes and interests in her classes. Thus, the project was successful in preventing this girl from being expelled from school and probably running away. This was accomplished with a very modest expenditure of staff time.

Case 2

Mark is a 7th grade boy referred by the local juvenile court for (a) incorrigibility—refusing to do chores, disobedient, defiant; (b) destructiveness—toys and family property were often impulsively destroyed; (c) stealing—both at school and at home; and (d) poor peer relations—he has few friends and frequently fights with his siblings. He lives with his natural parents and two younger sisters.

The case is particularly interesting because of the great difficulty the staff had in gaining parental cooperation. The mother and father seemed to be people who derived little from experience. The father handled all discipline problems with a combination of extended lectures and punishment. His whippings were commonly followed by some destructive act by Mark, but the father still would not reduce his corporal punishment. The mother was also prone to lecture Mark, as well as being quite vague and inconsistent in her expectations of him. The destructive acts around home were serious enough to require immediate attention. Money, praise (especially from father), and a new bicycle were found to be highly reinforcing to Mark. His allowance had been placed entirely contingent on report card grades at school, which meant long periods of nonreinforcement.

The parents were persuaded to reinstate the allowance contingent on daily nondestructive behavior at home. If he did destroy or damage something, he would lose money for that day, plus having to pay for repairs. In addition, Mark could earn points each day for the successful completion of chores at home, points that would accumulate toward the purchase of a bicycle in about six months. Regular assignments were encouraged from school so that Mark could be rewarded for studying at least 30 minutes after school. When father would arrive home from work he praised Mark for studying. Should he study each day of the week, father would "bonus" him with an extra allowance or special weekend outings together. Father was to ignore Mark on any day that he did not study. The parents kept daily records on these behaviors. The records were collected every other week.

At the end of seven weeks Mark had not committed a single destructive act, there had been no reports of stealing, he rarely missed completing a day of his chores, and he was studying at least one-half hour six nights a week. The parents were pleased, but informed the project that Mark did not need to be praised and rewarded for appropriate acts —this was just "bribery." It was so alien to the nature of these parents to use rewards to shape behavior that they were seriously considering dropping the plan despite its considerable success. Fortunately, report cards came out at this time and Mark showed improvement in both academic and behavior grades. Therefore, it was possible to persuade them to continue.

A disaster did occur several weeks later, though. Mark broke his eyeglasses. This prevented any studying for a week, but worse still it precipitated an infuriated reaction in his father because of the expense. Mark was castigated and the bicycle point-chart was indefinitely suspended.

Some six weeks passed before any consistent plan of action was reinstated. School work, intermittently reinforced with father's praise, was maintained at its prior high level. Two minor acts of destructiveness occurred at home (he broke some bathroom tile and a toy) and he exhibited some defiant behaviors toward his mother. Completion of chores began dropping again, and probably was most responsible for the parents again accepting the suggestion to make a chart for the chores and reward completion of them. The "back-up" (reward) would be interaction with father plus his praise. Earning money and the bicycle were still not allowed by the parents.

About five weeks were spent in keeping a daily chart on Mark's completion of chores. He would place a star on the chart and then the parents would praise him. The frequency of chore completion soon rose to 100 percent and this so pleased the father he decided to reinstate the bicycle point-chart. Completion of chores and obedient behaviors would then earn points, and when an arbitrary total was accumulated he would get a new bicycle. Mark got the new bicycle in 34 days. In this period he had 170 individual behaviors that could earn points, and he was reinforced on 168 of them.

The parents are fully persuaded as to the importance of making rewards contingent, and the efficacy of shaping behavior with positive reinforcement. No daily charts are now kept on Mark. A six-week followup shows no return to previous misbehaviors. Originally, he had earned two D's and an F in eight subjects on the midterm report card. His final report card had no mark below a C.

Case 3

Blaine is a 14-year-old boy whose limited ability (IQ in low 80's) had contributed to a number of adjustment problems at home and at school. His father referred him to the project because he had been setting fires in and around his home, and frequently messing up the home. The school complained of his antagonism toward peers and general incorrigibility. The father had tried occasional spankings, lectures, and restriction of TV (the most effective). The school had tried paddling, scolding, restriction of playground privileges, plus the principal inviting him to the gym to put on the boxing gloves!

The mother had died two years previously in an airplane crash. Blaine and his 12-year-old brother were cared for during the day by a neighbor, while the father worked as a policeman. The neighbor lady was capable of setting limits on Blaine, but was not a source of much reinforcement. The father was quite reinforcing and capable of using his reinforcers on contingency.

The most urgent matter of business was to stop the playing with matches. Several minor fires had been started by Blaine, and his father realistically feared a serious one. A daily chart was kept by the father and the babysitter. A star was put up each day that Blaine refrained from playing with matches. This was backed up daily by praise from his father and access to evening TV. A week of success also gained him 25 cents. If on any day he was caught playing with matches, he did not get his star, he lost his TV privileges and his quarter on the weekend. A second chart was simultaneously begun for the completion of chores (the details are unimportant here). No intervention was begun at school.

In the two weeks prior to intervention, Blaine had been caught playing with matches four times. Blaine continued on the chart system for nearly six months. He had 161 opportunities for reinforcement (no playing with matches) and he missed only one of them. Equally interesting. though, were the side effects that occurred after he was put on a positive schedule of reinforcement. Both Blaine and his brother began doing their chores regularly, thus receiving attention, praise, and money. The school reported a steady improvement in Blaine's attitude and behavior. No misbehavior incident was reported on him at school from the time following intervention. Recent followup showed no changes—the school was full of praise for his behavior and playing with matches had not recurred.

Case 4

The final case is particularly instructive because it demonstrates some of the strengths and limitations of behavior modification techniques. Loren is a 16-year-old boy who lives with his stepfather, mother, and two younger brothers. He was referred for (a) assaultive behavior—threatening to shoot his stepfather and trying to fist fight with both parents; (b) defiance of nearly all parental requests —coming home early at night, completing his household chores, mowing the lawn, not taking the car without permission; and (c) habitual truancy. Police had been called for several of these incidents, and referral was made from the local juvenile court.

Assessment of the family revealed that Loren was on an entirely aversive reinforcement schedule. He was denied allowance, restricted to the house, restricted from the car, continually threatened with the police, and verbally abused. None of these was effective. Money, use of the car, and nights out were considered positively reinforcing, but the parents were so angry with Loren they provided no clear way for him to earn these. An interview with Loren confirmed the latter.

Loren's parents were where many are at the point of referral—desperate. They had been meeting each infraction with punishment until a point of no return was reached. The thought of rewarding Loren for approximations of "good" behavior had not occurred to them and the suggestion was met with great skepticism. However, since they had exhausted their own repertoire of controls, the project staff member was able to persuade them to at least give his suggestions a try.

Two points in the family assessment were quite important. First, Loren apparently had never been given a clear idea of his parents' expectations. For example, instructions such as, "Be in at a decent hour," made for much uncertainty. Second, it became obvious that his stepfather wanted the boy out of the home and was trying to accomplish this through unrealistic and vacilating demands.

The intervention plan consisted of a carefully devised schedule—more nearly a contract—which would allow Loren to earn money for completion of chores and being obedient (e.g. on a weekend night he must be in by midnight). Failures brought not only a loss of money but also carried a fine in the form of 15-minute blocks of restricted time from use of the family car. For the first time he knew exactly how to earn money and time away from home, and exactly what the consequences would be for not conforming. The parents were not to hedge on the contingencies, and biweekly phone calls from our staff plus a posted copy of the "contract" were used to prevent this.

Rapid changes subsequently occurred in Loren's behavior. In the first 35 days, he was rewarded an average of 81 percent of the time in each of four areas of responsibility (range 75 to 89 percent). Prior to intervention he met these obligations rarely (0 to 10 percent).

At this point a second contract was drawn up because Loren's stepfather was continuing to nag him despite tremendous improvement and because Loren's car insurance had expired and his stepfather refused to renew it. The new contract was negotiated in the presence of both parents, Loren, and a project staff member. It allowed for points to be earned for chores and responsibilities which could be applied to the car insurance premium (stepfather agreed finally to this). Loren could earn a maximum of 50 points a week, and needed 250 for the premium. The first week he earned 22 points and then the full 50 on each week thereafter.

Loren began driving the car again, but only by meeting specific contingencies agreed to by his parents, himself, and staff. In addition, he reentered high school, achieved satisfactorily, was not truant, and had applied for an after-school job. The case was maintained at this level of success for 24 days, requiring only one phone call to the parents and two brief home visits. Loren's stepfather and mother expressed satisfaction over the changes and felt that he was doing so well that the "contract" should be abandoned. Our staff member vigorously tried to discourage this, feeling that such a drastic change was premature. However, the parents persevered and abruptly ceased abiding by the agreements and contingencies.

Events following the parents' return to preintervention conditions illustrate an unfortunate collapse of environmental controls. Loren was truant for the succeeding seven school days, and was arrested 11 days later for burglary. His parents refused to visit him during his two days at a detention home. In addition, they told the probation officer that Loren was "hopelessly" bad despite all the good things they had done for him. The court placed Loren on probation and reluctantly allowed him to return to his home. The project had recommended foster placement but none was available. His adjustment remains exceedingly tenuous at home, but the parents have refused further help.

Loren's case demonstrates the validity of behavior modification techniques—behavior can be changed by altering environmental consequences, while simultaneously exhibiting its limitations, and uncooperative parents can defeat productive change. Probation officers adopting operant techniques will thus have to accept a shortcoming common to all known forms of helping children, namely, bad parents yield bad results.

BEHAVIOR MODIFICATION AND JUVENILE PROBATION OFFICERS

What are the possible applications probation officers could make from these cases? The amount of time spent in devising intervention plans such as those used on the Behavioral Research

Project of the Southern Arizona Mental Health Center probably would not burden court staff (all of these were arranged in 3 or less interviews). Once the intervention plan is underway, staff contacts (by phone when possible) decrease steadily to three or four a month. Most importantly, though, the behavior modification techniques frequently *work,* and the probation officer can begin experiencing positive changes in behavior rather than just suppression of misbehavior.

The authors see juvenile probation officers as having the potential for becoming experts in behavior modification. They could continue to approach their delinquent charges as representatives of the courts, and as such they would still be dispensers of aversive control. The real change, though, would be that aversive methods would no longer be their only source of control. They could also be skilled in teaching parents how to put powerful positive rewards on contingency. The combination, in the hands of a trained person, is most effective. Psychologists are increasingly available to teach operant theory and its application, and thereafter can be available on a consultative basis to juvenile courts and field offices. The time has never been more right for the people in probation work to reach out for new techniques.

REFERENCES

Bandura, A.: Punishment revisited. *Journal of Consulting Psychology, 26:* 298-301, 1962.

Grossberg, J.M.: Behavior therapy: a review. *Psychological Bulletin,* 1964.

Jamieson, R. B.: Can conditioning principles be applied to probation. *Trial Judges' Journal,* vol. 4, no. 1, 1965.

Keller, F. S.: *Learning: Reinforcement Theory.* New York, Random House, 1954.

Schwitzgebel, R.: *Street Corner Research.* Cambridge, Harvard University Press, 1964.

Skinner, B. F.: *Science and Human Behavior.* New York Macmillan, 1953.

Ullman, L., and Krasner, L. (Eds.): *Case Studies in Behavior Modification.* New York, Holt, Rinehart and Winston, 1965.

Wolpe, J., Salter, A., and Reyna, L. J.: *The Conditioning Therapies: The Challenge in Psychotherapy.* New York, Holt, Rinehart and Winston, 1964.

Chapter 18

INDUCING BEHAVIOR CHANGE IN ADOLESCENT DELINQUENTS

ROBERT SCHWITZGEBEL *and* D. A. KOLB

> There is no more powerful therapeutic factor than the perform-
> ance of activities which were formally neurotically impaired or in-
> hibited. No insight, no emotional discharge, no recollection can be
> as reassuring as accomplishment in the actual life situation in which
> the individual failed.
>
> Alexander and French
Psychoanalytic Therapy

Reviews by Krasner (1958) and by Bandura (1961) show that
the majority of studies of operant conditioning with humans
have successfully altered specific response variables (e.g. plural
nouns, self-references, lever pulling) by the use of common
generalized reinforcers (e.g. head nod, "good," "mm-hmm"). The
subjects have typically been college students and hospitalized
psychiatric patients.

The use of delinquents or criminal offenders in conditioning
experiments has been reported much less frequently. Kadlub
(1956) found that "criminal normals" and "criminal psychopaths"
learned serial nonsense syllables with equal efficiency when cigarettes and verbal praise were used as reinforcers. Lykken (1957),
however, reported that institutionalized "primary sociopaths"
showed less anxiety than normals as measured by GSR and showed
less conditioning to electric shock. Cairns (1960) suggested that
"dependency-anxiety" among delinquents was positively related
to the effectiveness of social reinforcers. Johns and Quay (1962)

Reprinted with permission from *Behavior Research and Therapy*, *1*:297-304,
1964, (Pergamon Press).

found that psychopaths showed significantly less increase in reinforced pronoun response categories than did neurotics. None of these studies used operant conditioning as a therapeutic procedure, and all subjects were incarcerated at the time of the investigation.

In 1958, a juvenile court program was established in Cincinnati, Ohio, with a definite therapeutic orientation (Hahn, 1960). Young offenders were employed to participate in "milieu therapy" which included counseling and on-the-job work training. On a somewhat similar but more informal referral basis, a research project in Cambridge, Massachusetts, hired seven delinquents to take psychological tests and talk into a tape recorder as a means of introducing them to "intensive office treatment" (Slack, 1960). A mutual acquaintance of the delinquent and the therapist was used as a referral "contact." How to initiate cooperative attendance without the use of referrals remained a problem (Sidman, 1962). Even if it could be shown that most offenders would engage in counseling or other treatment by being paid, how could this be introduced where contacts were not available? And once participating was achieved, would what appeared to be successful treatment generalize to situations outside the office? The present study reports a procedure which was adopted whereby prospective employees were contacted directly on street corners, in pool halls, or at similar locations where delinquents spend much of their time. A storefront at the intersection of two busy city streets, donated by a local business firm, served as the first "street-corner research" laboratory.

SUBJECTS

Initial Contact

The initial contact with a prospective experimental subject was informal but direct. The experimenter would usually joke with prospective subjects, side with their defenses, readily admit his ignorance, and listen attentively to explanations. All this was done in the context of a legitimate job offer. The subject was told that the purpose of the job was to find out how teenagers feel about things, how they come to have certain opinions, and how they change. The employee's task would be to talk into a tape recorder about anything he wanted. For this job he would be paid a dollar an hour or sometimes more.

It did not seem necessary to engage in devious means or to make exaggerated promises. In simple terms, the experimenter wanted to hire a research subject, and the delinquent wanted to "make a fast buck." Neither party was required to sacrifice his social role of "research psychologist" or "delinquent," although the arrangement was admittedly somewhat unorthodox for both. (Perhaps one of the difficulties in getting delinquents into almost any intense relationship with a more law-abiding person is that the delinquent is usually required to sacrifice, in advance, what little identification or integrity he may feel he has. For the delinquent, it is often better to be "bad" than to be "nothing.")

The prospective subject was reassured that he did not have to talk about anything he did not want to, and that he could quit whenever he wished. He was also warned that some of the previous employees had changed their opinions about many things, but that this was not a condition of the job. The experimenter would then offer to take the prospective subject and several of his friends to a nearby restaurant of their choice and buy them refreshments. It was explained that one of the "qualifications" for the job and for going to the restaurant was that the person had a court record and had spent time in a reformatory or prison.

Although prospective subjects were often suspicious that the experimenter was a policeman, detective, homosexual, gangster, or even an escaped mental patient, they would usually go to the restaurant. Since it was a public place and they outnumbered the experimenter, it appeared that there was nothing to lose. Informal conversation in the restaurant about topics of the boys' interest would be followed by an offer to visit the laboratory just to look the place over and see if they might want a part-time job. A common response was, "Well I guess we don't have anything better to do." Once at the laboratory, the prospective subject and one or two of his friends played with the tape recorder, asked numerous questions about the equipment and the secretaries, and participated as a group in an unstructured recorded interview. At the conclusion of this initial interview, the subject was given an unexpected "bonus" of a dollar, and a time was set for an interview the next day. A subject was permitted to bring friends along for the first few interviews until he felt comfortable in the laboratory and with the experimenter.

Group Characteristics

The first twenty subjects employed by the project formed the experimental group. These twenty subjects were found to have the following characteristics. Their age range was 15 to 21 with a mean age of 17.8. The average age of the first arrest was 13.5; the average number of arrests was 8.2. The group averaged 15.1 total months of incarceration in reformatory and prison. Eleven of the subjects had histories of active refusal to participate in treatment programs. Only four subjects had held a full-time job longer than six months, and only one subject had completed secondary school. The majority of the subjects came from a lower-lower socioeconomic background; the predominant religious preference was Roman Catholic.

After the characteristics of the experimental group had been established and verified, a control group was formed by matching each experimental subject with another offender chosen from the records of state correctional agencies. None of the control subjects were interviewed by the experimenters. The pairs were matched on age of first offense, type of offense, nationality, religious preference, place of residence, and total number of months of incarceration. It was not possible to match the pairs on other variables such as the amount of school completed or the socioeconomic class since this information is seldom available from correctional records.

PROCEDURE

Shaping Attendance

Anna Freud (1958) has described adolescents as being difficult to get into treatment because they tend not to cooperate, to miss appointments, and are seldom punctual. She suggests that their rapidly changing emotional patterns leave little energy to be invested in the analyst. It may be that characteristics such as these, often ascribed to adolescents, are not necessarily descriptive of the age but artifacts of the treatment procedure. Our approach has been to shape dependable attendance and other behaviors by the use of strategies similar to those suggested by Skinner (1953).

Whenever a subject arrived at the laboratory for his second interview, regardless of the time, he was warmly welcomed and a Coke and some food was shared with him. If he did not arrive, the experimenter would go back to their original meeting place at a later date. In a few cases, it was necessary to meet subjects at locations successively closer to the laboratory.

For example, subject 11 was initially contacted in a pool hall. He failed to arrive for his second interview. The experimenter returned to the pool hall a couple days later and found the subject. The subject was somewhat bored and seemed glad to see the experimenter. The experimenter accompanied the subject to the laboratory via the subway. The third meeting was arranged outside the subway station nearest the pool hall, before the toll gate. The subject was reinforced by the experimenters paying the fares, offering the subject a cigarette, and by showing interest in some topic of conversation begun by the subject. The fourth meeting was arranged inside the subway station after the toll gate. In this case, part of the previous day's wage which the subject had earned was in the form of two subway tokens. (It was assumed that the subject would spend most of the cash he was given and therefore not be able to purchase a twenty-cent token the next day). This time the subject was reimbursed for the fare and the experimenter bought a candy bar for each of them. The next meeting was scheduled outside the subway station at the exit nearest the laboratory. Finally, the boy was met at the laboratory.

Several principles guided the experimenters in trying to shape attentance behavior.*

1. Reinforcers should be modest and natural. It would be better, the experimenters felt, to share a single orange with a subject than

---

*The research reported in this paper was exploratory in nature. Investigations are presently under way to gather more complete and systematic data regarding the effectiveness of various emyloyment procedures and reinforcement schedules.

to give him a dozen of them. "Charity" would probably offend the boy's pride.

2. Punishment should be avoided. Subjects were not reprimanded for missing a meeting or coming late. At most, they might lose some pay by not having a full hour to work.

3. Reinforcers should be given on a variable ratio schedule. Initially, subjects were reinforced every time they arrived for a meeting, but the amount and type of reinforcement varied (e.g. cigarettes, food, small change). After attendance became dependable, a variable-ratio, variable-interval schedule was used. The reinforcements for attendance became irregularly less frequent, and attention was focused on some other aspect of the subject's behavior. For example, a subject might arrive an hour late for tenth meeting. The experimenter would welcome him, mention that this was much better than the previous day when he was an hour and a half late. For the "good effort" the boy was given a twenty-five cent cash bonus. The next day the boy might arrive within fifteen minutes of the appointed time—hoping perhaps for a dollar bonus. The experimenter might mention nothing about his arrival, but the boy would be likely to call attention to the fact and ask about his bonus. It would then be explained that the employee can always expect to receive the basic wage but that bonuses depend entirely on the amount of money the experimenter happens to have and on his feelings at the time. The boy might be disappointed until, later in the hour, he receives a fifty-cent bonus for, say, showing curiosity about the meaning of a recurring dream. He might then realize that he could never be sure what he might receive a bonus for or what the bonus would be, but in general the whole thing seemed to be an interesting game. At the following meeting, the experimenter might take the subject to a restaurant for a sandwich if he arrived still more promptly.

Using the procedures we have outlined, it was possible to shape arrival to within a few minutes of the scheduled time for most subjects. The writers noticed on one occasion a boy waiting just outside the laboratory door for the chimes of a nearby church to ring in order that he might be exactly on time. Such extreme punctuality was not expected nor required. Fig. 18-1 shows the arrival times of a typical subject, S_2, for the first twenty-two meetings. For about ninety percent of the subjects, attendance became dependable within fifteen appointments and prompt within twenty-five appointments.

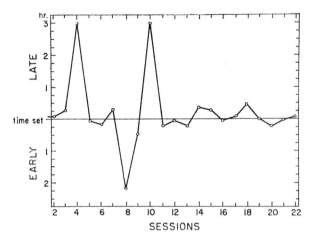

Fig. 18-1. Arrival times of experimental subject S_2 for initial twenty-two meetings.

Interviewing

The tape-recorded interviews were scheduled for one hour on an average of two or three times a week. Interviews were more frequent at the beginning of employment and less frequent toward the end. After a few hours of relating stories of their adventures and exploits, subjects often found that what appeared to be a "soft touch," i.e. getting paid for just talking, was actually a rather difficult task. In some cases, the experimenter's usual policy of attentive listening was modified to keep from arousing the subject's anxiety. The experimenter might suggest general topics to talk about, share with the subject some personal experiences, or shorten the length of the interview. While some anxiety in the interview situation was assumed to be unavoidable, the experimenter tried to avoid making the interview itself a punitive experience.

The direction and tone of the interviews were gradually shaped by giving small cash bonuses, unexpected privileges, or verbal praise for "good work." The professional orientation of the various experimenters (e.g. a clinical psychologist, a social worker, a Jesuit priest) was clearly reflected in the content of later interviews. The principal investigators believed that the process of exploration into one's own feelings was itself of value, and they tended to give bonuses for interviews where the subject talked about his own experiences in detail and with affect. Advice-giving was avoided, even when requested by the employee. It was believed that advice-giving generally prevents an individual from developing independent judgment—if the experimenter's advice should prove wrong, the employee escaped some personal responsibility; if the experimenter's should prove correct, the employee was robbed of a personal accomplishment.

After about two months of employment, subjects typically began to value the relationship with the project and the experimenter as much or more than their small salary. A sixteen-year-old subject reported the following conversation with a friend who wanted a job with the project (Schwitzgebel, 1960).

> I tell him to take the job. But there's no words for it. I tell him it starts out like a soft touch, but it isn't. I say "Things'll happen to you." But "things" isn't saying anything. He says, "yea," and he thinks to himself, "You're nuts." But he'll come around looking for the money.

In response to the common request to spend more than the scheduled hour at the laboratory, taped interviews were supplemented by activities such as preparing for driver's license tests, building simple electronic equipment, answering correspondence. The pay for this supplementary work was very small.

Termination of employment came gradually. Subjects would typically take part-time jobs in addition to the work at the laboratory. If the outside work went well, the frequency of the interviews decreased. If the outside work went poorly and the boy became discouraged, the experimenter would take the initiative to schedule more interviews. After nine or ten months of employment with the project (assuming they had not been incarcerated in the meantime), subjects left for full-time jobs, trade school, or armed services. Separation from the project seemed a natural event in view of the difference in ages, interests, and backgrounds of the experimenters and subjects.

RESULTS

Three years after termination of employment of the experimental group, an extensive follow-up of these twenty subjects showed a statistically significant reduction in the number of arrests and the number of months of incarceration as compared to the control group. Experimental subjects accumulated an average of 2.4 arrests during the follow-up period; the control group averaged 4.7 (t—33.0; a—0.025). The mean number of months of incarceration for experimental subjects was 3.5; the mean number of months for control subjects was 6.9 (t—2.79; a—0.05).

Experimental and control groups did not, however, show a significant difference (a—0.05) in the number of persons from each group returned to reformatory or prison. The recidivism rate for the experimental group was 35 percent; the recidivism rate for the control group was 45 percent.

It appears that the research procedure was effective in reducing, but not eliminating, delinquent behaviors. While some subjects of both groups continued committing illegal acts for which they were apprehended, the experimental subjects seemed to do so less frequently (reduced number of arrests) and the type of offense seemed less severe (reduced months of incarceration). For example, one experimental subject and a friend got into an argument with a cab driver regarding the fare they had been charged. They gave the driver ten dollars, pushed him out, and took the cab "for change." The boys were easily apprehended while randomly giving free rides to people in a neighboring city.

DISCUSSION

The evidence of the present study suggests that principles of operant conditioning may be effectively utilized in changing certain characteristic behaviors of adolescent delinquents. The frequency and severity of known crime was not reduced, in our opinion, by "direct attack." The tone of the project was clearly not one of "fighting" delinquency or delinquents but rather one of sympathy, firmness, and sharing. The experimenters attempted to establish conditions in which subjects could become secure enough to share experiences, to express honest opinions, and to explore new ways of feeling and living—in short, to become good employees. The fact that the job was both legitimate and difficult meant that good employees became quite involved and challenged by a noncriminal activity. In effect, delinquent behavior was counterconditioned by the reinforcing of competing behaviors. Seldom were any reinforcers given for simply staying out of trouble.

The strong personal relationship which developed in most cases between the subject and the experimenter seemed to gradually generalize to other persons whom the subject saw as being older, better educated, authorities, or employers. Once these and similar classes of people became less threatening to the subject, he found the usual social situations in which adolescents are involved (e.g. commercial employment, training programs, armed services) relatively attractive. He could earn considerably more money than the research project offered, and at the same time felt that he would be capable of making new friends. At this point the subject usually initiated his own voluntary termination from the project.

To the best of our knowledge, many of the undesirable side-effects often assumed to accompany conditioning of humans were not present. Generally, the concern is that conditioning (assuming it were effective) will somehow diminish man's freedom, initiative, privacy, creativity, spontaneity, and so forth. We shall mention briefly three values which we believe were sustained and supported in the course of the present behavior-change process.

1. *Recognition of individuality.* Each subject was offered a job at a wage assumed to be appropriate for his age and needs. Each subject was free to reject, accept, or bargain for his wages. Topics of the interviews were selected by the individual subjects. The failure of the experimenter to arbitrarily assign topics was, in fact, often a source of discomfort for the subjects.

The type as well as the amount of rewards and bonuses varied for each subject. Generalized reinforcers (e.g. food or money) were found to be effective initially, but gradually specific reinforcers (e.g. a particular brand of cigarettes which the subject liked but could seldom afford) were used more frequently, simply because they proved to be more effective. Reinforcers had to be empirically and operationally defined for each person. To the extent that individuals have different histories, the discovery of effective reinforcers always requires conditions which allow the subject honest freedom of expression and which permit the experimenter to exercise honest concern and attentiveness. We believe that the existential movement in psychology is of considerable value in reminding therapists of the unique history of each individual, the importance of free expression, and the value of relationships in which the therapist is "not being merely a shadowy mirror but an alive human being who is, at that hour, not concerned with his own problems but with understanding and experiencing, as far as possible, the existence (including the problems) of the patient (May, 1959) ."

2. *"Self-direction."* While the experimenters in the present study attempted to refrain from imposing many of their own idiosyncratic values on the subjects, they did overtly reinforce attempts of the subjects to explore feelings and solutions and to expand their capacity for self-direction. These values served as criteria for giving interview bonuses. "Self-direction" was defined as the ability of a person, through planning, to control his own reinforcers.

In general, we preferred subjects who were dominant, not submissive, in the process of their own behavior change. It is at this point that the traditional medical "treatment" paradigm may be the most inadequate in describing the conditioning procedure. Technically, operant conditioning requires an active organism; medical treatment may require a more passive or immobilized organism. Conditioning, as practiced in this research, did not require examinations, make formal diagnoses, promise cures, or assume legal responsibility for a subject's behavior or condition.

3. *Personal freedom.* All subjects of the present study were nonincarcerated volunteers. Referrals were not required and infrequently used. As mentioned previously in this paper, prospective subjects were warned that they might change their ideas and feelings about many things. They were told that this was their own affair and that they were always free to quit the job

whenever they wished. Literature about the project was available for the subjects to read or purposely shown to them in advance. Continuation of employment was not contingent on becoming nondelinquent. But if a subject became incarcerated, it was obvious that he would not be able to come to work at the laboratory. Subjects did not report feelings of coercion or construction. Most subjects looked on their experience favorably and recommended the project to their friends—with the warning, "Things'll happen."

One might try to measure "freedom" objectively in terms of the potential range of an individual's behaviors. Prior to employment by the project, for example, only four subjects had held full-time jobs longer than six months. Following the project, most subjects were legally self-supporting for about three years. It is assumed that subjects were still capable of irregular employment and criminal acts, but that they generally preferred to do something else.

We shall sidestep any theoretical discussion of determinism versus freedom. (Part of the complexity of this issue may be due to the diverse perspectives from which people may make predictions—in particular, whether a person making a prediction is himself part of the system about which the prediction is being made.)

As measured by results so far, the explicit use of a few elementary principles of operant conditioning to induce behavior change among adolescent delinquents has proven quite reinforcing for the experimenters. And concomitantly, certain apprehensions on the part of the experimenters regarding the "inhumanity" of the procedure have been strongly disconfirmed. Perhaps the most discouraging aspect of almost any research is the number of variables left uncontrolled or unmeasured. The extent to which the results of this particular study may be generalized to other experimenters, to other work situations, or to other subject populations would be largely speculation at this time.

REFERENCES

Bandura, A.: Psychotherapy as a learning process. *Psychol Bull, 58:*143-159, 1961.

Cairns, R.: The Influence of Dependency—Anxiety on the Effectiveness of

Social Reinforcers. Unpublished doctoral dissertation, Stanford University, 1960.

Freud, Anna: Adolescence. In *The Psychoanalytic Study of the Child,* vol. XIII, New York, International Universities Press, 1958, pp. 255-277.

Hahn, P.H.: Annual Report of the Work Therapy Dept. of the Court of Common Pleas, Juvenile Division, Cincinnati, Ohio, 1965.

Johns, J.H., and Quay, H.C.: The effect of social regard on verbal conditioning in psychopathic and neurotic military offenders. *J Cons Psychol,* *26:*213-220, 1962.

Kadlub, K.: The Effects of Two Types of Reinforcement on the Performance of Psychopathic and Normal Criminals. Unpublished doctoral thesis, University of Illinois, 1956.

Krasner, L.: Studies of the conditioning of verbal behavior. *Psychol Bull,* *55:*148-170, 1958.

Lykken, D.T.: A study of anxiety in the sociopathic personality. *J Abnorm Soc Psychol, 55:*6-10, 1957.

May, R.: The existential approach. In Arieti, S. (Ed.): *American Handbook of Psychiatry.* New York, Basic Books, 1959.

Schwitzgebel, R.: A new approach to understanding delinquency. *Fed Probation,* 1960, pp. 5-0.

Sidman, M.: Operant techniques. In Bachrach, A.J. (Ed.): *Experimental Foundations of Clinical Psychology,* New York, Basic Books, 1962, pp. 170-210.

Skinner, B.F.: *Science and Human Behavior.* New York, Macmillan, 1953.

Slack, C.W.: Experimenter-subject psychotherapy: a new method of introducing intensive office treatment for unreachable cases. *Ment Hyg* (New York), *44:*238-256, 1960.

Chapter 19

THE SUCCESSFUL APPLICATION OF AVERSION THERAPY TO AN ADOLESCENT EXHIBITIONIST

M. J. MacCULLOCH, C. WILLIAMS *and* C. J. BIRTLES

THE TERM exhibitionist derives from an article by Lasegue (1877) and has been defined by Kraft-Ebing (1912) as ". . . men who ostentatiously expose their genitals to persons of the opposite sex, whom in some instances they even pursue, without, however, becoming aggressive." This definition is still accepted in its essentials. Kraft-Ebing described two major categories of exhibitionist: patients in whom genital exhibition may be a symptom of a mental deterioration syndrome (organic psychosyndrome) and those in whom it is the outcome of an impulsive-compulsive drive.

Reports of successfully treated cases are relatively rare. In 1947 Sperling described a single case seen on five days per week for two and one-half years. The 600 sessions on analytically oriented psychotherapy resulted in the eventual marriage of the patient.

The use of conditioning techniques for the treatment of exhibitionism has been more recently described. Bond and Hutchinson (1960) successfully treated a single exhibitionist by reciprocal inhibition. A further single case (Kushner and Sandler, 1966) demonstrated the successful use of a partial reinforcement schedule with imaginal stimuli. Recovery was maintained at a follow-up period of 12 months. Evans (1968) treated 10 exhibitionists by a paradigm stated to be based on the anticipatory avoidance technique of Feldman and MacCulloch (1965). Their subjects were asked to phantasize aspects of their sexual deviation in response to

Reprinted with permission from *Journal of Behavior Therapy and Experimental Psychiatry*, 2:61-66, 1971. (Pergamon Press)

material projected on a screen. After a random delay period of 3 to 6 seconds, shock was administered, and terminated by the instrumental escape response of advancing the slide projector. Five of their 10 subjects, who reported normal heterosexual masturbatory phantasy prior to treatment, reached the success criteria after a median of four weeks. The remaining subjects, who had exhibitionistic masturbatory phantasies prior to treatment, required a median of 24 weeks' treatment to achieve the same degree of improvement. Evans highlights the importance of masturbatory learning trials in the genesis and maintenance of sexual exhibiting behavior.

The present paper reports the application of anticipatory avoidance aversion therapy to a single adolescent who showed persistent exhibiting behavior, using apparatus which represents a technical advance over previously published techniques.

CASE SUMMARY

K was referred at 12 years of age by his family doctor because of complaints from female neighbors in February, 1969. He was a reticent, neat, tidy, physically well-developed young man, who only divulged his inner thoughts as his confidence was gained over several exploratory sessions.

He was an adopted child whose developmental and emotional milestones appeared normal on retrospective questioning of the parents. He had suffered no separations, emotional or sexual traumata; neither did he have any physical illness or educational difficulties. At an interview, K said "I love women's bodies," and that female bras, pants, suspenders, petticoats and stockings sexually excited him. It seemed that he was highly preoccupied with women's bodies and underwear.

One month before we saw him a female neighbor had complained to the patient's mother that he had entered her house and searched for her teenage daughter's underclothes. K described the incident: "I went into the house through a door I knew would be open, looked at the daughter's clothes and went to the mother's room. I took off my clothes and went to dress in them [the mother's clothes]."

Just before we saw him, the patient had exhibited his genitals to two women of 25 years or more when he had been left alone at home for several hours. These acts had followed a characteristic sequence. When he was alone in the house, and particularly when bored, he experienced a compulsive thought to expose his erect penis to older women, i.e. women of more than 25 years, who, by preference, should have large breasts and buttocks and well-shaped legs. He experienced an inner sense of resistance to these thoughts which he regarded as "wrong." However, they were followed by a train of compulsive thoughts to undress and exhibit himself. He positioned himself naked behind the drape of the lounge curtains, and waited for a suitably attractive older female to walk past the house. As she drew level he stepped into view (at times actually out of the home front door) and achieved orgasm when the victim appeared startled. If orgasm did not occur, he masturbated to a phantasy of himself exhibiting to the female. He also masturbated twice daily to a phantasy of himself "handling" older women. His mother's underclothes were also masturbatory items.

Although he was interested in girls of his own age, he was shy and socially unskilled with them. It was decided, as a preliminary measure, to undertake psychotherapy aimed at reducing tension about approaching girls of approximately his own age in social situations. This enabled him to talk more freely about sex, but two months later he again exhibited himself to a woman of 25.

Five months after our first meeting he reported a three-month absence of further exhibitionist acts and exhibitionist masturbatory phantasy, and said that female peers were coming to occupy more of his thoughts.

Two months later a letter was received from the Chief Superintendent of Police of K's home area, stating that the patient had exhibited himself to the wife of a policeman. There seemed the strong possibility that this case might be brought to the notice of the Director of Public Prosecutions. A rapid means of suppressing further socially unacceptable (maladaptive) behavior was therefore sought to ward off a court appearance.

TREATMENT

The possibility of aversion therapy was put to the mother and the patient, who agreed to it after a full explanation of the technique and its implications. First, an analysis was made of the stimulus response sequences involved in the behavior, to render them compatible with the most effective form of aversion therapy at our disposal (Feldman and MacCulloch, 1964; MacCulloch and Feldman, 1968). It seemed probable that the initial stimulus to provoke sexual arousal and its consequent chain of exhibitionistic behavior was "seeing" or phantasising well-developed mature females. There was ample evidence that the patient masturbated to female lingerie, and to "pin-ups" of older women. There seemed to be a disproportion in his sexual interest between girls of his own age, and women over 25.

It was proposed to reduce the age of the patient's heterosexual approach objects: in short, to make women of over 25 years the CS_1 (stimulus to be associated with shock onset) and girls of his own age the CS_2 (stimulus to be associated with shock avoidance), and to apply the modified form of faradic anticipatory avoidance aversion therapy as described by Feldman *et al.* (1969).*

Measurement of Sexual Attitude

The Sexual Orientation Method (Feldman *et al.,* 1966) is a technique of assessing changes in sexual orientation during aversion therapy in homosexual subjects. In the present case, the object-choice of the patient was women over 25 years, and the aim of the treatment was to lower the age of preference to girls of his own age. The method was therefore modified by substituting "women of 25 years plus" for "men," and "girls of my own age" for "women." Apart from these changes, the adjective pairs and the scoring remained the same as the standard form of the method.

This modified questionnaire was completed by the patient just before the first session of anticipatory avoidance aversion therapy,

---

*The successful treatment of a similar case (of age-inappropriate heterosexual object choice) in a man in his early 20's is reported elsewhere (Feldman, MacCulloch and MacCulloch, 1968). In that case, the subject was capable of sexual arousal only by women of 35 plus years.

and repeated prior to sessions 3, 4, 5, 8 and 13; and at 6 and 14 weeks post-treatment.

Apparatus

Further refinements of the technical developments successively described in Feldman and MacCulloch (1964): Feldman and MacCulloch (1965) and Feldman *et al.* (1969), were as follows:

1. *Treatment.* A single Kodak Carousel 'S' projector was modified so that it could be operated by both the therapist and the patient. Three slides were used, a blank, the CS_1 and CS_2. Figure 19-1 shows the operating circuit.

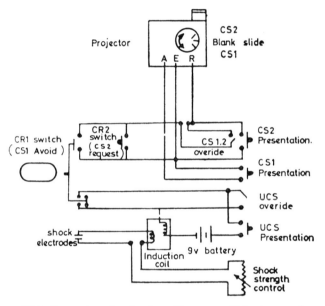

Figure 19-1. Operating circuit of avoidance conditioning equipment.

The projector was set to display the conditional stimuli onto a white desk top; in the between-trial intervals the projector was still running but using a blank slide. Presentation of the CS_1 and CS_2 was achieved by advancing or retarding the projector magazine.

2. *Data logging.* The projector operating switches were moni-

tored by a series of switches in mechanical parallel, whose output was recorded on 8-channel punched tape. The details of the encoder are reported elsewhere (MacCulloch, Birtles and Bond, 1970; Birtles, 1970.) *

Method

A series of slides (CS_1) of fully developed women of 20-plus years was prepared. The slides were rank-ordered by the patient using the method of paired comparisons (Woodworth and Schlosberg, 1962) ; and eight were used in treatment. A hierarchy of slides of a second group (CS_2) of sexually immature females of approximately the patient's age, was constructed in the same way; six were used in treatment.

The technique is described in detail by Feldman and MacCulloch (1965) together with preliminary results on the first 19 patients. Essentially, the method relation to HS/S represents the application to the treatment situation of laboratory-derived escape-avoidance learning.

The slides of older females and young females were arranged in ascending and descending orders of attractiveness. The former signalled shock onset and hence anxiety, which was avoided if the patient removed the slide from the screen within 8 seconds; the onset of the latter was associated with shock avoidance, and consequent anxiety relief. The technique thus combined aversion to older females and desensitization to young ones within the same treatment system.

Once the patient was avoiding consistently, he was placed on a treatment program comprising three types of trial: (a) reinforced (R), in which his avoidance response succeeds immediately; (b) delayed (D), in which, by special arrangement of the circuitry, the patient's attempts to switch off fail for a period of time within the 8-second period which elapses between the onset of the older female slide and recurrence of shock. He does eventually succeed before 8 seconds have elapsed. The length of time for which he is delayed may be either $4\frac{1}{2}$, 6 or $7\frac{1}{2}$ seconds, after the

---

*Details of the aversion/data logger "hybrid" apparatus, together with the computer program (MACRO 9) are available from the authors.

onset of the slide, varied randomly; (c) *NR,* the patient's attempts to switch off are not allowed to succeed and he has to sit out the 8 seconds and receive a brief shock of aversive strength. The shock and the slide terminate simultaneously. The program consists of one-third of each type of trial, varied randomly.

When the patient reported that (a) his previous attraction to the current older female slide had been replaced by indifference or even actual dislike, and (b) he attempted to switch off within 1 to 2 seconds of its appearance, we proceeded to the next older female slide and repeated the process.

As mentioned above, we also attempted to associate relief from anxiety with the introduction of the young female slide. However, such a slide was not introduced at every trial, to preserve what we consider to be the important principle of reducing generalization decrement—that is, reducing the disparity between the treatment situation and the real-life situation, in which of course, attempts to approach the desired females are not always likely to meet with success. We allowed the patient to request the return of the young female slide after it had been removed. (The young female slide was always removed by the therapist and not by the patient.) The patient was provided with a switch, which he could use in order to bring the young female slide back to the screen. However, his request was met in an entirely random manner, sometimes being granted and sometimes not, so that he could not predict the consequences of his attempting to switch off the older female slide, nor of his "asking" for the return of the young slide. The whole situation was designed to lead to the acquisition of two responses: avoidance of older females and approach to young females.

Figure 19-2 summarizes the treatment sequence.

The patient was given 18 20-minute sessions of anticipatory avoidance aversion therapy, using eight CS_1 and six CS_2 slides.

RESULTS

Clinical. The prime aim of this therapy was to prevent all further exhibitory behavior in order to avoid legal proceedings against the patient; he was therefore interviewed before each aversion therapy session. After three sessions he reported a gradual in-

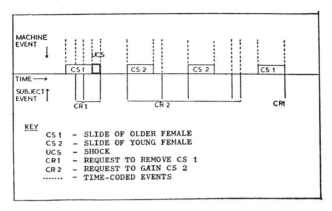

Figure 19-2. Sequence of treatment operations.

crease in the ease with which he could prevent such exhibitory phantasy, and the phantasy of older women during masturbation. At the completion of treatment he was able to control the start of the cognitive chain which had previously led to the exhibitory behavior, although 25 percent of his masturbatory phantasy was still concerned with older women. At six weeks' follow-up he reported that his masturbatory phantasy exclusively concerned girls of his own age and the compulsive ideas about exhibiting himself were absent. The situation remains unchanged at the latest follow-up at five months. His heterosexual skills are improved, he has a 13-year-old "girlfriend" who visits his home, and he reports a lessening of anxiety in heterosexual relationships.

Psychometric: Sexual Orientation Measure. The scoring system for the Sexual Orientation Measure is so designed as to give scores between 6 and 48 on the two stimulus classes—in this case "women of 25 plus years" and "girls of my own age," where high scores indicate the direction of sexual orientation of the patient. From Figure 19-3 it will be seen that on first presentation K attained a maximum score on both scales indicating a high positive attitude to both girls of his own age and women over 25 years.

This high scoring on both scales was maintained through the first two treatment sessions, but by the fifth session his score on the women over 25 years concept began to drop, reaching the mini-

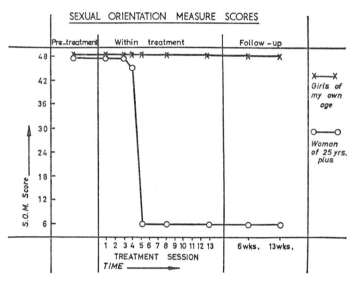

Figure 19-3. Sexual orientation measure scores.

mum score by the eighth session, where it has remained up to the latest follow-up.

The fall in score in relation to women of 25 plus years paralleled the increase in the patient's ability to control his compulsive thought.

We would like to suggest that aversion therapy of this type is a potent component of the behavior therapist's repertoire provided that it is judiciously used. The main usefulness of aversion therapy appears to be in situations where maladaptive approach behavior cannot be relieved.

REFERENCES

Birtles, C. J.: A data logging system for behavioral studies. M.Sc. Thesis, University of Birmingham, 1970.

Bond, I. K. and Hutchinson, H. C.: Application of reciprocal inhibition therapy to exhibitionism. *Can Med Ass J, 83:*23-25, 1960.

Evans, D. R.: Masturbatory fantasy and sexual deviation. *Behav Res & Therapy, 6:*17-19, 1968.

Feldman, M. P. and MacCulloch, M. J.: A systematic approach to the treatment of homo-sexuality by conditioned aversion. Preliminary report. *Am J Psychiat, 121:*167-172, 1964.

Feldman, M. P. and MacCulloch, M. J.: The application of anticipatory avoidance learning to the treatment of homosexuality. I. Theory, technique and preliminary results. *Behav Res & Therapy,* 2:165-183, 1965.

Feldman, M. P. and MacCulloch, M. J., Mellor, V. and Pinschof, J. M.: The application of anticipatory avoidance learning to the treatment of homosexuality, III. The sexual orientation method. *Behav Res & Therapy, 4:* 289-299, 1966.

Feldman, M. P., MacCulloch, M. J. and MacCulloch, M. L.: The aversion therapy treatment of a heterogeneous group of five cases of sexual deviation. *Acta Psychiat Neurol Scand, 44:*113-123, 1968.

Feldman, M. P., MacCulloch, M. J., Orford, J. F. and Mellor, V.: The application of anticipatory avoidanve learning to the treatment of homosexuality. Developments in treatment technique and response recording. *Acta Psychiat Neurol Scand, 45:*109-117, 1969.

Feldman, M. P. and MacCulloch, M. J.: *Homosexual Behaviour: Therapy and Assessment.* Oxford, Pergamon Press, 1970.

Kraft-Ebing, R. Von: *Psychopathia Sexualis,* 12th ed. New York, Rebman, 1912.

Kushner, M. and Sandler, J.: Aversion therapy and the concept of punishment, *Behav Res & Therapy,* 4:179-186, 1966.

Lasegue, E C.: Les exhibitionistes.' troisieme serie, L'union medicale, France, 1877.

MacCulloch, M. J. and Feldman, M. P.: Aversion therapy management of 43 homosexuals, *Brit Med J, 2:*594-597, 1967.

MacCulloch, M. J. and Feldman, M. P.: Personality and the treatment of homosexuality. *Acta Psychiat Neurol Scand, 43:*300-317, 1967.

MacCulloch, M. J., Birtles, C. J. and Bond, S.: A free space-time traversal data-logging system for two human subjects. *Med & Biol Engng, 7:*593-599, 1969.

Sperling, M.: The analysis of an exhibitionist. *Int J Psychoanal, 28:*32-45, 1947.

Woodworth, R. S. and Schlosberg, H.: *Experimental Psychology.* New York, Holt, Rinehart and Winston, 1962.

Chapter 20

COVERT SENSITIZATION

JOSEPH R. CAUTELA

FROM A BEHAVIORAL STANDPOINT, maladaptive behavior can be divided into maladaptive avoidance responses and maladaptive approach responses. Maladaptive avoidance responses, such as phobias, fear of failure, fear of criticism, have been treated effectively by reciprocal inhibition procedures developed by Joseph Wolpe (1958). These procedures include desensitization, assertive training, and the use of sexual responses. Other methods of dealing with the anxiety components of this type of response involve thought-stopping and aversion-relief therapy.

The treatment of such maladaptive approach responses as obsession, compulsion, homosexuality, drinking, and stealing has employed aversive stimulation in the reduction and/or elimination of the frequency of the faulty approach behavior. In the usual technique of aversive stimulation, shock is presented contiguously with a socially undesirable stimulus (e.g. a picture of a homosexual is flashed on a screen at the same time a shock is delivered to the feet (Thorpe, Schmidt, and Castell, 1963) or shock is administered in the presence of a fetish object (Marks, Rachman, and Gelder, 1965).

Recently I have developed a new procedure for treating maladaptive approach behavior (Cautela, 1966). This procedure is labeled "covert sensitization." It is called "covert" because neither the undesirable stimulus nor the aversive stimulus is actually presented. These stimuli are presented in imagination only. The word "sensitization" is used because the purpose of the pro-

Reprinted with permission from *Psychological Reports*, *20:*459-468, 1967. (Southern Universities Press)

cedure is to build up an avoidance response to the undesirable stimulus.

DESCRIPTION OF PROCEDURE

The patient is taught to relax in the same manner as used in the desensitization procedure (Wolpe, 1958, pp. 139-155). He is asked to raise his index finger when he can relax completely without any tension. This usually takes no more than three or four sessions. When the patient is able to relax completely, he is told that he is unable to stop drinking in excess (or eating, or whatever is the problem to be treated) because it is a strong, learned habit which now gives him a great amount of pleasure. He is also told that the way to eliminate his problem is to associate the pleasurable object with an unpleasant stimulus. The patient is then asked (while relaxed with his eyes closed) to visualize very clearly the pleasurable object (e.g., food, liquor, homosexual). When he can do this, he is told to raise his index finger. After he signals, he is told to next visualize that he is about to take the object (commit the compulsive act). If the object is liquor, for instance, he is asked to visualize himself looking at the glass with the alcoholic beverage in it. Then he is to visualize a sequence of events: holding the glass in his hand, bringing it up to his lips, having the glass touch his lips. When he imagines this latter scene, he is told to imagine that he begins to feel sick to his stomach. In imagination, he begins to vomit. The vomit goes all over the floor, the drink, his companions and himself. He is then asked to visualize the whole scene by himself and to raise his finger when he can picture it and actually feel nauseous when he had the intention of drinking, gradually getting sicker as he touches the glass, raises it, etc.

A feeling of relief is provided in scenes when he turns away from the pleasurable object. He is told to imagine that as he rushes outside into the fresh clean air, or home to a clean, invigorating shower, or whenever he is tempted to drink and refuses to do it, the feeling of nausea goes away and he no longer feels ill.

After several practice trials in the therapist's office, the patient is instructed to continue treatment on his own twice a day by means of "homework" assignments which are 10 to 20 repetitions of the trials experienced in the office. He is also carefully instructed to imagine immediately that he has just vomited on his drink whenever he is tempted to drink, or about to order one, or about to ingest it. Patients report that treatment is quite effective whenever it is followed conscientiously. As therapy progresses, the use of this procedure as a self-control technique usually continues, and the patients are able to monitor their behavior very well. It is important to note that, when anxiety is an essential part of the maladaptive response, desensitization is also utilized.

THEORETICAL BASIS

Since the individual is asked to imagine an aversive situation as soon as he has thought of drinking or is about to drink, this is a punishment procedure. An aversive stimulus is made to follow the response to be reduced. Evidence indicates that punishment is quite effective in reducing the frequency of responses and that this reduction can be long-lasting or permanent (Kushner and Sandler, 1966). Certain conditions should be carefully arranged to produce a decrease in response frequency. The noxious stimulus should be contiguous with that response. The response should have a history of positive reinforcement (e.g. drinking). The aversive stimulus should be presented on a continuous basis, at least initially, after which a partial schedule can be presented. The level of punishment should be clearly noxious but not so intense as to immobilize the organism.

Since the patient is usually told that the nausea and vomiting behavior decreases and he feels better as soon as he turns away from the undesirable object (e.g. beer, food, homosexual), this is analogous to an escape procedure which occurs when a particular behavior terminates the presentation of a noxious stimulus. Eventually, avoidance behavior occurs, as evidenced by the fact that the patients report they no longer have the urge or the temptation for the particular stimulus. The cues which have been previously associated with the noxious stimulation of nausea and vomiting now have become discriminatory stimuli for avoidance behavior (Hall, 1966, p. 212).

TREATMENT OF SPECIFIC MALADAPTIVE APPROACH RESPONSES

Treatment of Alcoholic Problems

Besides the usual brief history taken in all behavior therapy cases, special attention is paid to certain characteristics of the client's drinking behavior. With the use of a specially constructed questionnaire and interviews, the following factors are determined: (a) history of the drinking problem, (b) frequency of present drinking behavior, (c) where subject usually does his drinking, (d) what subject drinks, and (e) antecedent conditions that are followed by drinking behavior.

A client may, for example, do most of his drinking in a barroom and may usually drink straight whiskey and sometimes beer. The covert sensitization sessions will then consist of scenes in which the client is about to drink whiskey in a barroom. If he drinks alone at home, scenes concerning the home will also have to be included. Essentially we try to cover all the applicable kinds of drinking and all the places where the particular drinking behavior occurs.

A practical problem still exists concerning whether to proceed first with the kind of drinking he does most often in the most usual situations or to begin covert sensitization with the type of drinking and its situations which occur the least often. For the most part, I have used the first method. The primary advantage of the second method, however, is the provision of some measure of success since it involves the least amount of habit strength and will make the client more eager to continue treatment. A description of the procedure is as follows:

> You are walking into a bar. You decide to have a glass of beer. You are now walking toward the bar. As you are approaching the bar you have a funny feeling in the pit of your stomach. Your stomach feels all queasy and nauseous. Some liquid comes up your throat and it is very sour. You try to swallow it back down, but as you do this, food particles start coming up your throat to your mouth. You are now reaching the bar and you order a beer. As the bartender is pouring the beer, puke comes up into your mouth. You try to keep your mouth closed and swallow it down. You reach for the glass of beer to wash it down. As soon as your hand touches the glass, you can't

hold it down any longer. You have to open your mouth and you puke. It goes all over your hand, all over the glass and the beer. You can see it floating around in the beer. Snots and mucous come out of your nose. Your shirt and pants are all full of vomit. The bartender has some on his shirt. You notice people looking at you. You get sick again and you vomit some more and more. You turn away from the beer and immediately you start to feel better. As you run out of the barroom, you start to feel better and better. When you get out into clean fresh air you feel wonderful. You go home and clean yourself up.

An important characteristic of the covert sensitization procedure is that its effects are very specific. If one treats for aversion to beer, there will be very little generalization to wine and whiskey. Avoidance to wine and whiskey must be treated separately. Sometimes I combine a covert sensitization trial for wine, beer and whiskey by having the client see a glass of wine, a glass of beer, and a glass of whiskey on a table. As in the manner described above, he is told that he is sick and he vomits over all three beverages.

Treatment of Obesity

Approach. The client is requested to write down everything he eats or drinks from session to session. Other details of his eating behavior are determined in a manner similar to that used in treating an alcoholic patient. A questionnaire has also been constructed for this purpose. Covert sensitization sessions are not begun until two or three weeks have passed, in order to obtain some kind of baseline in terms of the eating habits. The therapist is especially concerned with four factors when he reads over the client's eating behavior of the previous week: (a) nature of the food, (b) when he eats (with special concern for eating between meals), (c) how much he eats, and (d) where he eats.

At first covert sensitization is applied to sweets of all types, especially to foods with heavy carbohydrate content, and then to between-meal eating. The amount of food is usually the prime concern after the kinds of food and the time of eating has been considered. If the therapist finds that the patient is eating too much apple pie or pastry for dessert, for instance, he can proceed in the following manner:

I want you to imagine you've just had your main meal and you are about to eat your dessert, which is apple pie. As you are about to reach for the fork, you get a funny feeling in the pit of your stomach. You start to feel queasy, nauseous and sick all over. As you touch the fork, you can feel food particles inching up your throat. You're just about to vomit. As you put the fork into the pie, the food comes up into your mouth. You try to keep your mouth closed because you are afraid that you'll spit the food out all over the place. You bring the piece of pie to your mouth. As you're about to open your mouth, you puke; you vomit all over your hands, the fork, over the pie. It goes all over the table; over the other peoples' food. Your eyes are watering. Snot and mucous are all over your mouth and nose. Your hands feel sticky. There is an awful smell. As you look at this mess you just can't help but vomit again and again until just watery stuff is coming out. Everybody is looking at you with shocked expressions. You turn away from the food and immediately start to feel better. You run out of the room, and as you run out, you feel better and better. You wash and clean yourself up, and it feels wonderful.

In addition to the scenes (about ten per session) in which the patient gives in to the temptation and vomits, scenes in which the patient is initially tempted and then decides not to eat the food are also included in equal number. An example of such a scene is as follows:

You've just finished eating your meal and you decide to have dessert. As soon as you make that decision, you start to get that funny feeling in the pit of your stomach. You say, "Oh, oh; oh no; I won't eat the dessert." Then you immediately feel calm and comfortable.

Homework. The patient is asked to repeat the scenes presented during the therapy session twice a day until the next therapeutic session. He is also asked to imagine he is vomiting on a particular food whenever he is tempted to eat it. For instance, if he is tempted to eat potato salad, he is told immediately to imagine that the potato salad has vomit all over it.

Some general comments on the treatment of obesity. A physical examination, including an investigation of thyroid activity and metabolic rate, is required of all patients prior to treatment. Each week they are asked about their general health and well being in order to ensure that no physical harm is being done.

The patients are weighed at the beginning of each session. If there is indication that eating food is a mechanism of anxiety reduction, the patient is also treated to reduce the sources of anxiety.

After they have lost 15 pounds, the patients are often asked to perform simple neck and arm exercises to avoid loose skin in these regions. They are also encouraged to walk as much as possible. After the patient has reached the weight desired, as determined by height-weight charts taking the body frame into consideration, the same eating habits which have occurred during the past two or three weeks are encouraged. Subject continues to be monitored in therapeutic sessions for another month. He is then asked to keep track of his own eating habits, and he is taught when and how to apply covert sensitization to himself whenever he finds he is nearing the maximum weight assigned to him. If he finds that he cannot do this on his own, he can call the therapist for a "booster" session. This happens rarely, however. Most of the patients are able to control their weight very well. The patients report that they still enjoy the food they eat.

Of all the syndromes treated, covert sensitization seems to be most effective in dealing with the problems of obesity. This treatment is also very specific in its effects.

Treatment of Homosexuality

In the treatment of the behavior disorders indicated above, the task of the therapist is to somehow break the relationship between the stimulus (alcohol or food) and the response (drinking or eating). In the case of homosexuality, the stimulus is an individual of the same sex who elicits a response of sexual approach behavior. The therapist then attempts to identify individual characteristics which are sexually attractive and under what conditions. For example, some individuals prefer obese sexual objects, some prefer short, young, or intellectual ones.

Approach. The following instructions may be given:

I want you to imagine that you are in a room with X. He is completely naked. As you approach him you notice he has sores and scabs all over his body, with some kind of fluid oozing from them. A terrible foul stench comes from his body. The odor is so strong it makes you sick. You can feel food particles coming up your throat. You can't help yourself and you vomit all over the place, all over the floor, on your hands and clothes. And now that even makes you sicker and you vomit again and again all over everything. You turn away and then you start to feel better. You try to get out of the room, but the door seems to be locked. The smell is still strong, but you try desperately to get out. You kick at the door frantically until it finally opens and you run out into the nice clean air. It smells wonderful. You go home and shower and you feel so clean.

One essentially builds up a hierarchy of the desirable sexual objects and the available contacts of likely sexual stimulation. Covert sensitization is applied to all items in the hierarchy, with the most desirable sexual object usually being treated first.

Scenes are also presented in which the patient sees pictures of homosexuals and vomits on them. Homework similar to that given in the treatment of the other disorders is given in this case as well. The homosexual patient is also told that if he sees someone and becomes sexually attracted to him or whenever he starts to have a sexual fantasy about an undesirable sexual object, he is immediately to imagine that the object is full of sores and scabs and he vomits on the object.

Examples. This method has been only recently applied to homosexuals. I have treated two cases; one case has been treated at Temple Medical School.

One of my cases was a delinquent in a training school. According to his reports and those of the staff and of other boys in the training school, he has not engaged in homosexual behavior since the termination of covert sensitization treatment and has now been released from the training school.

My second case was a member of the Armed Forces. This individual's behavior was primarily vicarious. All his sexual fantasies, with and without masturbation, were homosexual in nature. This behavior has been reduced to about four temptations a week which last about a second. This is still in the process of treatment.

In the Temple Medical School case, it has been four months since the last therapeutic session, and the patient has not engaged in any homosexual behavior to date, according to his own reports and those of his wife. He is continuing with the homework.

All in all, the preliminary results are promising, although much work still remains to be done in this area.

Treatment of Juvenile Offenders

Since March of this year (1966), I have been using behavior therapy procedures in individual and group settings with juvenile offenders at the Rhode Island Medical Center. My preliminary guess, based on his experience, is that the usual behavior therapy procedures, such as relaxation, desensitization, and "thought-stopping," can be effective in the treatment of juvenile offenders. I have also used covert sensitization where applicable. In one case, it was used in the treatment of homosexuality as I reported above. Currently under treatment is a boy with a severe alcoholic problem. His juvenile offenses have always occurred while he was drinking. Covert sensitization seems to be quite effective with this boy. He is allowed to go home on weekends. Reports from him and his mother indicate that his drinking has been drastically reduced on these weekends at home when previously he used to drink himself into a two-day stupor.

I have also treated stealing behavior (car stealing and breaking and entering offenses). Car stealing is one of the most frequent offenses of juvenile offenders. In the treatment of this type of behavior, the boy is asked what cars he prefers to steal and under what conditions. A hierarchy is then constructed from that information. A typical scene is as follows:

> You are walking down a street. You notice a real sharp sports car. You walk toward it with the idea of stealing it. As you're walking toward it you start to get a funny feeling in your stomach. You feel sick to your stomach and you have a slight pain in your gut. As you keep walking, you really start to feel sick, and food starts coming up in your mouth. You're just about to reach for the handle of the door and you can't hold it any longer. You vomit all over your hand, the car door, the upholstery inside, all over your clothes. The smell starts to get to you and you keep puking from it. It's all over the place. It's dripping from your mouth. You turn around and run away and then you start to feel better.

I've also treated some cases of glue sniffing in a similar manner. My main surprise in working with juvenile offenders is that most of them will cooperate well with the behavior therapy procedures. Group relaxation also seems usable without too much difficulty.

EXPERIMENTAL DATA

In behavior therapy our procedures are usually derived from the results of controlled laboratory studies. We also try to test the validity of our techniques by appropriate experimentation.

Donner and Ashem,* at the New Jersey Neuro-psychiatric Institute in Princeton, attempted an experimental test of the efficacy of covert sensitization in the treatment of institutionalized alcoholics. Preliminary data indicate that three out of four of the nontreated controls resumed drinking after a six-month follow-up. Only two out of seven of the covert sensitization group resumed drinking after a six-month follow-up. All treated subjects received nine sessions. These data are only preliminary, since more subjects remain to be followed up. Investigators are waiting for the six-month period to be completed.

In this study, one subject had to be eliminated after some training sessions because the mere mention of alcohol made him actually vomit. This is important to note because the treatment of covert sensitization should be explicitly applied to the individual's *desire* to drink alcohol, not just to the alcohol itself. All of the covert sensitization subjects were also given relaxation training. Study is needed to determine whether relaxation is necessary for effective treatment; I have used it to help develop clear imagery.

Forward and backward covert sensitization groups were included in the study. In the backward covert sensitization group, individuals were asked to imagine vomiting before they took the alcohol. No differences were found between the backward and forward conditioning covert sensitization groups. One can easily hypothesize that the backward conditioning group was not truly backward conditioned, since the nausea could still be present from a previous trial.

Another study, using aversive electric stimulation (MacCulloch *et al.*, 1966), has reported no success in the treatment of four cases of alcoholism. These results are somewhat puzzling, since using the same procedure, they were able to successfully treat homosexuals (MacCulloch *et al.*, 1965). There are a number of

---

*L. Donner and B. Ashem. Unpublished research data from a study at the Neuro-psychiatric Institute in Princeton, New Jersey, 1966.

possible procedural differences that either individually or collectively might account for the efficacy of covert sensitization as compared to the use of electrical stimulation as an aversive stimulus in the treatment of alcoholism. One of the crucial procedural differences is that in covert sensitization the patients are taught to apply the procedure to themselves outside of the office situation in a prescribed manner. Patients are usually told to practice the procedure 10 to 20 times a day. Also, they are told to apply the procedure any time they have a temptation to drink. This assigned "homework" accomplishes three important behavioral effects. In the first place, more conditioning trials are used (there are more reinforcements). Secondly, the patient now has a procedure under *his* control that can be applied whenever the temptation actually occurs. So a lot of *in vivo* conditioning occurs when an individual is tempted in particular situations. Thirdly, according to reports by patients, just knowing they have a procedure they can use whenever they need it, reduces the overall anxiety level. Another difference between the procedures is that the aversive stimulus used in covert sensitization (vomiting) has stimulus and response properties that have probably been presented quite often when the patient has been drinking. With the covert sensitization procedure, we are using a behavior that has already accompanied the stimulus to drink and the response of drinking. We have some conditioning trials even before we start our formal treatment procedure.

A major difference between procedures that has yet to be explored systematically is the difference in effect of presenting the aversive stimulus in imagination or in actuality. In *a priori* speculation, one would assume that the actual presentation of the aversive stimulus would be more effective than the imaginary presentation of the stimulus, since in the actual presentation of the stimulus there is more control over the intensity and occurrence of the aversive stimulus. Also, the actual presentation of the stimulus probably results in greater perceived pain.

Perhaps none of the above differences in procedure is responsible for the apparent difference in results when using covert sensitization as compared to electrical stimulation. Perhaps the procedure of MacCulloch *et al.* (1966) simply needs modification for effective results. For example, the interval between the CS and the US can be varied; or the number of conditioning trials per session can be an important factor; also the intensity of the electrical stimulation used may not be the most appropriate.

Covert sensitization, as I have used it, is a relatively new procedure. But, of course, the use of aversive stimulation to overcome faulty approach behavior is not new. I have applied by procedure to a wide variety of behaviors and the technique looks quite promising. One of the reasons for its effectiveness is probably the sense of control the individual feels over his own behavior. So far, the treatment of obesity appears to show the greatest promise in terms of probability of remission and number of sessions required for change. Treatment of alcoholic problems appears the most difficult in terms of prognosis and number of treatment sessions necessary. There are two factors that could account for this.

The habit strength for the alcoholic responding is much higher because of the large number of reinforcements possible within a given day. The number of homosexual contacts one can make, or the number of times a car can be stolen are relatively small by comparison. The drive-reducing properties of alcohol are quite strong because of the physiological effect alcohol has on the nervous system. So even though one could argue that, if you count every mouthful of food as a reinforcement, it is possible to have as many reinforcers in a given day as are possible with drinking, it is unlikely that food as a rule has the strong reducing properties of alcohol.

More controlled studies are needed in this area, such as the one carried out by the Neuro-psychiatric Institute.

REFERENCES

Cautela, J. R.: Treatment of compulsive behavior by covert sensitization. *Psychol Rec, 16:*33-41, 1966.

Hall, J. F.: *The Psychology of Learning.* Philadelphia, Lippincott, 1966.

Kushner, M. and Sandler, J.: Aversion therapy and the concept of punishment. *Behav Res Ther, 4:*179-186, 1966.

MacCulloch, M. J., Feldman, M. P., Orford, J. F. and MacCulloch, M. L.:

Anticipatory avoidance learning in the treatment of alcoholism: a record of therapeutic failure. *Behav Res Ther, 4:*187-196, 1966.

MacCulloch, M. J., Feldman, M. P. and Pinschof, J. M.: The application of anticipatory avoidance learning to the treatment of homosexuality: avoidance response latencies and pulse rate changes. *Behav Res Ther, 3:*21-44, 1965.

Marks, I. M., Rachman, S., and Gelder, M. G.: Methods for the assessment of aversion treatment in fetishism with masochism. *Behav Res Ther, 3:* 253-258, 1965.

Thorpe, J. G., Schmidt, E. and Castell, D.: A comparison of positive and negative (aversive) conditioning in the treatment of homosexuality. *Behav Res Ther, 1:*357-362, 1963.

Wolpe, J.: *Psychotherapy by Reciprocal Inhibition.* Stanford, Stanford Univer. Press, 1958.

Chapter 21

ACHIEVEMENT PLACE: TOKEN REINFORCEMENT PROCEDURES IN A HOME-STYLE REHABILITATION SETTING FOR PREDELINQUENT BOYS

ELERY L. PHILLIPS

ALTERNATIVES are being sought to the placement of juvenile delinquents in large state reformatories. While reformatories are steadily increasing their standards, they still have had less than adequate records of success (Block and Flynn, 1966; Berelson and Steiner, 1964).

The current trend away from the reformatory can be seen in the establishment of small home-style, residential treatment programs by individual communities. These often involve a pair of house-parents and from three to eight youths. The adjudicated youths live in these homes, attend the local schools, and continue to participate in their communities.

Achievement Place, the program described in this report, is an example of a home-style, community based, treatment facility. The treatment program at Achievement Place employed a "token economy" based on those described by Cohen, Filipczak, and Bis

Reprinted with permission from *Journal of Applied Behavior Analysis, 1*:213-223, 1968. (University of Kansas, Department of Human Development)

I wish to thank Montrose M. Wolf for his advice and guidance throughout this research. I am also indebted to Elaine Phillips for assistance in conducting the experiments and in preparing this manuscript. This study is based on a thesis submitted to the Department of Human Development in partial fulfillment of the requirements of the Master of Arts degree. The research was partially supported by a grant (HD 03144) from the National Institute of Child Health and Human Development to the Bureau of Child Research and the Department of Human Development, University of Kansas.

(1965), and Burchard (1967) for institutionalized delinquents; by Ayllon and Azrin (1965) for institutionalized psychotics; and by Wolf, Giles, and Hall (1968), Clark, Lachowicz, and Wolf (1968), and Birnbrauer, Wolf, Kidder, and Tague (1965) for classroom management.

The aim of the present research was to develop and evaluate the effects of a token economy (based on naturally available reinforcers) in a home-style, residential treatment program for "predelinquent" boys.

PROGRAM
Subjects

Three boys who had been declared dependent-neglected by the County Court and placed in Achievement Place served as subjects. The boys, all from low-income families, had committed minor offenses ("thefts," "fighting," and "general disruptive behavior") and had histories of "school truancy" and "academic failure."

Jack was 13 years old. His school records reported an IQ of 85 and a second-grade reading level. Concern had been noted regarding a "speech problem," "poor grammar," "aggressiveness," "poor motivation," and "a general lack of cleanliness."

Don was 14 years old. School records indicated that academically he was performing two years below his grade placement, but that he had a normal IQ rating. Reports from school also described this youth as "possessing an inferior attitude," "rejected" by his classmates, and "aggressive."

Tom, who was 12, was described as having an IQ of approximately 120. His disruptive behavior in school had resulted in his being placed in the fifth grade, three years below his level of achievement as indicated by the Iowa Basic Skills Test. School records also noted that he was "dangerous to other children" and "openly hostile toward teachers."

Facilities and Routine

The purpose of Achievement Place was to provide a home situation in the community for boys who had been termed predelinquents by local juvenile authorities (boys who had committed only minor offenses thus far, but whom the Court felt would probably advance to more serious crimes unless steps were taken to modify their behavior). The author and his wife were the house-parents.

The daily routine was similar to that of many families. The boys arose at 7:00 A.M. They showered, dressed, and cleaned their bedrooms and bathrooms. After breakfast, some of the boys had kitchen clean-up duties before leaving for school. After school the boys returned home and prepared their homework, after which they could watch TV, play games, or engage in other recreational activities if these privileges had been earned via the token economy. Some boys were assigned kitchen clean-up duties after the evening meal. Bedtime was 9:30 P.M. Trips, athletic events, and jobs, both around the home and away from the home, were scheduled for weekends and school holidays.

The Target Behaviors and the Token Reinforcement System

Target behaviors were selected in social, self-care, and academic areas considered to be important to the youths in their current or future environment. A further requirement was that a target behavior had to be definable in terms of observable events and measurable with a high degree of interobserver agreement.

Token reinforcers were used which could be easily and rapidly administered and thus could bridge the delay between the target behavior and the remote back-up reinforcing events. The tokens took the form of points. The boys earned points for specified appropriate behavior and lost points for specified inappropriate behavior. Points were tallied on 3 by 5 inch index cards that the boys always carried with them. Thus, the points could be earned or lost immediately and points later redeemed for the back-up reinforcers.

Items and events which were naturally available in the home and which appeared to be important to the boys were the back-up reinforcers. Access to these privileges was obtained on a weekly basis. At the end of each week, the boys could trade the points they had earned that week for privileges during the next week. Some of the privileges are described in Table 21-1.

TABLE 21-I
PRIVILEGES THAT COULD BE EARNED EACH WEEK WITH POINTS

Privileges for the Week	Price in Points
Allowance	1000
Bicycle	1000
TV	1000
Games	500
Tools	1000
Snacks	500
Permission to go downtown	1000
Permission to stay up past bedtime	1000
Permission to come home late after school	1000

The prices of the privileges were relatively constant from week to week, although they were occasionally adjusted as their importance appeared to vary. For example, during the winter the price of television was increased.

The economy of the system (the relationship between the total number of points that could be earned and the total cost of all the privileges) was arranged in such a manner that if a youth performed all the tasks expected of him and lost a minimum of points in fines, he could expect to obtain all the privileges without performing any extra tasks.

There was another set of privileges for "one-of-a-kind" opportunities which had no fixed price but which were instead sold to the highest bidder, auction style. One example was the "car privilege" which entitled the purchaser to his choice of seating in the car for the week. Another auctioned privilege was the opportunity for a boy to obtain authority over the other boys in the execution of some household chore. Each week these managerships were auctioned. The purchaser was made responsible for the maintenance of the basement, the yard, or the bathrooms. Each manager had authority to reward or fine the other boys under his direction for their work at the task. The manager, in turn, earned or lost points as a result of the quality of the job done (as judged by the house-parents) .

Most of the behaviors which earned or lost points were formalized and explicit to the extent of being advertised on the bulletin board. Rewards and fines ranged from 10 to 10,000 points. Some of the behaviors and approximate points gained are indicated in Table 21-II.

TABLE 21-II

BEHAVIORS AND NUMBER OF POINTS EARNED OR LOST

Behaviors That Earned Points	*Points*
1) Watching news on TV or reading the newspaper	300 per day
2) Cleaning and maintaining neatness in one's room	500 per day
3) Keeping one's person neat and clean	500 per day
4) Reading books	5 to 10 per page
5) Aiding house-parents in various household tasks	20 to 1000 per task
6) Doing dishes	500 to 1000 per meal
7) Being well dressed for an evening meal	100 to 500 per meal
8) Performing homework	500 per day
9) Obtaining desirable grades on school report cards	500 to 1000 per grade
10) Turning out lights when not in use	25 per light

Behaviors That Lost Points	*Points*
1) Failing grades on the report card	500 to 1000 per grade
2) Speaking aggressively	20 to 50 per response
3) Forgetting to wash hands before meals	100 to 300 per meal
4) Arguing	300 per response
5) Disobeying	100 to 1000 per response
6) Being late	10 per min
7) Displaying poor manners	50 to 100 per response
8) Engaging in poor posture	50 to 100 per response
9) Using poor grammar	20 to 50 per response
10) Setaling, lying, or cheating	10,000 per response

A few other contingencies were less formalized but still resulted in point consequences. For example, even though there was no formal rule the boys would sometimes earn or lose points as a result of their overall manners while guests were in the home.

EXPERIMENT I: AGGRESSIVE STATEMENTS

One behavior pattern that had led to the classification of these youths as deviant juveniles had been the "aggressiveness" they exhibited. The terms "aggression" and "aggressiveness" were noted in school records, psychological test reports, court notes, and in general comments from individuals who were familiar with the youths. Inquiry into the nature of this "aggressiveness" revealed it to be inferred almost completely from comments the boys emitted such as, "I'll smash that car if it gets in my way" or "I'll kill you." The following experiment describes the house-parents' program to measure and to reduce the aggressive verbal behavior.

Procedures and Results

"Aggressive" phrases were recorded for the three boys simultaneously for three hours each day (one session) while the youths were engaged in woodworking activities in the basement workshop.

Response Definition

Phrases or clauses emitted by the youths were considered to be aggressive statements if they stated or threatened inappropriate destruction or damage to any object, person, or animal. For example, the statement "Be quiet" was not counted as an aggressive response, while "If you don't shut up, I'll kill you" was recorded as an aggressive statement. Over 70 percent of the aggressive statements were from a list of 19 phrases used repeatedly.

Conditions

BASELINE. No contingencies were placed on the youths' responses.

CORRECTION. The boys were told what an aggressive statement was and that such statements were not to be used. A corrective statement by one of the house-parents, such as "That's not the way to talk," or "Stop that kind of talk," was made contingent on the youths' responses. An arbitrary period of approximately 3 to 5 sec. was allowed to elapse after a response (or responses) before the corrective comment was made. This meant that a correction did not follow every aggressive statement; sometimes many responses were emitted before a corrective statement was made. The delay interval was employed in order to increase the chance that the boy would have completed his speech episode before correction was administered by the parent.

FINES. A fine of 20 points was made contingent on each response. The fines, like the corrections of the previous condition, were not delivered until approximately 3 to 5 sec. had passed without a response. No announcement of this condition was made in advance.

NO FINES. No fines or corrections were levied on responses. This condition was introduced unannounced. There were occasional threats to reinstate the fines condition if the rate of responding did not decrease. The threats were worded approximately as follows: "If you boys continue to use that aggressive talk, I will have no other choice but to take away points." These threats were not carried out.

FINES. This condition was identical to the first fines condition except that fines were 50 points instead of 25. The onset of this condition was announced.

In Figure 21-1 it can be seen, by comparing correction rate with the baseline rate, that correction reduced the responding of only one boy, while fines (20 points per response) produced an immediate and dramatic decline in each youth's aggressive statements. Responses gradually returned when fines were no longer levied but were eliminated when the fines condition was reinstated. Although the first threat (indicated by the arrows) in the no fines condition did appear to have a large suppressive effect on the rate of behavior, the last two threats appeared to have much less, possibly due to the fact that the first threat had not been carried out.

Interobserver agreement about the occurrence of aggressive statements was measured by the use of a second observer during 14 of the 75 sessions. Agreement averaged 92 percent.

EXPERIMENT II: BATHROOM CLEANING

The youths in the home were assigned a number of household chores, such as aiding in the upkeep of the yard and cleaning their rooms and bathrooms. They originally failed to complete these chores in most instances. Programs involving the point system were designed to increase the boys' contribution to the maintenance of these areas. The cleaning of the bathrooms was studied under a number of conditions.

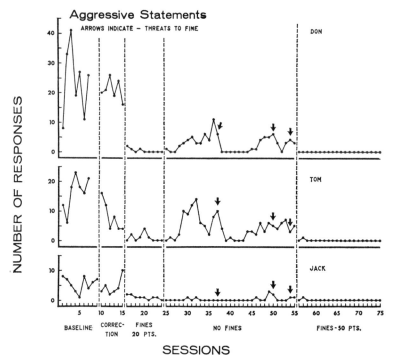

Figure 21-1. Number of aggressive statements per 3-hr session for each youth under each condition.

Procedures and Results

Sixteen cleaning tasks in the bathroom involving the sinks, stools, floors, etc. were scored as accomplished or not accomplished. The bathrooms were scored every day between 12:00 and 12:30 P.M., except in the baseline condition, where recording was done as soon as the boys reported that the cleaning had been completed (usually before noon). Consequences, if there were any, were levied immediately after inspection.

Response Definition

As stated above, the bathroom cleaning was divided into 16 tasks. In order to obtain a high degree of interobserver agreement, each task had a specified set of criteria to be met in order to be considered accomplished. For example, one of the 16 tasks was described in the following manner:

> Floor and Rugs—The floor has to be clear of all objects greater than ¼ by ¼ by ¼ inch and clear of all visible water. If rugs were removed for cleaning, they should be replaced and centered under the sink within one foot of the wall.

Conditions

BASELINE. The baseline condition consisted of instructing all the boys to clean the bathrooms. No consequences were contingent on their behavior other than the instruction that they clean the bathrooms again, if fewer than four of the tasks had been accomplished.

MANAGER. During the manager condition one boy was given the responsibility for cleaning the bathrooms daily. He picked the individual, or individuals, to clean the bathrooms each day, and then paid or fined the workers (20 points lost or gained per task) according to the quality of their work as judged by him. Later, when the bathrooms were checked by the house-parents, the manager received or lost points (20 points per task). The manager earned points only if 75 percent or more of the tasks were completed. The privilege of being manager was auctioned each week.

GROUP. The group condition consisted of all boys being responsible for cleaning the bathrooms and subject to the same fines. There was no manager. The boys were fined when less than 75 percent of the 16 tasks were completed. The amount of the fines varied from 25 to 300 points.

MANAGER. This condition was identical to the first manager condition.

GROUP. Identical to the first group condition except that the fines were 100 points.

MANAGER. Identical to the first and second manager conditions.

The point contingencies levied by the manager under the manager condition were more effective than the fines administered by the house-parents under the group condition, even when the values of the fines under the group condition were greater than those administered by the manager. The greater effectiveness of

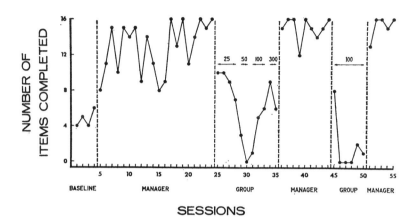

Figure 21-2. Number of tasks accomplished per session for each condition. The numerals above the arrows indicate the possible number of points lost or gained for the sessions indicated by the horizontal arrows.

the manager condition may have been the result of the differential contingencies for each boy administered by the manager.

Table 21-III shows the average number of points lost per boy each day under each condition. Table 21-III shows clearly that the managership was not purchased because it was possible to earn a large number of points as a manager. The manager consistently lost more points than the workers he supervised.

TABLE 21-III
AVERAGE NUMBER OF POINTS LOST PER SESSION BY WORKERS AND MANAGER UNDER EACH CONDITION

	Baseline	First Manager	First Group	Second Manager	Second Group	Third Manager
Worker	0	18	73	13	100	0
Manager	0	64	—	20	—	16

Item by item, inter-observer agreement about the accomplishment of the bathroom cleaning tasks for 20 sessions ranged from 83 to 100 percent agreement and averaged 97 percent.

EXPERIMENT III: PUNCTUALITY

One of the boys in particular failed to respond to instructions about promptness. This led to an analysis over a series of behaviors, of the effectiveness of point contingencies on punctuality.

Procedures and Results

Promptness was recorded for three separate behaviors:

1. Returning home from school.
2. Going to bed.
3. Returning home from errands.

Instructions were posted which stated times to be home from school and to retire to their bedrooms at night. When a boy was sent on an errand, the time he was due to return was determined before he departed.

The house-parents recorded the number of minutes late or early up to 30 minutes.

Conditions

BEFORE FINES. If the boy was late from school or an errand, he was reprimanded by one of the house-parents, "Why are you late? You know what time I told you to be here." Tardiness in going to their bedrooms resulted in a reminder every 10 minutes, "Go to bed; it's past your bedtime." No other contingencies were involved.

FINES. The youths were fined 20 points for every minute that they were late. Other than being initially informed of the change in contingencies, they were given no reminders or verbal reprimands. The fines were dispensed when the youths returned home or departed for bed. There were no programmed consequences for being early.

Punctuality for school was dealt with first. The termination of the baseline (before fines) involving school marked the beginning of the baseline of errands. Completion of the baseline for errands corresponded to initiation of the baseline for bedtime behavior.

The development of Tom's punctuality in all three areas can be seen in Figure 21-3. The other two boys had a consistent

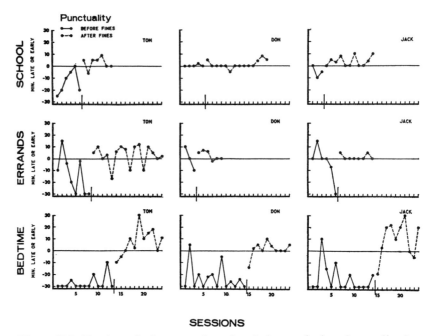

SESSIONS

Figure 21-3. Number of minutes early or late before and after the application of point contingencies. Each youth's punctuality was measured for school, errands, and bedtime.

punctuality problem only at bedtime, and this disappeared at the onset of the fines condition. The fines were very specific in their effect on the subjects' behavior. Fining tardiness from school had no apparent effect on promptness in returning from errands, and punishing lateness from errands did not seem to produce punctuality at bedtime. Interobserver agreement was greater than 95 percent for the 53 checks which occurred throughout the study.

EXPERIMENT IV: HOMEWORK

Failure in school is frequently associated with juvenile delinquency. The school records of the boys sent to Achievement Place all contained accounts of truancy and lack of academic success throughout the boys' school years. One apparently severe deficiency in their school repertoires involved their failure to prepare routine classroom assignments and homework. This experiment compared the effect of several contingencies on preparation of homework tasks.

Procedures and Results

The study was carried out during the summer, when the youths were not in school. Daily assignments were described on 3 by 5-inch index cards which were available after 8:00 A.M. each morning. The work was scored at 5:00 P.M. of the same day. Each boy was instructed that failure to pick up an assignment card during the day would result in a fine equal to the number of points he would have received if he had completed the assignment. None of the youths ever failed to pick up his assignment card. The house-parents were available to aid in the preparation of the assignments during two periods each day, 10:00 to 11:00 A.M. and 2:00 to 3:00 P.M.

Response Definition

The assignments were pages out of self-teaching workbooks which required approximately 1 hour to complete. The workbooks used were *The Practice Workbook of Arithmetic,* Grade 5 and 6. Treasure Books, Inc., 1107 Broadway, New York, N.Y., and *The Practice Workbook of Reading,* Grades 2 and 3, also by Treasure Books, Inc.

The assignments, usually two or three pages, were divided into five approximately equal parts on the assignment cards. Each part required an accuracy of 75 percent to be considered complete. The boys received one-fifth of the maximum number of points, money, or time obtainable for each assignment completed, as explained below.

Conditions

MONEY. Under this condition, each boy could earn 25 cents for each day's assignment if he had completed the assignment with less than 25 percent errors. The youths had the choice of receiving the money daily or at the end of the week. All three chose the latter, and the amount of money they earned was accumulated on an index card carried by each boy.

WEEKLY LATE-TIME. The boys had the opportunity to earn up to 1 hour of late-time per assignment. Late-time could be spent on the weekends to stay up beyond the youths' normal bedtime (9:30 P.M.). A maximum of 7 hours could be spent by a boy during a weekend and the boys could share their late-time with each other.

DAILY LATE-TIME. Throughout this condition the boys could use the late-time the same day earned or save it for the weekend.

POINTS. The points phase allowed the youths to earn 500 points per assignment.

MONEY. This was the same as the first money condition.

POINTS. This was the same as the first points condition.

Figure 21-4 shows that the points condition was by far the most effective in producing homework preparation. Daily late-time compared favorably to other conditions. Money, at the one value tested, yielded relatively poor results.

It should be noted that no effort was made to equate the points

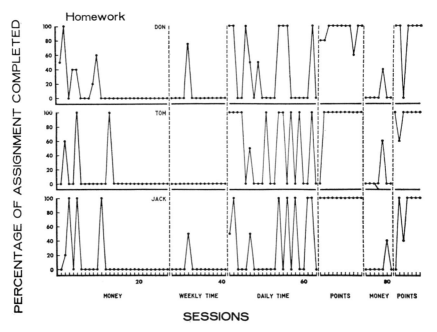

Figure 21-4. Percent of homework assignment completed by each boy under each of several conditions.

with the money, and it seemed quite likely that at some higher value money would have been as effective as points. It was thought that the low rate of behavior in the first money condition might have been due to the youths' lack of experience in using money. Thus, after the first condition, an allowance of $1.50 was given each week until the second money condition (a period of seven weeks). During this interim the youths spent their money and appeared to understand what could be obtained with money. However, the reinstatement of the money condition produced no better performance than the original money condition.

Observer agreement in scoring the assignments was measured for four separate sessions, one in each of the first four conditions. The agreement on the proportion of the assignment completed was 100 percent.

EXPERIMENT V: "AIN'T"

Poor grammar was an obvious problem for one of the boys. The present study describes a program designed to correct a grammatical problem both with and without manipulation of the point system.

Procedure and Results

The verbal response "ain't" was recorded for one boy for 3 hours (one session) each day. The 3 hours were not consecutive, nor the time of day consistent. Responses were registered on a silent counter which appeared to be unnoticed by the youth.

Response Definition

It was necessary to differentiate between "ain't" used in normal conversation and the "ain'ts" used in discussions about the incorrect responses. Thus, "ain'ts" used as verbs were considered responses, while "ain'ts" employed as nouns or other parts of speech were not recorded.

Conditions

BASELINE. No contingencies were placed on the youth's responses.

CORRECTION. The correction procedure consisted of either house-parent's interrupting the boy's conversation, informing him of his error, suggesting an appropriate alternative, and requiring the youth to repeat the sentence using the correction. The house-parents corrected the mistake in a matter-of-fact manner. The subject's peers were also encouraged to assist in informing the boy of his errors.

CORRECTION AND FINES. This condition was identical to the previous phase except that a 20-point fine was levied on each response heard throughout the day. The "ain'ts" from each 3-hour session were recorded as above. Also, the total number of responses fined for the entire day was available by tallying the entries noted on the point card. Again, the other boys were told to inform the house-parents of any responses which occurred when they were not present. These responses were also fined.

POST CHECK. One month after the final session of the correction and fine condition the response was again recorded for five days (3 hours each day).

As can be seen in Figure 21-5, no effect was evident from the correction condition but when the 20-point fine was made contingent on the youth's behavior, there was an immediate and consistent decline in the frequency of the inappropriate behavior, until by the end of the second week, the response, "ain't," was eliminated. It was the impression of the house-parents that this effect was not accompanied by any noticeable decline in the youth's overall rate of speech. The dashed line in Figure 21-5 indicates the course of the decline in "ain'ts" recorded throughout each day during this condition.

The post-check condition, 30 days after the elimination of "ain'ts," revealed no trace of the response.

Observer reliability was recorded for over one-fourth of the sessions. The observer recorded data simultaneously with the primary recorder, but recording was independent. Agreement was never less than 93 percent, and the overall average was 99 percent.

DISCUSSION

The token economy (point system), which was designed to deal with a variety of social, self-care, and academic behaviors in

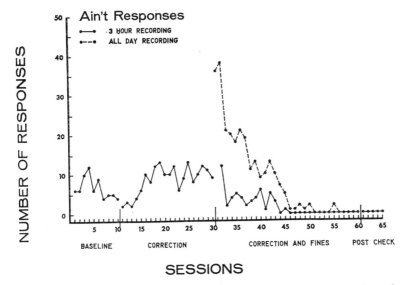

Figure 21-5. Number of responses per day (3-hr. session) for one youth under: (a) no consequences (baseline); (b) correction by the house-parents and other boys; and (c) correction and a 20-point fine for each response. Post-checks of the behavior were taken 30 days later, The dashed line indicates the total number of responses for the entire day.

the homestyle treatment program for predelinquent boys, proved to be practicable, economical, and effective. The points seemed almost as convenient to administer as verbal consequences. In the series of experiments presented, the house-parents removed or presented points by requesting the youth's point card and recording the consequence. Subsequent to these studies, the youths themselves have performed the recording tasks equally well. The house-parents have simply instructed the boys to "take off" or "give yourself" points. Cheating has not appeared to be a problem, possibly because of the extremely heavy fine if caught. The privileges for which the points were traded cost nothing, since they were all naturally available in the home as they would be in almost any middle-class home. Since the privileges could be purchased only for a week at a time, they were available over and over again as reinforcers, thus providing an almost unending supply.

The programs involving the point system successfully modified aggressive verbal behavior, bathroom tidiness, punctuality, homework preparation, and poor grammar. The research goals remain of expanding the program to include more boys and more behaviors as well as developing means of transferring the newly established repertories to the natural contingencies of reinforcement. If these goals can be achieved, token reinforcement procedures should become a basic feature of home-style treatment programs for delinquents.

REFERENCES

Ayllon, T. and Azrin, N. H.: The measurement and reinforcement of behavior of psychotics. *Journal of the Experimental Analysis of Behavior,* 2:357-383, 1965.

Berelson, B. and Steiner, G. A.: *Human Behavior: An Inventory of Scientific Findings.* New York, Harcourt, Brace & World, Inc., 1964.

Birnbrauer, J. S., Wolf, M. M., Kidder, J. D., and Tague, C. E.: Classroom behavior of retarded pupils with token reinforcement. *Journal of Experimental Child Psychology,* 2:219-235, 1965.

Bloch, H. A. and Flynn, F. T.: *Delinquency: The Juvenile Offender in America Today.* New York, Random House, 1956.

Burchard, J. D.: Systematic socialization: a programmed environment for the habilitation of antisocial retardates. *The Psychological Record,* 17:641-476, 1967.

Burchard, J. D. and Tyler, V. O.: The modification of delinquent behavior through operant conditioning. *Behavior Research and Therapy,* 2:245-250, 1965.

Clark, M., Lachowicz, J., and Wolf, M. M.: A pilot basic education program for school dropouts incorporating a token reinforcement system. *Behavior Research and Therapy,* 6:183-188, 1968.

Cohen, A. K. and Short, J. F.: Juvenile delinquency. In Melton, R. E. and Nisbet, R. A. (Eds.): *Contemporary Social Problems.* New York, Harcourt, Brace & World, 1961, pp. 77-126.

Cohen, H. L., Filipczak, J. A., and Bis, J. S.: Case project: contingencies application for special education. Progress Report, U.S. Department of Health, Education, and Welfare, 1965.

Glueck, S. and Glueck, E.: *Unraveling Juvenile Delinquency.* Cambridge, Mass., Harvard University Press, 1950.

McCord, W., McCord, J., and Zola, I. K.: *Origins of Crimes: A New Evaluation of the Cambridge-Sommerville Youth Study.* New York, Columbia University Press, 1959.

Powers, E. and Witmer, H.: *An Experiment in Prevention of Delinquency: The Cambridge-Sommerville Youth Study.* New York, Columbia University Press, 1951.

Schwitzgebel, R. K.: *Street Corner Research: An Experimental Approach to Juvenile Delinquency.* Cambridge, Mass., Harvard University Press, 1964.

Slack, C. W.: Experimenter-subject psychology: a new method of introducing intensive office treatment for unreachable cases. *Mental Hygiene, 44:* 238-256, 1960.

Staats, A. W. and Butterfield, W. H.: Treatment of non-reading in a culturally deprived juvenile delinquent: an application of reinforcement principles. *Child Development, 36:*925-942, 1965.

Thorne, G. L., Tharp, R. G., and Wetzel, R. J.: Behavior modification techniques: new tools for probation officers. *Federal Probation,* June, 1967.

Wetzel, R.: Use of behavioral techniques in a case of compulsive stealing. *Journal of Consulting Psychology, 30:*367-374, 1966.

Wolf, M. M., Giles, D. J., and Hall, R. B.: Experiments with token reinforcement in a remedial classroom. *Behavior Research and Therapy, 6:* 51-64, 1968.

Chapter 22

BEHAVIORAL CONTRACTING WITHIN THE FAMILIES OF DELINQUENTS

RICHARD B. STUART

Aɴʏ ɪɴᴛᴇʀᴠᴇɴᴛɪᴏɴ program intended for use with delinquents must first define a specific subpopulation as a target group. Delinquents may be subdivided according to whether their predominant offenses are or are not classifiable as adult crimes, whether they are initial or chronic offenders, and whether or not they reside in environments replete with constructive resources which can be mobilized to their advantage. For many delinquents, i.e. for 24 percent of the adolescent male wards of one Michigan county juvenile court (Huetteman, Briggs, Tripodi, Stuart, Heck and McConnell, 1970), violations of parental authority and other uniquely juvenile offenses (e.g. possession of alcoholic beverages and failure to attend school) constitute the only "crimes" ever recorded. Many engage in chronically dysfunctional interactions with their families and schools, both of which settings contain the rudiments of effective behavioral controls.

A continuum of short- to intermediate-term dispositional goals is available for working with this group (see Fig. 22-1). Ranging from maintaining the youth in his natural home environment, through a series of semi-institutional settings, to institutionalization in correctional or psychiatric settings, the points along the continuum vary according to the extent to which they provide social structure and make use of natural forces of behavioral control in the community. Recent studies have shown that the more potent the influence of the natural environment throughout treat-

Reprinted with permission from *Journal of Behavior Therapy and Experimental Psychiatry*, 2:1-11, 1971. (Pergamon Press)

ment, the greater the likelihood that behavioral changes will be maintained following treatment. For example, it has been shown that two groups of delinquents, who spent an average of 131.6 days in psychiatric settings or 91.8 days in correctional settings of every year that they were wards of the juvenile court, actually committed more offenses than another very similar group who were not institutionalized (Huetteman *et al.,* 1970). Even stronger support of the need for community treatment is found in a large-scale review of many rehabilitation programs, which concluded with the following finding:

> . . since severe penalties do not deter more effectively, and since prisons do not rehabilitate, and since the criminal justice system is inconsistent and has little quantitative impact on crime, the best rehabilitative possibilities would appear to be in the community (Harlow, 1970, pp. 33-34).

Community treatment for large numbers of delinquents will be possible only when techniques have been developed which (a) are effective, (b) require comparatively little time for administration, (c) can extend family influence to control behavior in a number of different situations, and (d) can be administered by paraprofessionals. It is suggested that behavioral contracting, to be described and illustrated in this paper, is one technique which meets each of these requirements and can be employed as a tactic in every instance in which efforts are made to strengthen the place of an adolescent in a natural, foster, or group home environment.

RATIONALE

At the core of the effort to use behavioral contracting to combat delinquency are two assumptions. First, it is assumed that the family plays a critical role in the etiology of delinquency when certain dysfunctional family interaction patterns coexist with a paucity of opportunities for acceptable performance in the community (Rodman and Grams, 1967) and when peer pressures are conducive to deviant behavior (Burgess and Akers, 1969). The family may function as a pathogen in two ways. First, the family may model and differentially reinforce patterns of antisocial behavior (Bandura and Walters, 1963). Second, the family may inadequately reinforce prosocial behavior in comparison with the reinforcement of antisocial behavior available in the community. Stuart (1970a) showed that the family of delinquents could be differentiated from the families of nondelinquents on the basis of their low rate of positive exchanges, while Patterson and Reid (1971) demonstrated that interactional patterns of coercion are more common within delinquent families than patterns of reciprocity.

The second assumption is that the family in many instances is a potentially powerful if not the only force available to aid the delinquent in acquiring prosocial responses. Over 15 years ago, Katz and Lazarsfeld (1955) clearly showed that in studies of attitude formation and change the family accounts for over two-thirds of the observed variance. Modern sociologists such as Schafer and Polk (1967) have shown that most social agencies, including schools in particular, are more oriented toward removing than rehabilitating the delinquent. Therefore it is essential to both eliminate the pathogenic elements of the family and to harness its vast power in order to mount constructive programs to aid delinquents.

BEHAVIORAL CONTRACTS

A behavioral contract is a means of scheduling the exchange of positive reinforcements between two or more persons. Contracts have been used when reciprocal patterns of exchange have broken down within families (Carson, 1969; Tharp and Wetzel, 1969) or in efforts to establish reciprocal exchanges from the out-

    —— 1. Own home, strong controls
    —— 2. Own home, weak controls
    —— 3. Foster, home, strong controls
    —— 4. Foster home, weak controls
    —— 5. Structured living situation, adults present
    —— 6. Unstructured living situation, adult monitoring
    —— 7. Group home (semi-institution)
    —— 8. Institution

Figure 22-1. Continuum of dispositional goals for the treatment of juvenile delinquents.

set in formal relationships in therapeutic (Sulzer, 1962) and scholastic (Homme, Csanyi, Gonzales and Rechs, 1969) settings. Contracts structure reciprocal exchanges by specifying: who is to do what, for whom, under what circumstances. They therefore make explicit the expectations of every party to an interaction and permit each to determine the relative benefits and costs to him of remaining within that relationship (Thibaut and Kelley, 1959). Furthermore, by making roles explicit for family members, contracts enhance the likelihood that responsibilities will be met, and by postulating reciprocal exchanges within families, contracts contribute to interactional stability. Finally, because privileges and responsibilities are fairly well-standardized across families, the execution of behavioral contracts in time-limited, high-pressure settings is quite feasible.*

Behavioral contracting with families rests upon four assumptions. First, the following is assumed.

Receipt of positive reinforcements in interpersonal exchanges is a privilege rather than a right.

A privilege in this sense is a special prerogative which one may enjoy at the will of another person upon having performed some qualifying task. For example, states bestow driving privileges upon citizens who qualify for this privilege by passing certain performance tests and by driving with standard prudence. In contrast, a right implies undeniable and inalienable access to a prerogative. Furthermore, a right cannot be denied, no matter what an individual might do. In modern society there are virtually no rights beyond the right of the individual to think as he may choose. For example, people in a democratic society have the privilege to say what they think, but not to shout "fire" in a crowded theater no matter how hard it is to find a seat.

Within families it is the responsibility of one person to grant the privileges requested by another on a reciprocal basis. For example, an adolescent, might wish free time—this is his privilege —and it is his parents' responsibility to provide this free time.

---

*Behavior Change Systems (3156 Dolph Drive, Ann Arbor, Michigan 48103) makes available behavioral contracting kits, including code book and computer compatable code forms in addition to standardized materials for use with clients.

However, the parents may wish that the adolescent attend school each day prior to going out in the evening—the adolescent's school attendance is their privilege and it is his responsibility to do as they ask. Privileges may, of course, be abused. Thus a parent might wish to know where his adolescent goes when he leaves home, but if the parents attack the adolescent when they learn of his plans, they have failed to meet their responsibility, i.e. use the information constructively. Thus it is appropriate to consider as a part of the definition of a privilege the conditions for its appropriate use.

A second assumption underlying the use of behavioral contracts is the following.

Effective interpersonal agreements are governed by the norm of reciprocity.

A norm is a "behavioral rule that is accepted, at least to some degree, by both members of the dyad (Thibaut and Kelley, 1959, p. 129)." Norms serve to increase the predictability of events in an interaction, permit the resolution of conflicts without recourse to power and have secondary reinforcing value in and of themselves (Gergen, 1969, pp. 73–74). Reciprocity is the norm which underlies behavioral contracts. Reciprocity implies that "each party has rights and duties (Gouldner, 1960, p. 169)," and further, that items of value in an interchange must be exchanged on an equity or *quid pro quo* ("something for something [Jackson, 1965, p. 591]") basis. Therefore, inherent in the use of behavioral contracts is acceptance of the notion that one must compensate his partner fairly for everything which is received, that is, there are no gifts to be expected within contractual relations.

The third principle basic to the use of behavioral contracts states the following:

The value of an interpersonal exchange is a direct function of the range, rate, and magnitude of the positive reinforcements mediated by that exchange.

Byrne and Rhamey (1965) have expressed this assumption as a law of interpersonal behavior postulating that one's attraction to another will depend upon the proportion and value of positive reinforcements garnered within that relationship. In a similar vein, Mehrabian and Ksionsky (1970) have reviewed many years of social psychological research supporting the conclusion that "Situations where affiliative behavior increases positive reinforcement . . . induce greater affiliative behavior (p. 115) ."

In the negotiation of behavioral contracts, through a process of accommodation (Gergen, 1969, p. 73) , each party seeks to offer to the other the maximum possible rate of positive reinforcement, because the more positive reinforcements which are emitted, the more will be received. In this sense, each positive offered represents an individual's "investment" in a contract, and each privilege received represents "return on an investment." Therefore a good intrafamilial contract encourages the highest possible rate of mutual reinforcement as represented by the following diagram (Fig. 22-2) in which CO_{fma} implies the optimal choice for father, mother and adolescent, CO_{fma} the optimal choice for father which the mother and adolescent will accept, etc., and k a value-determining constant.

$$CO_{FMA} = f \left[CO_{F/MA} + CO_{M/FA} + CO_{A/FM} \right] + k$$

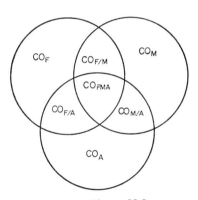

Figure 22-2.

The following is the fourth and final assumption basic to the concept of behavioral contracting.

Rules create freedom in interpersonal exchanges.

When contracts specify the nature and condition for the exchange of things of value, they thereby stipulate the rules of the interaction. For example, when an adolescent agrees that she will visit friends after school (privilege) but that she will return home by 6:00 P.M. (responsibility), she has agreed to a rule governing the exchange of reinforcers. While the rule delimits the scope of her privilege, it also creates the freedom with which she may take advantage of her privilege. Without this rule, any action taken by the girl might have an equal probability of meeting with reinforcement, extinction or punishment. If the girl did not have a clear-cut responsibility to return home at 6:00 P.M., she might return one day at 7:00 P.M. and be greeted warmly, return at 6:00 P.M. next day and be ignored, and return at 5:30 P.M. the following day and be reprimanded. Only by prior agreement as to what hour would be acceptable can the girl insure her freedom, as freedom depends upon the opportunity to make behavioral choices with knowledge of the probable outcome of each alternative.

Just as contracts produce freedom through detailing reciprocal rule-governed exchanges, so must contracts be born of freedom, since coerced agreements are likely to be violated as soon as the coercive force is removed. Therefore effective behavioral contracts must be negotiated with respect to the following paradigm.

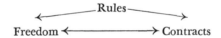

ELEMENTS OF BEHAVIORAL CONTRACTS

Good behavioral contracts contain five elements. First, the contracts must detail the privileges which each expects to gain after fulfilling his responsibilities. Typical privileges used in behavioral contracts in the families of delinquents include free time with friends, spending money, choice of hair and dress styles and use of the family car for the adolescent. Second, good contracts must detail the responsibilities essential to securing each privilege. Again, in the families of delinquents, responsibilities typically include maintenance of minimally adequate school attendance and performance, maintenance of agreed-upon curfew hours, completion of household chores and keeping parents informed about the adolescent's whereabouts. Every effort is made to restrict privileges to prosocial behaviors and to keep responsibilities to a minimum. The former is necessary if the family is to effectively serve as an agent of social control. The latter is necessary because the parents of teenage children control comparatively few salient reinforcements and must use those which are controlled with sufficient care to maintain desired behavior. If the number of responsibilities is increased without comparable increase in the value of privileges offered, little or no reinforcement will be provided for the new responsibilities and they are unlikely to be met, weakening the general credibility of the contract.

As an added requirement, the responsibilities specified in a family contract must be monitorable by the parents, for if the parents cannot determine when a responsibility has been fulfilled, they cannot know when to properly grant a privilege. Therefore there are some things which are beyond the scope of behavioral contracts, such as where an adolescent goes when he is not at home or whom he sees as friends. The single exception to this rule is the possibility of using school attendance and performance as responsibilities. While it can be argued that classroom behavioral management is the primary responsibility of teachers (Stuart, 1970b), it is often not possible for a behavior modifier to gain access to *any* or all of an adolescent's teachers (Bailey, Phillips and Wolf, 1970), so he may be required to attempt to control behavior in school with reinforcements mediated in the home. When this is done, it is essential to arrange for systematic feedback to be provided by the teacher to the parent describing the teenager's attendance and performance in class. A simple card brought for a teacher's signature every day or every week by the teenager is a sufficient and very practical means of securing this feedback (see Fig. 22-3).

The third element of a good behavioral contract is a system of sanctions for failure to meet responsibilities. While in one sense the possibility of time out from privileges should be adequate to insure the completion of responsibilities, there are obviously periods in the course of family life when this is not the case. At all times, behavior is under multiple contingency control (Stuart, 1970c), and in certain instances it is more reinforcing to violate

SCHOOL PERFORMANCE CHART

Name of Student:..   Date:...................

In order to keep my parents posted on my progress in school, I am asking all my teachers to grade my work in all of my major subjects at the end of each class period. Would you please rate my performance as: A = excellent, B = above average, C = average, D = below average, E = failing.
PLEASE USE INK and initial any corrections. THANK YOU.

Subject	Attendance	Homework	Tests and/or class discussion	Signature

Figure 22-3.

the contract and to forfeit a subsequent privilege than to garner the rewards of adhering to the terms of the contract. At these times the existence of sanctions may tip the balance of a behavioral choice toward compliance with contractual obligations. Furthermore, sanctions have an added advantage: they provide the aggrieved party with a temperate means of expressing his displeasure. In families without explicit or understood behavioral contracts, the failure of a child to meet curfew is often met with threats of long-term "grounding." Faced with the threat of not being permitted to go out for weeks on end, the teenager is often persuaded to violate his contract even further and remain out later because the magnitude of the penalty is fixed and not commensurate with the magnitude of his violation.

When sanctions are built into the contract, they may be of two types. One is a simple, linear penalty such as the requirement that the adolescent return home as many minutes early the following day as he has come in late on the preceding day. The second type of sanction is a geometric penalty which doubles or triples the amount of make-up time due following contract violations. It is probably best to combine both types of sanctions, making certain that lateness does not reach a point of diminishing return when it would actually be impractical for the adolescent to return home at all because he would incur no greater penalty for continued absence.

The fourth element in a good behavioral contract is a bonus clause which assures positive reinforcement for compliance with the terms of the contract. Much behavior control within families consists of "negative scanning" (Stuart, 1969) or the extinction of positive responding (by ignoring it) coupled with the severe punishment of negative responding. The effect of this punishment is, of course, to strengthen negative behavior as a consequence of the facts that attention follows negative behavior and does not follow positive responses (Madsen, Becker, Thomas, Kosar and Plager, 1968). To counteract this, bonuses calling for permission to remain out longer than usual, extra money or extraordinary privileges such as the opportunity to have a party or to take a trip with friends are built into contracts as contingencies for extended periods of near-flawless compliance with contractual responsibilities.

When behavioral contracts are well executed, each member of the family is assured of receiving the minimum level of positive reinforcement (privileges) necessary to sustain his participation in the interaction. Furthermore, each party to the agreement is provided with a means of responding to contract violations and each is reinforced for long chains of desirable responses. The contract is not complete, however, unless a means is also built in for keeping track of the rates of positive reinforcements given and received. This is accomplished through feedback systems which serve two functions. First, they cue each individual as to how to respond in order to earn an additional inducement. Second, they signal each person when to reinforce the other. Furthermore, the provision of feedback in this context also sets the occasion for positive comments which themselves strengthen prosocial behavior. The exchange of feedback is facilitated by the use of a behavioral monitoring form calling for each person to check off the fulfillment of his own responsibilities (which includes provision of the privileges of the others).

ILLUSTRATION

A behavioral contract constituted the primary treatment procedure in the management of a 16-year-old girl who was referred to the Family and School Consultation Project by the local juvenile court. At the time of referral, Candy Bremer* had been hospitalized as an inpatient at a local psychiatric hospital following alleged promiscuity, exhibitionism, drug abuse and home truancy. Associated with these complaints was an allegation by her parents that Candy engaged in chronically antagonistic exchanges within the family and had for a year done near-failing work in school. Owing to the cost of private psychiatric care, the parents sought hospitalization at state expense by requesting that the juvenile court assume wardship. After initiating this action, the parents were informed by a court-appointed attorney representing their daughter that the allegations would probably not stand up in court. The parents accordingly modified their request to a petition that the court place Candy on the consent docket affording quasi-ward status without termination of parental rights.

At the time of referral, Mr. and Mrs. Bremer were 64 and 61 years old respectively, and both were physically ill—Mr. Bremer suffering from emphysema and Mrs. Bremer from a degenerative bone disease in her hip. Both holding college degrees, Mr. Bremer performed scholarly work at home on a part-time basis while Mrs. Bremer worked as a medical secretary. Candy, the third of their three children, was 20 years younger than her oldest sister. The Bremers resided in a very small ranch-type home which lacked a basement, so privacy could only be found in the bedrooms.

Initially, Mr. and Mrs. Bremer wished to maintain virtually total control over Candy's behavior. They were reluctantly willing to accept her at home but established as conditions that she adhere to a punishing curfew which allowed her out of the home for periods averaging 2 to 3 hours per summer day. Great effort was expended to convince the parents of the need to modify their expectations and to modify a continuous chain of negative interactions. However, when both of these efforts failed, it was decided to execute a behavioral contract anyway, because the problems

*Pseudonym

expected at home seemed less negative than the probable consequences of continued institionalization and because it was hoped
that a more realistic contract could be effectuated as time progressed. Within three weeks of the start of the contract, Candy
was reported to be sneaking out of her bedroom window at night,
visiting a local commune and returning home before dawn. It
was found that over a 24-day period there were eight major contract violations, and the probability of an extended series of days
of contract compliance was quite small* (see Fig. 22-4). While
is was deemed vital to introduce more privileges for Candy, it
seemed imprudent to do this as a contingency for her having
violated her contract in the past. Finally it was decided to do two
things. A new contract, which was far more permissive, was introduced (see Table 22-I), accompanied by a new monitoring sheet
(see Fig. 22-5), but a new court order was requested and granted
which proscribed Candy from entering the communes. Candy was
made to understand that should she be found in either commune,
not she but the commune members would be liable to prosecution
for contributing to the delinquency of a minor as they had been
officially informed of the limitation placed upon Candy's activities.

As seen in Figure 22-4, this modified contract was quite ef-

---

*These and subsequent data were evaluated using a Markovian chain designed
to make predictions of future behavior based upon observation of past behavior in
24-day blocks. For an extended discussion of this procedure, see Kemeny, Mirkil, Snell and Thompson (1959). In simplified form, the analysis is completed
through the following *steps:* (a) write the series of dichotomous observations as a
series of +, — notations (+ — — ++ — +, etc.); (b) count the number of + +,
+ —, — + and — — sequences, recording the totals in a 2 × 2 table; (c) compute
the proportion of + + vs + vs — — sequences and enter these decimals
in the appropriate cells of a 2× 2 table; (d) draw as many Markovian tree forms
as needed following the illustration in Fig. 3; (e) for each + +, + —, — + and
— — series, write in the proportions obtained in step 3; (f) multiply all such entries in each series. *Checks:* (1) entries at each pair of branching alternatives

(C+ $\overset{0\cdot6 \quad C+}{\underset{0\cdot4 \quad C-}{\diagdown}}$) must total 1·00 (0·6 + 0·4). (2) The probability of all series

must total 1·00.

Interpretation. The obtained values may be interpreted as the probability that each
series (e.g. + + — —) will occur, relative to all other series, assuming constant
conditions.

FIG. 4. CANDY BREMER—CURFEW MAINTENANCE
THREE 24-DAY BLOCKS.

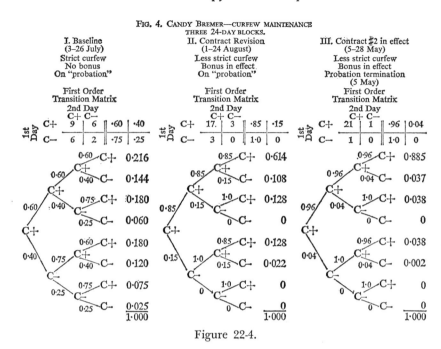

I. Baseline	II. Contract Revision	III. Contract #2 in effect
(3–26 July)	(1–24 August)	(5–28 May)
Strict curfew	Less strict curfew	Less strict curfew
No bonus	Bonus in effect	Bonus in effect
On "probation"	On "probation"	Probation termination
		(5 May)

Figure 22-4.

Days of Month

	1/17	2/18	3/19	4/20	5/21	6/22	7/23	8/24	9/25	10/26	11/27	12/28	13/29	14/30	15/31	16/—
Chores: Set table, etc.																
Dishes, kitchen, etc.																
Bathroom																
Vacuum, FR, LR, halls																
Cat boxes																
Other:																
Other:																
Curfew: Time leave afternoon																
Phone after school																
Time arrive home from school in afternoon																
Time leave in evening																
Destination approved																
Time return in evening																
Time leave afternoon																
Lateness																
Lateness made up																
Bonus Time: Bonus 1 earned																
Bonus 1 spent																
Bonus 2 earned																
Bonus 2 requested																
Bonus 2 spent																

Figure 22-5. Behavioral contract: monitoring form.

TABLE 22-1
BEHAVIORAL CONTRACT

Privileges	Responsibilities
General In exchange for the privilege of remaining together and preserving some semblance of family integrity, Mr. and Mrs. Bremer and Candy all agree to	concentrate on positively reinforcing each other's behavior while diminishing the present overemphasis upon the faults of the others.
Specific In exchange for the privilege of riding the bus directly from school into town after school on school days	Candy agrees to phone her father by 4:00 P.M. to tell him that she is all right and to return home by 5:15 P.M.
In exchange for the privilege of going out at 7:00 P.M. on one weekend evening without having to account for her whereabouts	Candy must maintain a weekly average of "B" in the academic ratings of all of her classes and must return home by 11:30 P.M.
In exchange for the privilege of going out a second weekend night	Candy must tell her parents by *6:00* P.M. of her destination and her companion, and must *return home by* 11:30 P.M.
In exchange for the privilege of going out between 11 A.M. and 5:15 P.M. Saturdays, Sundays and holidays	Candy agrees to have completed all household chores *before* leaving and to telephone her parents once during the time she is out to tell them that she is all right.
In exchange for the privilege of having Candy complete household chores and maintain her curfew	Mr. and Mrs. Bremer agree to pay Candy $1.50 on the morning following days on which the money is earned.
Bonuses and Sanctions If Candy is 1–10 minutes late	she must come in the same amount of time earlier the following day, but she does not forfeit her money for the day.
If Candy is 11–30 minutes late	she must come in 22–60 minutes earlier the following day and does forfeit her money for the day.
If candy is 31–60 minutes late	she loses the privilege of going out the following day and does forfeit her money for the day.
For each half hour of tardiness over one hour, Candy	loses her privilege of going out and her money for one additional day.
Candy may go out on Sunday evenings from 7:00 to 9:30 P.M. and either Monday or Thursday evening	if she abides by all the terms of this contract from Sunday through Saturday with a total tardiness not exceeding 30 minutes which must have been made up as above.
Candy may add a total of two hours divided among one to three curfews	if she abides by all the terms of this contract for two weeks with a total tardiness not exceeding 30 minutes which must have been made up as above and if she requests permission to use this additional time by 9:00 P.M.

Monitoring

Mr. and Mrs. Bremer agree to keep written records of the hours of Candy's leaving and coming home and of the completion of her chores.

Candy agrees to furnish her parents with a school monitoring card each Friday at dinner.

fective, increasing the rate of compliance to the contract terms to a very respectable high rate. When court wardship was terminated and the contract was the sole behavioral prosthesis, Candy's behavior actually continued to improve.

DISCUSSION

Behavioral contracting served as a very useful means of structuring a constructive interaction between Candy and her parents. By removing from the realm of contention the issues of privileges and responsibilities, the eliciters of many intrafamilial arguments were eliminated. When fights did occur, they tended to be tempered by the options available through the contract. The contract itself cannot account for a change in Candy's behavior; but the contract apparently served to assure the use of privileges such as free time and money as contingencies in the truest sense of the term.

The process of negotiating a contract through accommodation of each other's wishes (Gergen, 1969) might have been characterized as an "experience in form" by John Dewey. It appears to have laid the groundwork for a more effective interaction and in this case was adequate in and of itself. In other instances, it is likely that behavioral contracting could profitably be supplemented with interaction training for the parents, tutoring or vocational guidance for the adolescent or financial assistance for the family. The decision about which additional techniques should be employed is discretionary, but it is suggested that behavioral contracting be made a part of every plan to improve the interaction between an adolescent and his parents.

REFERENCES

Bailey, J., Phillips, E. and Wolf, M.: Home-based reinforcement and the modification of predelinquents' classroom behavior. Proceedings of the 78th Annual Convention of the American Psychological Association, vol. 5, 1970, 751-752 (Summary).

Bandura, A. and Walters, R.H.: Social Learning and Personality Development. New York, Holt, Rinehart and Winston, 1963.

Burgess, R.L. and Akers, R.L.: A differential association-reinforcement theory of criminal behavior. In Cressey, D.R., and Ward, D.A. (Eds.): *Delinquency, Crime and Social Process*. New York, Harper & Row, 1969.

Byrne, D. and Rhamey, R.: Magnitude of positive and negative reinforcements as a determinant of attractions. *J Pers Soc Psychol, 2*:884-889, 1965.

Carson, R.C.: *Interaction Concepts of Personality*. Chicago, Aldine, 1969.

Gergen, K.J.: *The Psychology of Behavior Exchange*. Reading, Massachusetts, Addison-Wesley, 1969.

Gouldner, A.W.: The norm of reciprocity; A preliminary statement. *Amer Soc Rev, 25*:161-178, 1960.

Harlow, E.: Intensive intervention: An alternative to institutionalization. *Crime and Delinquency Literature, 2*:3-46, 1970.

Homme, L., Csanyi, A.P., Gonzales, M.A. and Rechs, J.R.: *How To Use Contingency Contracting in the Classroom*. Champaign, Ill., Research Press, 1969.

Huetteman, M.J., Briggs, J., Tripodi, T., Stuart, R.B., Heck, E.T., and McConnell, J.V.: A descriptive comparison of three populations of adolescents known to the Washtenaw County Juvenile Court: Those referred for or placed in psychiatric hospitals, those placed in correctional settings, and those released following hearings. Unpublished manuscript, Family and School Consultation Project, Ann Arbor, Michigan.

Jackson, D.D.: Family rules. *Arch Gen Psychiatr, 12*:589-594, 1965.

Katz, E., and Lazarsfeld, P.F.: *Personal Influence*. Glencoe, Ill., Free Press, 1955.

Kemeny, J.G., Mirkil, H., Snell, J.L. and Thompson, G.L.: *Finite Mathematical Structures*. Englewood Cliffs, New Jersey, Prentice-Hall, 1959.

Madsen, C.H., Jr., Beckers, W.C., Thomas, D.R., Kosar, L., and Plager, E.: An analysis of the reinforcing function of "sit down" commands. In Parker, R.K. (Ed.): *Readings in Educational Psychology*. Boston, Allyn and Bacon, 1968.

Mehrabian, A. and Ksionsky, S.: Models of affiliative behavior. *Psychol Bull, 74*:110-126, 1970.

Patterson, G.R. and Reid, J.: Reciprocity and coercion: Two facets of social systems. In Neuringer, C. and Michael, J.: *Behavior Modification in Clinical Psychology*. New York, Appleton-Century-Crofts, 1971.

Rodman, H. and Grams, P.: Juvenile delinquency and the family: A review and discussion. In President's Commission on Law Enforcement and Administration of Justice, Task Force on Juvenile Delinquency, *Task Force Report: Juvenile Delinquency and Youth Crime*. Washington, D.C., U. S. Government Printing Office, 1967.

Schafer, W.E. and Polk, K.: Delinquency and the schools. In President's Commission on Law Enforcement and Administration of Justice, Task Force on Juvenile Delinquency, *Task Force Report: Juvenile Delin-*

quency and Youth Crime. Washington, D.C., U.S. Government Printing Office, 1967.

Stuart, R.B.: Operant-interpersonal treatment for marital discord. *J Consult Clin Psychol, 33*:675-682, 1969.

Stuart, R.B.: Assessment and change of the communicational patterns of juvenile delinquents and their parents. In Rubin, R.D. (Ed.): *Advances in Behavior Therapy 1969.* New York, Academic Press, 1970a.

Stuart, R.B.: Behavior modification techniques for the education technologist. In Sarri, R.C. (Ed.): *Proceedings of the National Workshop on School Social Work, 1969-70.* New York, National Association of Social Workers, 1970b.

Stuart, R.B.: Situational versus self-control in the treatment of problematic behaviors. In Rubin, R.D. (Ed.): *Advances in Behavior Therapy, 1970.* New York, Academic Press, 1970c.

Sulzer, E.S.: Research frontier: Reinforcement and the therapeutic contract. *J Counsel Psychol, 9*:271-276, 1962.

Tharp, R.G. and Wetzel, R.J.: *Behavior Modification in the Natural Environment.* New York, Academic Press, 1969.

Thibaut, J.W., and Kelley, H.H.: *The Social Psychology of Groups.* New York, J. Wiley, 1959.

AUTHOR INDEX

SUBJECT INDEX